The Simple API for XML

THE BOOK OF SAX

THE SIMPLE API FOR XML

W. Scott Means and Michael A. Bodie

NO STARCH PRESS

San Francisco

THE BOOK OF SAX. Copyright ©2002 by W. Scott Means and Michael A. Bodie.

All rights reserved. No part of this work may be reproduced or transmitted in any form or by any means, electronic or mechanical, including photocopying, recording, or by any information storage or retrieval system, without the prior written permission of the copyright owner and the publisher.

✪ Printed in the United States of America on recycled paper

1 2 3 4 5 6 7 8 9 10 – 05 04 03 02

No Starch Press and the No Starch Press logo are registered trademarks of No Starch Press, Inc. Other product and company names mentioned herein may be the trademarks of their respective owners. Rather than use a trademark symbol with every occurrence of a trademarked name, we are using the names only in an editorial fashion and to the benefit of the trademark owner, with no intention of infringement of the trademark.

Publisher: William Pollock
Editorial Director: Karol Jurado
Cover and Text Design: Octopod Studios
Composition: 1106 Design, LLC
Copyeditor: Judy Ziajka
Proofreader: Vanessa Mason
Indexer: Kevin Broccoli

Distributed to the book trade in the United States by Publishers Group West, 1700 Fourth Street, Berkeley, CA 94710; phone: 800-788-3123; fax: 510-658-1834.

Distributed to the book trade in Canada by Jacqueline Gross & Associates, Inc., One Atlantic Avenue, Suite 105, Toronto, Ontario M6K 3E7 Canada; phone: 416-531-6737; fax 416-531-4259.

For information on translations or book distributors outside the United States and Canada, please contact No Starch Press, Inc. directly:

No Starch Press, Inc.
555 De Haro Street, Suite 250, San Francisco, CA 94107
phone: 415-863-9900; fax: 415-863-9950; info@nostarch.com; http://www.nostarch.com

The information in this book is distributed on an "As Is" basis, without warranty. While every precaution has been taken in the preparation of this work, neither the author nor No Starch Press, Inc. shall have any liability to any person or entity with respect to any loss or damage caused or alleged to be caused directly or indirectly by the information contained in it.

Library of Congress Cataloguing-in-Publication Data

```
Means, W. Scott.
   The book of SAX : the simple API for XML / W. Scott Means and
   Michael A. Bodie.
     p. cm.
 Includes index.
   ISBN 1-886411-77-8
   1.  XML (Document markup language) 2.  Application
software--Development. 3.  User interfaces (Computer systems)  I.
Bodie, Michael A. II. Title.
   QA76.76.H94 M437 2001
   005.7'2--dc21
                             2001045243
```

DEDICATION

To Dorothy Bell Davis,
for instilling a love of reading and writing
and mainly for always treating me like a grown-up.
–W.S.M.

To W.R. Crickenberger,
a giant of a man whose gentle memory endures.
–M.A.B.

ACKNOWLEDGMENTS

A book doesn't grow fully-formed on the shelves of your local Barnes & Noble (although those of us who write them sure wish they did sometimes). We'd like to take a moment to thank a few of them right now. If you're not one of those people, I predict that you will skip ahead after reading this sentence. That's OK, we do the same thing for books that don't have our names in them.

Scott would first love to thank his lovely wife Celia for her unflagging support and encouragement. Without her organizational skills, a good bit of this book would probably have to have been written by candlelight (because I would have forgotten to pay the electric bill). Also, my two lovely children Selene and Skyler provide me with many hours of enjoyment. Unfortunately several of those hours seem to be scheduled in the middle of the night and interfere with normal sleep patterns, but still . . .

Mike would like to thank, first and foremost, his wife Cindy and son Brandon, for providing support, balance, and unpredictability in his life. Without them, life would be a moot point and much less exciting. Mike also thanks the technical staff of the now-defunct Celeris Financial for their invaluable input on this project. Finally, Mike would like to thank his co-author, Scott Means, for completely (and knowingly) misrepresenting the magnitude of work involved in writing a book.

Both Mike and Scott would like to thank David Setzer and the team at VirtualConnect.net for the great site design they did for this book's web site, www.bookofsax.com. As always, they came through when we needed them the most.

We'd also like to thank Bill Pollock, Amanda Staab, and Karol Jurado at No Starch for their hard work on this project. A book is really a collaborative effort, and the team at No Starch has gone above and beyond the call of duty to get this book out of our heads and onto the shelves.

BRIEF CONTENTS

Chapter 1
Introduction
1

Chapter 2
A Complete SAX Application
5

Chapter 3
Handling Errors
17

Chapter 4
Working with InputSources
25

Chapter 5
Capturing DTD Information
33

Chapter 6
Namespace Support
39

Chapter 7
Advanced SAX Concepts
45

Chapter 8
Migrating SAX 1.0 Applications
49

Chapter 9
Parser Support
55

Chapter 10
SAX 2.0 API Reference
63

Chapter 11
Deprecated SAX 1.0 API
239

Index
285

CONTENTS IN DETAIL

1
INTRODUCTION

Tree-based APIs	2
Simple API for XML (SAX)	2
About This Book	3
How to Use This Book	4

2
A COMPLETE SAX APPLICATION

What Is SAX?	6
Where Do I Get It?	6
Configuring Your Environment	7
Basic SAX Application Flow	7
The XShell Sample Application	8
Using the XMLReader Interface	9
Implementing the ContentHandler Interface	10
Parsing and Processing	11
Accessing Attribute Values Using the Attributes Interface	15
Wrapping Up	16

3
HANDLING ERRORS

Running the Application	18
Catching SAXExceptions	18
The ErrorHandler Interface	18
SAX Property and Feature Exceptions	21
Handling Multiple Errors	22
Moving On	23

4
WORKING WITH INPUTSOURCES

InputSource Overview	26
Using the InputSource Class	26
Public and System IDs	27
Character Encoding	28
Custom Entity Resolvers	28
The Locator Interface	31
Moving On	32

5
CAPTURING DTD INFORMATION

The DTDHandler Interface	34
Unparsed Entities	34
A Typical Application	35
Tracking NOTATION and ENTITY Declarations	36
Processing Entity References	37
Moving On	37

6
NAMESPACE SUPPORT

Namespace Terminology	40
Checking Parser Capabilities	41
Recognizing Namespaces at Parse Time	42
Tracking Namespace Prefixes	43
Moving On	44

7
ADVANCED SAX CONCEPTS

The XMLFilter Interface	46
Extending XMLFilter	47
Filter Chaining	48
Moving On	48

8
MIGRATING SAX 1.0 APPLICATIONS

Differences between SAX 1.0 and 2.0   50
Migration Strategies   50
The XMLReaderAdapter Class   52
Replacing Deprecated Code   53
Using Old Parsers   54
Moving On   54

9
PARSER SUPPORT

Using the DefaultHandler Class   56
Working with the InputSource Class   57
SAX Features and Properties   60
Namespace Tracking   60
The LocatorImpl Class   61
Error Handling   62
Where to Go from Here   62

10
SAX 2.0 API REFERENCE

Attributes Interface   64
AttributesImpl Class   76
ContentHandler Interface   95
DefaultHandler Class   105
DTDHandler Interface   117
EntityResolver Interface   120
ErrorHandler Interface   121
InputSource Class   125
Locator Interface   136
LocatorImpl Class   139
NamespaceSupport Class   145
ParserAdapter Class   154
SAXException Exception   170
SAXNotRecognizedException Exception   174
SAXNotSupportedException Exception   175
SAXParseException Exception   176
XMLFilter Interface   183
XMLFilterImpl Class   185
XMLReader Interface   205
XMLReaderAdapter Class   222
XMLReaderFactory Class   236

11
DEPRECATED SAX 1.0 API

AttributeList Interface	239
AttributeListImpl Class	245
DocumentHandler Interface	255
HandlerBase Class	262
Parser Interface	272
ParserFactory Class	281

Index
285

1

INTRODUCTION

Unless you've spent the past five years in outer space, XML has probably become a regular part of your programming repertoire. Almost every industry and type of application is starting to use XML for everything from transmitting invoices to drawing pictures. There are many different APIs available for working with XML documents, but if you've never heard of SAX, it might just be the solution to problems you didn't even realize you had (yet).

Every day there are more and more ways for programmers to incorporate XML documents into the systems they are building. Unless writing an XML parser sounds appealing, in most cases you will need to use a third-party XML parser and some type of XML API.

Tree-based APIs

One of the most popular XML APIs at the moment is the *Document Object Model*, which is a standard that was developed by the World Wide Web Consortium (www.w3c.org). DOM is what is known as a *tree-based* API, which means that all of the information and content from the original document must be read into memory and stored in a tree structure before it can be accessed by a client program. Figure 1-1 shows the basic flow of an application that uses a tree-based API (like DOM) to access XML document content.

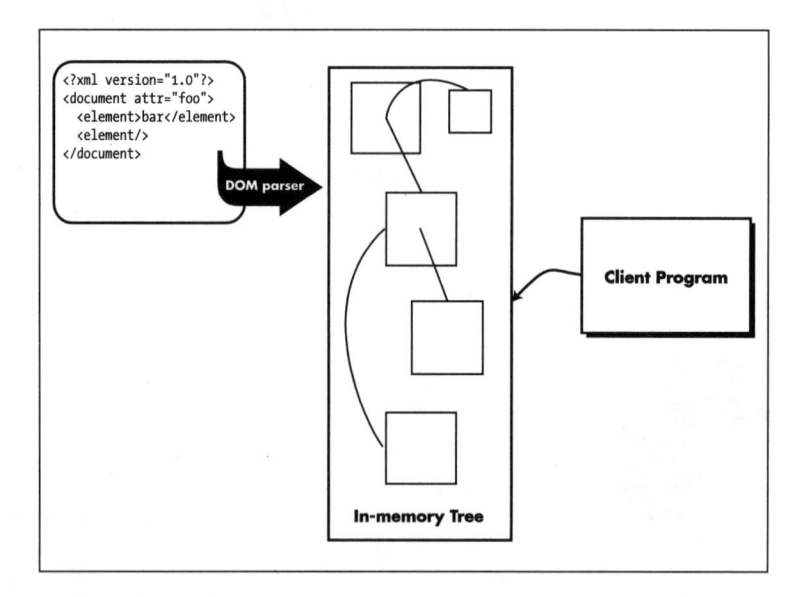

Figure 1-1: Typical flow of a tree-based XML application

Once the document has been parsed and stored as an in-memory tree structure, the client application has full access to its contents. It is simple to follow references from one part of the document to another. It is also easy to modify the document by adding and removing nodes from the tree.

While this approach has some obvious advantages, it has some equally obvious disadvantages. The size of the document affects the performance (and memory consumption) of the program. If the document is very large, it may not be possible to store the entire thing in memory at one time. Also, the whole document must be successfully parsed before any information is available to the client program.

Simple API for XML (SAX)

It was to solve these and other problems that the members of the XML-DEV mailing list (www.xml.org) developed the Simple API for XML (SAX). Unlike DOM, SAX is an *event-driven* API. Rather than building an in-memory copy of the document and passing it to the client program, the client program registers

```
          XML Document                Event Notifications
   ┌─────────────────────────┐   ┌──────────────────────────────┐
   │  <?xml version="1.0"?> ─┼───┼─→ startDocument()            │
   │  <document attr="foo"> ─┼───┼─→ startElement()             │
   │                         │   │ ┌→ startElement()            │
   │    <element>bar</element>┼──┼─┤                            │
   │                         │   │ └→ characters()              │
   │                         │   │ ┌→ endElement()              │
   │    <element/> ──────────┼───┼─┘                            │
   │                         │   │ ─→ endElement()              │
   │  </document> ───────────┼───┼─→ endDocument()              │
   └─────────────────────────┘   └──────────────────────────────┘
```

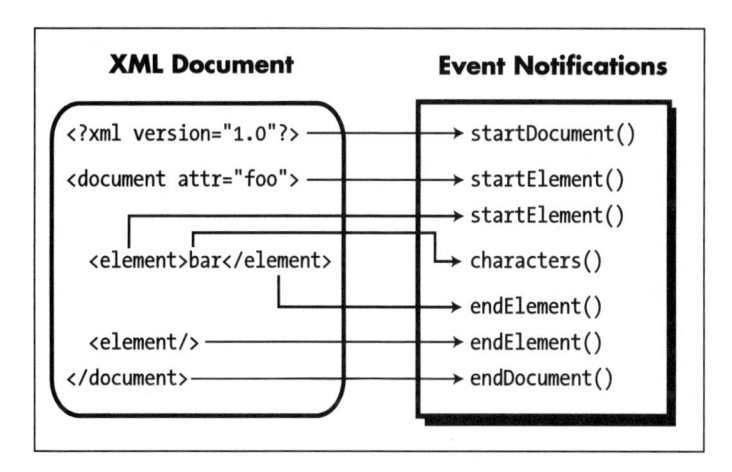

Figure 1-2: Event-based XML application flow

itself to receive notifications when the parser recognizes various parts of an XML document. Figure 1-2 shows the flow for a typical event-driven XML application.

In the event-driven scenario, the API itself doesn't allocate storage for the contents of the document. The required content is passed to the event notification method, and then forgotten. This means that whether the document was 10 kilobytes or 10 megabytes, the application's memory usage and relative performance will remain constant.

Unlike in the tree-based approach, notifications are received as the document is parsed. This means that the client application can begin processing before the entire document has been read. For many Internet-based applications, where bandwidth may be an issue, this can be extremely useful.

There are, of course, drawbacks to this approach. The application developer is responsible for creating his own data structures to store any document information he will need to reference later. Since no comprehensive model of the document is available in memory, SAX is unsuitable for sophisticated editing applications. Also, for applications where random access to arbitrary points of the document is required (such as an XSLT implementation), a tree-based API would be more appropriate.

About This Book

This book is meant to be a complete introduction, tutorial, and reference for the Simple API for XML. The chapters in Part I progressively introduce the interfaces and classes that make up a standard SAX distribution. They should be read in order, as each chapter builds on the concepts explained in the preceding chapters.

This book attempts to introduce concepts in the order that you need to use them in a real-world application. Chapter 2 starts by showing you how to build a complete, functioning SAX application. Chapter 3 explains the SAX error handling process. Chapter 4 introduces the concept of the SAX InputSource class, which enables more sophisticated handling of document content. Chapter 5 explains how to capture the meta-information from the XML document type definition (DTD).

Chapter 6 explains the SAX support for the Namespaces in XML standard. Chapter 7 explains advanced SAX concepts, such as the support for SAX filter classes. Chapter 8 is intended to assist programmers who have developed applications for SAX version 1.0 to migrate to the new (and very different) SAX 2.0 API. The final tutorial chapter, Chapter 9, explains the issues that face programmers who want to write their own SAX implementations.

Part II is a complete reference to the org.xml.sax and org.xml.sax.helpers packages. Each of the classes, interfaces, and exceptions that make up a standard SAX distribution are documented. Part II is organized into two major sections: Chapter 10, "SAX 2.0 API Reference" and Chapter 11, "Deprecated SAX 1.0 API Reference."

SAX is still a very young—though well-supported—API, and the differences between versions 1.0 and 2.0 reflect the changes in XML itself. The one major change between 1.0 and 2.0 is the incorporation of full support for XML namespaces. When writing new SAX applications, only the classes and interfaces in Chapter 10 of Part II should be used. The other section is provided for historical purposes, and includes tips for quickly converting old applications to the new 2.0 API.

How to Use This Book

If you are new to SAX and have never written a SAX application before, you will probably want to continue directly to Chapter 2 and build your first application. Since each subsequent chapter introduces progressively more specialized functionality, you may find everything you need within the first two or three chapters you read. Don't feel compelled to read the entire tutorial section at once before getting started. The best way to learn SAX (or any programming concept) is by trying it out.

Once you become familiar with SAX, you will probably be more interested in using the reference material in Part II. This book makes sure to include language-specific bindings for both Java and the Microsoft MSXML implementations of SAX for all of the classes and interfaces in Part II. There are also functioning examples that demonstrate the use of each object and method given.

Now let's get started and build our first SAX application!

2

A COMPLETE SAX APPLICATION

This chapter walks you through the process of writing your very first SAX application.

This chapter discusses the following topics:

- What is SAX?
- Selecting a SAX implementation.
- Configuring SAX to work with your environment.
- Basic SAX application flow.
- The XShell sample application.
- Using the `XMLReader` interface.
- Implementing the `ContentHandler` interface.
- Parsing and processing.
- Accessing attribute values using the `Attributes` interface.

What Is SAX?

In reality, SAX is nothing more than a set of Java class and interface descriptions that document a system for writing event-driven XML applications. The SAX specification (along with the source code for a set of Java interfaces and classes) lives on its own Web site (www.saxproject.org) and is still maintained and extended by the members of the XML-DEV mailing list.

But to actually write a SAX application, you need an XML parser that has a concrete implementation of the various interfaces and classes that make up the `org.xml.sax` and `org.xml.sax.helpers` Java packages.

Where Do I Get It?

Before we get into the nitty-gritty details of writing a SAX application, you'll need to install an XML parser distribution that supports SAX. Although SAX was originally designed for Java programmers, implementations of the SAX interfaces have been written for many other programming languages such as Perl, C++, and Visual Basic. For the rest of this book, we'll assume that you're writing Java applications that use the Xerces parser distribution that is supported by the Apache Foundation's XML Project (http://xml.apache.org).

After downloading the Xerces package from the Apache XML Project Web site, you'll need to follow the installation instructions that go with the specific version you will be using. The examples in this book have been tested with Xerces version 1.4.0, but they should work with any other parser that supports the SAX 2.0 standard. The installation process for 1.4.0 amounts to no more than unzipping the package in a directory on the local hard drive using either the Java `jar` utility or the unzipping program of your choice (we use WinZip 8.0 on our Windows machines).

You will also need a copy of the Java 2 SDK to compile and execute your SAX application. The examples in this book were compiled using the JDK version 1.2.2 that is installed by default by the Borland JBuilder version 3.0 Java Integrated Development Environment (IDE).

> ### What Version Number Was That?
> Observant readers will notice that the version numbers for the products mentioned in this section are (in some cases) one or two major revision numbers out of date. This is actually a conscious decision (if a somewhat unconventional one). After reviewing the additional features and bug fixes that were available for newer versions of these products, the trouble spent upgrading seemed to outweigh the value that would be gained by using the more recent version. Since we may be using an older version of these tools than you are, they should be forward compatible with more recent versions. If we had used the most recent versions, the reverse would probably not have been true.

The examples in this book were developed using the Borland JBuilder Foundation 3.0 IDE. Although it was lacking in a few areas, it is an excellent value for the money (the lowest-end version of JBuilder is available for download from Borland at no cost). It can be obtained from the Borland Web site (www.borland.com). Although an IDE (such as JBuilder) can certainly make software development less tedious, there is no requirement that you use one. The examples in this book could just as well have been developed using a basic text editor and command-line tools.

Configuring Your Environment

The following instructions assume that you're using the Xerces parser. If you're not, you'll need to follow the instructions that come with your parser to add the `org.xml.sax` and `org.xml.sax.helpers` packages to your system's Java `CLASSPATH` environment variable.

If you are using Xerces, you should add the *xerces.jar* file in the root of the distribution directory to your system's `CLASSPATH` environment variable. This can be done through the System applet of the Control Panel for most versions of Windows. This will allow *java.exe* (the JDK Java runtime) to locate the SAX classes at runtime without your needing to supply their location on the command line.

Basic SAX Application Flow

Every SAX application needs to go through the same basic steps to process XML documents:

1. Obtain a reference to an object that implements the `XMLReader` interface.
2. Create an instance of an application-specific object that implements one or more of the various SAX *Handler (`DTDHandler`, `ContentHandler`, and `ErrorHandler`) interfaces.
3. Register the object instance with the `XMLReader` object so that it will receive notifications as XML parsing events occur.
4. Call the `XMLReader.parse()` method for each XML document that needs to be processed by the application. The object instance that was registered in step 3 will receive notifications progressively as the document is parsed.

It is up to the application-specific object (or objects) to track and process the information that is delivered via the various event notification methods that it implements. For example, an application that wants to strip markup out of an XML document and leave only the text content would need to implement the `ContentHandler` interface and implement its specific processing in the `characters()` event callback method. Even though the setup for every SAX application is almost identical, the data structures and algorithms that process the event notifications will vary widely depending on what the application is designed to do.

The XShell Sample Application

To illustrate the various features (and pitfalls) of SAX, we will be developing a complex example throughout the tutorial chapters. This example will implement a simple command-line shell interface (similar to command.com or cmd.exe) where the commands are encoded as XML elements. Keep in mind that our goal is not to build a full-featured command-line interpreter, but to show off the various features of SAX that make it ideally suited to interactive XML applications. Whenever a trade-off between application functionality and clarity of SAX usage needs to be made, SAX will always come out the winner.

⊕ The full source code for this application (as well as other goodies) is available at this book's Web site (www.bookofsax.com). Throughout the book, we will call attention to complementary information that can be found at the Web site through the use of the Web site icon.

For now, we will define the XShell application as a Java program that accepts zero or more XML document URIs from the command line, and parses each given document, and executes the recognized batch commands within. If no URIs are given on the command line, the XML commands will be read from the System.in InputStream. Input will be batched one line at a time, until a blank line is detected. The batch will then be parsed using the same algorithm that is used to parse documents read from URIs. Input will be terminated by an empty batch (no XML content).

Listing 2-1 shows the basic skeleton of the XShell class, including the main() method that acts as the command-line entry point.

Listing 2-1: The XShell class skeleton

```
public class XShell extends DefaultHandler {
...
  /**
   * Command line entry point.
   */
  public static void main(String[] args)
  {
    // create a new XShell session object and set the output to go to stdout
    XShell xbSession = new XShell(System.out);

    try {
      if (args.length > 0) {
        // user provided document URIs on the command line
        for (int i = 0; i < args.length; i++) {
          InputSource is = new InputSource(args[i]);

          xbSession.doBatch(is);
        }
      } else {
        // no command line argument provided, read from stdin
```

X implementation is the XMLReader interface.

- Controlling how the underlying XML parser will operate (validating versus nonvalidating, and so on).
- Enabling or disabling specific SAX features (such as namespace processing).
- Registering object instances to receive XML parsing notifications (via the handler interfaces).
- Initiating the parsing process on a specific document URI or input source (via the parse() methods).

Before an application can use the XMLReader interface, it must first obtain a reference to an object that implements it. How the XMLReader interface is supported is a decision that is left up to the implementers of the particular SAX distribution. For instance, the Xerces package supplies a class called org.apache.xerces.parsers.SAXParser that implements the XMLReader interface. Any application that uses Xerces to provide SAX support can simply create a new instance of the SAXParser class and use it immediately.

The SAX specification does define a special helper class (from the org.xml.sax.helpers package) called XMLReaderFactory that is intended to act as a class factory for XMLReader instances. It has two static methods for creating a new XMLReader object instance:

```
XMLReaderFactory.createXMLReader();
XMLReaderFactory.createXMLReader(String className);
```

Of course, both of these methods require that the class name of the class that supports the XMLReader interface be known in advance. Since all that these methods do is use the class name given to create a new object instance, this helper class is, at best, of questionable utility.

A Complete SAX Application **9**

The XShell constructor obtains a reference to an XMLReader class instance by directly instantiating the SAXParser class from the Xerces package inside its constructor:

```
m_xrShell = (XMLReader)new org.apache.xerces.parsers.SAXParser();
```

Now that we have an XMLReader object instance to work with, we can register our class to receive XML parse callback notifications.

Implementing the ContentHandler Interface

The most interesting interface in the SAX package, from the application author's standpoint, is the ContentHandler interface. This interface provides notification of:

- documents starting and ending
- element start and end tags recognized
- character data found
- namespace prefixes going in and out of scope
- processing instructions found
- ignorable whitespace read

For normal XML applications, XML element and text content are the most important types of data that will be processed. That is why almost every SAX application will want to implement the ContentHandler interface and register to receive its notifications. It is a rather large interface, however, and many applications will neither need nor want to receive all of the notifications it offers.

To save application writers from having to implement half a dozen methods that they have no intention of using, SAX provides the DefaultHandler class. This class provides a default empty implementation of all of the callback interfaces supported by SAX 2.0, including the EntityResolver, DTDHandler, ContentHandler, and ErrorHandler interfaces. By deriving your SAX application object from DefaultHandler, you can immediately register to receive any of the callback notifications without writing empty methods to satisfy the various Java interface specifications. The XShell class is derived from the DefaultHandler class directly, like this:

```
public class XShell extends DefaultHandler { . . .
```

Then, in the XShell constructor, it registers itself to receive ContentHandler notifications using the XMLReader object instance it just created:

```
m_xrShell = (XMLReader)new org.apache.xerces.parsers.SAXParser();
m_xrShell.setContentHandler(this);
```

Now that the XShell instance is ready to receive content notifications, the application is ready to parse an XML document.

Parsing and Processing

Whether the XML command-line instructions come from an external document or from System.in, both cases end up calling the doBatch() method:

```
/**
 * Given an InputSource object, parses and executes the commands given.
 */
public void doBatch(InputSource is) throws IOException
{
  try {
    m_xrShell.parse(is);
  } catch (SAXException se) {
    // we just eat it, we already notified the user
  }
}
```

This very simple method calls the parse() method of the XMLReader instance that was created by the XShell constructor. The parse() method does not return until either the document referenced by the passed InputSource has been completely parsed, or a fatal parsing error occurs. In either case, no indication of the result is returned to the application by the parse() method. Error handling is covered thoroughly in Chapter 3.

🌐 After the XML parser has been invoked, the SAX interface begins calling notification methods for the object instances that were registered by the set*Handler() methods of the XMLReader interface. To help you understand the sequence in which notifications are sent by SAX, we've developed a simple utility called com.bookofsax.SAXAnimate that prints the interface and method names of every SAX callback for a given XML document. Given the following simple XML document:

```
<?xml version="1.0" encoding="UTF-8"?>
<root>
  <element xmlns="http://namespaces.bookofsax.com/null">
    <message>Hello, SAX.</message>
  </element>
</root>
```

The SAXAnimate utility generates the following list of notification calls:

```
ContentHandler.setDocumentLocator()
ContentHandler.startDocument()
ContentHandler.startElement()
ContentHandler.characters()
ContentHandler.startPrefixMapping()
ContentHandler.startElement()
ContentHandler.characters()
ContentHandler.startElement()
ContentHandler.characters()
ContentHandler.endElement()
ContentHandler.characters()
ContentHandler.endElement()
ContentHandler.endPrefixMapping()
ContentHandler.characters()
ContentHandler.endElement()
ContentHandler.endDocument()
```

By reading through this trace and matching it to the content in the XML document, you should be able to more easily understand how SAX sequences notifications to ensure that your application has an accurate picture of the XML document at any point in time. For instance, the namespace prefix mapping notification is sent *before* the corresponding element declaration, since elements and attributes can use a namespace as soon as it is declared.

Now, given this understanding, how will the XShell application process notifications to ensure that it will have the appropriate information available when it needs it? How much (or how little) information needs to be preserved from the data that is delivered by the ContentHandler interface?

To answer this question, we will need to define exactly how the XShell will function. The pseudo-code for the application is:

```
while more-documents-to-process or more-interactive-commands
   while more-child-elements-of-root
     read-complete-child-element
     if element-name-recognized then
        execute-named-command
     end if
   end while
end while
```

It's a bit simplistic, but that's basically all that most command-line interpreters do. The additional complication that we will face is that the read-complete-child-element step is not as straightforward as it seems. As we can see from the output of the SAXAnimate class, the information we need will be passed to us a little bit at a time. It is our job to determine how much and which of the given content we are to keep, and how to store it.

The hierarchical nature of XML data makes the stack a very popular structure for storing arbitrary levels of document information. The simplest possible notification sequence for a simple leaf element that contains some character data is:

```
ContentHandler.startElement()
ContentHandler.characters()
ContentHandler.endElement()
```

Based on this, our program will need to preserve the data that is passed in by the startElement() and characters() notifications, and act on that data when the corresponding endElement() notification is received. The method signature for the startElement() notification is:

```
public void startElement(java.lang.String namespaceURI,
                         java.lang.String localName,
                         java.lang.String qName,
                         Attributes atts)
```

Of all of this information, the only part we really need to preserve are the attributes. The endElement() method will be given the same namespaceURI, localName, and qName parameters when the element close tag is parsed (or immediately, if it is an empty element). Since elements can be nested, we will need to use the java.util.Stack object to keep track of the attributes that are valid for the element we are currently processing. As long as the attributes are pushed on the stack in the startElement() method and popped off in the endElement() method, the stack is always guaranteed to be accurate. To support this, we will need to add two members to the XShell class and write a startElement() method that looks like this:

```
/**
 * Attribute stack.
 */
Stack m_stAtts = new Stack();

/**
 * Accumulated character data on stack.
 */
Stack m_stChars = new Stack();
...
/**
 * Sets up attribute and character data stacks for processing later by the
 * endElement() method.
 */
```

(continued on next page)

```
public void startElement(java.lang.String namespaceURI,
    java.lang.String localName, java.lang.String qName, Attributes atts)
{
  // save the attributes for this element, for use later in endElement()
  m_stAtts.push(new AttributesImpl(atts));

  // create new, empty string buffer to capture character data
  m_stChars.push(new StringBuffer());
}
```

Look at the `startElement()` method; the first push operation actually pushes a new `AttributesImpl` object rather than a reference to the object that was passed in as a parameter. The object that was passed in is not guaranteed to be valid outside the scope of the `startElement()` method. This is generally true for any of the data that is passed to a SAX notification method. Anything that you need to preserve will need to be copied to a new object instance that your program controls. In this case, the `AttributesImpl` object is an object provided in the `org.sax.helpers` package. It implements a copy constructor that can be used to duplicate the contents of an object that supports the `Attributes` interface for later use.

The second push operation provides a new, empty Java `StringBuffer` object instance that will be used to capture any character data this element might contain. Once again, since elements can be nested, a new `StringBuffer` instance must be created for every element open tag. The `characters()` notification method appends any character data it receives to the `StringBuffer` on the top of the `m_stChars` stack.

```
/**
 * Appends new characters to the StringBuffer on top of the
 * character data stack.
 */
public void characters(char[] ch, int start, int length)
{
  ((StringBuffer)m_stChars.peek()).append(ch, start, length);
}
```

Finally, when the `endElement()` notification is received, we can examine the element name and decide what action, if any, to take. At this point, we are saving *all* of the element content for *every* element we encounter. We are going on the assumption that this content is valid and will be used later. One possible future optimization would be to set flags and ignore attribute and character data for unrecognized elements, but since we will be expanding our application to incorporate additional commands in the future, we will capture everything now and deal with it later. The `endElement()` notification method looks like this:

```java
/**
 * Pops saved data off of stack and executes the given
 * command.
 */
public void endElement(String namespaceURI, String localName, String qName)
{
  Attributes atts = (Attributes)m_stAtts.pop();
  String strCharData = ((StringBuffer)m_stChars.pop()).toString();

  // dispatch the message, based on the localName (XML tag name)
  if (localName.equals("echo")) {
    doEcho(atts, strCharData);
  } else if (localName.equals("dir")) {
    doDir(atts, strCharData);
  } else if (localName.equals("cd")) {
    doCD(atts, strCharData);
  }
}
```

🌐 This method recognizes the three command elements that the shell currently supports (echo, dir, and cd) and dispatches the cached attribute and character data to the worker methods that implement the actual shell logic. In the interest of space, we will not show the implementations of all three of the doEcho(), doDir(), and doCD() methods here. They are available (along with the rest of the application source code) on this book's Web site. We will show the implementation of the doCD() method because it does show the basic usage of the Attributes interface.

Accessing Attribute Values Using the Attributes Interface

The attributes interface provides access to the XML attributes that are included (either directly or through implicit values in the DTD) in an element's open tag. There are two basic methods for accessing attribute values: by name or by index.

It is illegal to have two attributes on a single element with the same qualified name (meaning that the namespace URIs and local parts match). Therefore, retrieving attribute values by name is very common when processing XML documents. The Attributes interface provides the getType() method for getting an attribute's type (CDATA, ID, IDREF, and so on), and the getValue() method for getting an attribute's string value. Both methods can use either the attribute's qualified name or its namespace URI and local name. Since no guarantees are made that attribute values will be made available in the same order in which they appear in the element tag, referencing by name is the only safe way to ensure that your application is reading the attribute you intend.

When enumerating attributes, however, the `getLength()`, `getQName()`, and `getValue()` methods can be used to get information about all of the attributes that are available for a particular element. The `Attributes` interface is not completely symmetric, and certain methods are accessible only using an attribute's index (such as the `getURI()` method for retrieving the attribute's namespace URI). The `getIndex()` methods are provided to perform a reverse lookup from an attribute's qualified name or namespace/local part to its corresponding index number.

Many of these methods are not particularly useful until an application becomes namespace aware. Information about how SAX deals with namespaces and qualified names is thoroughly covered in Chapter 6, "Namespace Support."

Wrapping Up

We have now built a completely functional SAX application. It parses documents, handles notification events, and even does (some) useful work. Download the application (complete with source code) from this book's Web site and try the test script you find there. Try running it in interactive mode and enter some invalid XML. You'll probably find that the default error handling leaves something to be desired. We'll tackle that next, in Chapter 3, "Handling Errors."

3

HANDLING ERRORS

In the previous chapter, we built a complete, functioning SAX application. This chapter explains how SAX handles various types of errors, and how to incorporate error handling into your application.

This chapter discusses the following topics:

- Catching `SAXException`s.
- Implementing the `ErrorHandler` interface.
- Property and feature exceptions.
- Handling multiple errors.

Running the Application

Now that we've built our application, let's try putting it through its paces to see how it works. Start XShell in interactive mode by executing it without any command-line arguments:

> **NOTE** *Before running the application, you must make sure that the root output directory (XShell/classes if you're using JBuilder) of the compiled program is on the system classpath. This is set through the CLASSPATH environment variable when using Windows.*

```
java com.bookofsax.xshell.XShell
```

If everything has been compiled correctly and the Java CLASSPATH is correct, the application will enter a loop waiting for input from the standard input file. Let's try a simple dir command first (note the second carriage return that is required to submit the batch of commands to the interpreter):

```
<dir>↵
↵
```

It seems that, for some reason, the doDir() method was never called. Since our application doesn't yet have any error-handling facilities, the program itself can't give us much help. Implementing basic error handling is certainly a good first step toward finding out what went wrong.

Since standard Java programming practice is to throw an exception when something unexpected happens, let's look at the org.xml.sax package. We can see that SAX provides the definitions for four different exceptions. The one called SAXException directly extends the java.lang.Exception class. The other three exceptions are subclasses of the generic SAXException class. This arrangement offers a convenient way to provide a blanket catch statement that deals with any exceptions that come from SAX, without having to provide specialized processing for each different error.

Catching SAXExceptions

Let's take a closer look at the code in the XShell.doBatch() method. Since the XMLReader.parse() method is declared to throw a SAXException, we wrapped it in an empty try...catch block. That's not a very good practice, though, so let's modify it to at least print any exceptions we might be getting from the XML parser:

```
public void doBatch(InputSource is) throws IOException
{
  try {
    m_xrShell.parse(is);
  } catch (SAXException se) {
    System.err.println(se);
  }
}
```

Now let's recompile and try our sample command again:

```
java com.bookofsax.xshell.XShell↵
<dir>↵
↵
org.xml.sax.SAXParseException: The element type "dir" must be terminated by the
matching end-tag "</dir>".
```

NOTE *As a standard convention throughout Part I of this book, program output will always be shown in boldface type. This differentiates it from user input.*

That's much better. XML doesn't allow unmatched open element tags. When the XML parser notified the SAX implementation about this well-formedness error, SAX threw a `SAXParseException` back to our application. Let's try the command again, this time with a valid XML fragment:

```
<dir/>↵
↵
<dir path="E:\TheBookOfSAX\BOS-CH3\classes">
    <file name="com" size="0"/>
    <file name="dependency cache" size="0"/>
</dir>
```

This time the XML command batch was parsed correctly, and the `endElement()` notification method was able to successfully call the `doDir()` method. Catching the `SAXException` thrown from the `parse()` method is certainly better than no error handling at all, but SAX provides a mechanism for receiving error notifications directly during parsing.

The ErrorHandler Interface

The `ErrorHandler` interface is another callback interface provided by SAX that can be implemented by an application to receive information about parsing problems as they occur. The `ErrorHandler` interface specifies three notification functions to be implemented by a client application:

warning() Called for abnormal events that are not errors or fatal errors.

error() Called when the XML parser detects a recoverable error. For instance, a validating parser would throw this error when a well-formed XML document violates the structural rules provided in its DTD.

fatalError() Called when a non-recoverable error is recognized. Non-recoverable errors are generally violations of XML well-formedness rules (for instance, forgetting to terminate an element open tag).

The process for registering to receive notifications on the `ErrorHandler` interface is similar to that for registering the `ContentHandler` interface. First, an object that implements the `ErrorHandler` interface must be instantiated. The new instance then needs to be passed to the `XMLReader.setErrorHandler()` method so that the SAX parser will be aware of its existence.

For the XShell application, implementing the `ErrorHandler` interface is not a problem. The `DefaultHandler` helper class already implements `ErrorHandler` and provides default, do-nothing implementations of the three notification methods. Since the XShell class extends `DefaultHandler`, we can just register with the `setErrorHandler()` method and implement the callback methods we are interested in at the time. To register, we add a call to `setErrorHandler()` to the XShell constructor:

```
public XShell(PrintStream ps)
{
  m_xrShell = (XMLReader)new org.apache.xerces.parsers.SAXParser();
  m_xrShell.setContentHandler(this);
  m_xrShell.setErrorHandler(this);
  m_psStdout = ps;
}
```

We will also want to implement one of the notification methods as well. Since none of the XML we have been parsing until now has been valid (meaning that it has a DTD or XML schema associated with it), the only type of error we will be receiving is the fatal well-formedness error. So let's implement the `fatalError()` notification:

```
public void fatalError(SAXParseException exception) throws SAXException
{
  System.err.println("fatal error: line " + exception.getLineNumber()
      + ": column " + exception.getColumnNumber() + ": "
      + exception.getMessage());
}
```

This will print a slightly more informative error message that includes the line and column number from the input document, as well as the exception message text. Let's try it by duplicating the error we had at the beginning of the chapter:

```
E:\TheBookOfSAX\BOS-CH3\classes>java com.bookofsax.xshell.XShell↵
<dir>↵
↵
fatal error: : line 2: column 10: The element type "dir" must be
terminated by the matching end-tag "</dir>".
org.xml.sax.SAXException: Stopping after fatal error: The element
type "dir" must be terminated by the matching end-tag "</dir>".
```

It looks like our `fatalError()` method was called correctly, but that didn't stop SAX from throwing a `SAXException` back to the `XMLReader.parse()` method. Since our `doBatch()` method dumps any `SAXExceptions` it sees, we end up with two error messages instead of one. The simplest solution is to remove the output code from the `catch()` block of the `doBatch()` method and rely on our notification messages to provide any required feedback to the user.

Dealing with a fatal error is relatively straightforward. Since parsing cannot continue, the only valid option is to abort processing of the offending document. But the strategy for dealing with nonfatal errors isn't as obvious. A common type of nonfatal error is a validity error that is generated when an XML document contains content that doesn't match its DTD.

SAX Property and Feature Exceptions

By default, the Xerces SAX parser is nonvalidating. This means that even if a document contains a DTD, the parser doesn't check the document contents to make sure that they conform to its rules. Enabling validation requires the use of the `XMLReader.setFeature()` method. SAX offers this method to provide different sets of features in an extensible way. To enable validation, we'll add the following line to the `XShell` object constructor:

```
m_xrShell.setFeature("http://xml.org/sax/features/validation", true);
```

But checking the API documentation for `XMLReader.setFeature()` shows that the method may throw two different SAX-specific exceptions:

SAXNotRecognizedException   The SAX implementation doesn't recognize the feature name given.

SAXNotSupportedException   Although the feature name was recognized, this particular SAX implementation doesn't support it.

⊕ Before we can compile the application, we need to add a `try...catch` block that will catch these exceptions (or the blanket `SAXException`, from which both exceptions are derived). Once those changes have been made and the program has been successfully compiled, it should be possible to validate incoming documents using a DTD. To test this, we'll create a simple DTD (shown in Listing 3-1) called *XShellScript.dtd* that describes the structure of a valid XShell script.

Listing 3-1: XShellScript.dtd

```
<!ELEMENT batch (cd | echo | dir)+>

<!ELEMENT cd EMPTY>
<!ATTLIST cd
  path  CDATA #IMPLIED
>

<!ELEMENT echo (#PCDATA)>

<!ELEMENT dir EMPTY>
<!ATTLIST dir
  path  CDATA #IMPLIED
>
```

To use the new DTD, we'll need to create a test document that includes a <!DOCTYPE> declaration. A simple test script is shown in Listing 3-2, which is available on this book's Web site as *XShellTestScript.xml*.

Listing 3-2: XShellTestScript.xml

```
<?xml version="1.0" encoding="UTF-8"?>
<!DOCTYPE batch SYSTEM "XShellScript.dtd">
<batch>
  <cd path="/"/>
  <dir/>
  <bogus/>
  <echo>Done processing!</echo>
</batch>
```

Handling Multiple Errors

Note that the next-to-the-last element in the top-level `<batch>` element is not valid, according to the DTD. This will cause the SAX parser to call the nonfatal `error()` notification method, to report the invalid content. To make sure that this happens, we will provide our own `error()` method implementation for the XShell object:

```java
public void error(SAXParseException exception) throws SAXException
{
  System.err.println("error: line " + exception.getLineNumber()
      + ": column " + exception.getColumnNumber() + ": "
      + exception.getMessage());
}
```

After recompiling, let's run XShell in noninteractive mode, by passing in the name of the test script on the command line:

```
E:\TheBookOfSAX\BOS-CH3\classes>java com.bookofsax.xshell.XShell
    ..\XShellTestScript.xml ↵
<dir path="/">
    <file name="TheBookOfSAX" size="0"/>
</dir>
error: line 6: column 11: Element type "bogus" must be declared.
Done processing!
error: line 8: column 10: The content of element type "batch" must match
    "(cd|echo|dir)+".
```

Note that the SAX parser notified our application of two different validity errors and continued parsing the rest of the document.

Moving On

Now that our application is better able to deal with errors both internal and external, it is time to start thinking about the different ways in which the user should be able to submit scripts for execution. The application already supports the entry of scripts by using standard input and execution of scripts from files. To go beyond these basic mechanisms, we need to explore the way in which SAX uses the `InputSource` class to provide character data to the XML parser.

4

WORKING WITH INPUTSOURCES

More sophisticated applications may want more control over the source of the XML content that will be parsed.
This chapter discusses the following topics:

- Basic `InputSource` usage.
- Public and system IDs.
- Character encoding issues.
- Extending the `InputSource` class.
- Resolving external entities.
- Using the `Locator` interface.

InputSource Overview

Although the file and stream handling facilities of Java are extremely rich and flexible, a simple `InputStream` or `Reader` class doesn't provide enough information to allow an XML parser to do its job. To provide this additional information, the authors of SAX created the `InputSource` object.

An InputSource object instance can be thought of as a wrapper for an open Java `Stream` or `Reader` object. In addition to providing the parser with a source for character input, it also allows the user to provide additional information about the input, such as:

- The public ID
- The system ID
- The underlying character encoding (for byte streams)

The additional information in an `InputSource` object allows the parser to produce more accurate error messages, perform correct character translations, and, when possible, automatically retrieve content that is identified by a URL (system ID) or through a directory of well-known documents (using a public ID).

Also, having the system and/or public ID available at parse time allows SAX to throw more meaningful error messages when parsing problems occur. If only the Java file I/O object were available, it wouldn't always be possible to identify the original source of the characters being read (due to the frequently used technique of chaining streams and readers together).

Another important function is extensibility. SAX application developers may extend the `InputSource` class directly. This is useful when the source of the characters to be parsed is nonstandard, such as a TCP/IP socket. We will be looking at that functionality later in this chapter.

Using the InputSource Class

The two primary uses of `InputSource` objects in the SAX framework are:

- As an argument to the `parse()` method of the `XMLReader` class.
- As a return value from a custom `EntityResolver` class.

It is not always necessary to create an `InputSource` object. If the document your application needs to parse can be read using an `http:` or `file:` URL, there is an `XMLReader.parse()` method that can be called with the system ID as a string. But if you want to provide a custom value for the system ID, a public ID, or a specific character encoding, you'll need to create an `InputSource` object manually.

There are several ways to construct a new `InputSource` object, depending on what type of underlying Java stream you will be using. The four available constructors are:

InputSource()
This default, no-argument constructor cannot be used until a byte stream, character stream, or system ID is provided using one of the set*() methods.

InputSource (java.io.InputStream byteStream)
This constructor indicates that the underlying source of data is a raw byte stream. The parser will attempt to identify the character encoding if none is given using the setEncoding() method.

InputSource (java.io.Reader characterStream)
Since the Java Reader interface already exposes incoming data as Unicode characters, setting character encoding is not necessary when using this constructor.

InputSource (java.lang.String systemId)
The new InputSource object will attempt to open a connection to the URI given and fetch its content.

Depending on which of these options is selected, you should also provide your new InputSource object with a public ID, a system ID, or possibly both.

Public and System IDs

The difference between public and system IDs is one of the least clear portions of the XML specification. So, unsurprisingly, it is one of the least understood aspects of XML parsing tools (like SAX).

The system ID is the better understood of the two. A system ID is nothing more or less than a Uniform Resource Identifier (as defined in IETF RFC 2396). Although the full URI specification is much more comprehensive, the most common type of URI is the lowly URL (Uniform Resource Locator).

A URL is composed of a protocol (such as http:) and a protocol-specific identifier. For HTTP URLs, this is usually a server name (or IP) followed by a path to a specific document on the server. Another popular URL protocol is the file: protocol, which can be used to access documents stored on a computer's local storage devices (hard drives, CDs, floppy drives, and so on).

A public ID is less crisp and well defined. The primary purpose of a public ID is to allow well-known documents to be distributed throughout the Internet without requiring every user to retrieve them from the same location. For example, the public ID for HTML 4.0 is:

```
-//W3C//DTD HTML 4.0 Transitional//EN
```

Any HTML document that includes this public ID is testifying that it conforms to the DTD that is associated with this public ID on the W3C Web site (or any other mirrored location). The major problem with public IDs is that no organization seems to have the global authority to manage them. This can lead to confusion when different companies or organizations declare public IDs that match.

In operation, an XML parser is supposed to look up the public ID in some sort of directory and map it to a concrete URI that can actually be read. In reality, most documents provide both the public ID and the system ID for a given document because some parsers don't perform this function.

Character Encoding

Character encoding is one of those things that is completely invisible to programmers most of the time. Basically, character encoding is the mapping between the binary numbers stored in a text document and the actual human characters they represent. Most modern operating systems support basic ASCII encoding (the characters from 0 to 127 that represent the Latin alphabet, numbers, some diacritics, and punctuation). Since the UTF-8 encoding of Unicode is byte-for-byte compatible with ASCII, authoring XML documents that are portable between different systems is usually not a big problem.

But, particularly when dealing with legacy data and older platforms, character encoding can become a significant issue. Many text files were created using Microsoft's special character set (Cp1252, also known as Windows ANSI), which included special box-drawing characters and other symbols in addition to the basic ASCII characters. Attempting to directly include this type of content can cause confusion if the XML parser is not warned in advance. One way to ensure that the parser correctly identifies the character set of a given file is to open the file manually using a Java `Reader` class and specify the encoding name directly. The resulting reader can then be used to construct an `InputSource` object that can be parsed. The following code fragment shows how a document that was saved in Cp1252 could be opened and parsed:

```
InputStreamReader isr = new InputStreamReader(
    new FileInputStream(args[i]), "Cp1252");
InputSource is = new InputSource(isr);
```

In this case, Java itself is supporting the Cp1252 character set, and the XML parser simply reads Unicode characters that have already been translated. Another way to support alternate character sets is through the use of the XML declaration or text declaration encoding attribute:

```
<?xml version="1.0" encoding="ISO-8859-1"?>
```

The XML parser would know that the rest of the document had been encoded using the Latin-1 character set, and could convert it to Unicode appropriately.

Custom Entity Resolvers

External entities are XML's equivalent of the #include C/C++ preprocessor directive. It is possible to construct an XML document that is contained in multiple separate physical files by declaring and referencing external entities, like so:

```xml
<!DOCTYPE batch SYSTEM "XShellScript.dtd" [
<!ENTITY ext-command SYSTEM "ext-command.xml">
]>
<batch>
  &ext-command;
  <echo>Done processing!</echo>
</batch>
```

This causes the contents of the file *ext-command.xml* to be included and parsed as part of the primary script. The `<!ENTITY>` declaration specifies where the external content is located, in this case by using the SYSTEM keyword and a URI. Most XML parsers support the `http:` and `file:` protocols when used in URLs, but through the SAX `EntityResolver` interface we can implement our own special protocols to make this feature even more useful.

For example, what if we could create our own special entity resolver that would allow us to include content from Java system properties? That would be a useful feature for a command-line interpreter. To do this, we'll define our own special URL syntax that we'll recognize in our `EntityResolver`:

```
x-env:java_system_property_name
```

Any time an entity is declared with a URL that uses the x-env: protocol, our handler will intercept it and return the corresponding Java property. To provide this functionality, we need to implement our own `entityResolver()` method that can recognize our "special" protocol and return system properties, yet otherwise provide the default entity resolution behavior:

```java
public InputSource resolveEntity(String publicId, String systemId)
{
```

Now, based on our requirement that we only process URIs that use our special protocol, we need to do some simple parsing of the system ID provided:

```java
if (systemId == null) {
  return null;
}

int iSep = systemId.indexOf(':');
if (iSep < 0) {
  return null;
}

String strProtocol = systemId.substring(0, iSep);
String strPath = systemId.substring(iSep+1);
```

Note that if no system ID was provided, or if the system ID doesn't seem to have a protocol, our `resolveEntity()` method returns `null`. This causes the SAX parser to go ahead and process the entity normally. Next, the method checks to see if the URL is for us, and if it is, processes it:

```
if (strProtocol.equalsIgnoreCase("x-env")) {
  StringReader sr = new StringReader(System.getProperty(strPath));
  return new InputSource(sr);
} else {
  return null;
}
```

Notice that once again we create a new `InputSource` object to contain our special `Reader` instance. Now, before our new method will be called, we need to modify the XShell constructor to call the `setEntityResolver()` method of our `XMLReader` object:

```
m_xrShell.setEntityResolver(this);
```

To test this new functionality, we need to create a simple test script that uses our new entity functionality:

```
<?xml version="1.0" encoding="UTF-8"?>
<!DOCTYPE batch SYSTEM "XShellScript.dtd" [
<!ENTITY vendor SYSTEM "x-env:java.vendor">
]>
<batch>
  <echo>The vendor of this Java implementation is &vendor;</echo>
</batch>
```

When this script is saved and executed with the newly compiled XShell application, we see the following output:

```
java com.bookofsax.xshell.XShell ..\XShellTestScript.xml
The vendor of this Java implementation is Sun Microsystems Inc.
```

Obviously this technique could be extended to provide all sorts of interesting entity types such as real-time stock quotes, et cetera.

The Locator Interface

One issue that comes up frequently when parsing a document is how to pinpoint a particular location in the source so that it can be communicated to the user. In the case of parsing errors, this information is provided through the SAXParseException class, but during normal parsing there hasn't been any way to retrieve the current location of an element start tag, a section of character data, and the like.

Although it is not mandatory, SAX implementers may choose to provide programs with a SAX Locator object instance that can be used to retrieve the current URL, line, and column number in the XML source document being parsed. To get this object instance, it is necessary to implement the setDocumentLocator() callback method of the ContentHandler interface:

```
Locator m_locCur = null;
. . .
public void setDocumentLocator(Locator locator)
{
   m_locCur = locator;
}
```

Now that we have saved the locator information, we can start reporting problems more accurately. For example, take the case where an invalid path attribute is given to the <dir> command. Currently, the code doesn't check for an error, and a null pointer exception is generated. It would be much friendlier if we could report the file, line, and column number of the offending script line to the user. To do this, we need to make the following changes to the doDir() method:

```
if (files == null) {
   if (m_locCur != null) {
      m_psStdout.println("invalid &lt;dir&gt; path: URL "
         + m_locCur.getSystemId() + ": line " +
         m_locCur.getLineNumber() + ": column "
         + m_locCur.getColumnNumber());
   }
} else {
   for (int i = 0; i < files.length; i++) {
      m_psStdout.println("   <file name=\"" + files[i].getName()
         + "\" size=\"" + files[i].length() + "\"/>");
   }
}
```

Now whenever anyone attempts to obtain a directory listing of an invalid path, they'll see an error message like this:

```
<dir path="bogus">
invalid &lt;dir&gt; path: URL
    file:///C:/BookOfSAX/BOS-CH4/XShellTestScript.xml: line 7: column 22
</dir>
```

This type of feature is excellent for reporting application-specific errors in an XML document that aren't validity errors, but still must be caught and corrected. It isn't possible to create an XML schema that will check to make sure that the value of an attribute maps to a physical directory on a given machine, but it is possible for the application itself to inform the user about the problem in a friendly fashion.

Moving On

Now that you've learned how to extend the power and reach of our SAX application beyond the world of simple file URLs, we can start exploring some of the more advanced features of XML itself. The next chapter introduces the `DTDHandler` interface and shows how it can be used to further extend the interaction between SAX and your particular application.

5

CAPTURING DTD INFORMATION

So far, we have not dealt directly with XML validation issues in our application. If a particular script included a DTD, we allowed the SAX parser to validate it and we reported any resulting errors. But SAX does provide access to additional information from the document type definition through the `DTDHandler` interface, as we'll see in this chapter.

This chapter discusses the following topics:

- The `DTDHandler` interface.
- Using unparsed entities.
- A typical application.
- Tracking `NOTATION` and `ENTITY` declarations.
- Processing entity references.

The DTDHandler Interface

As the `ContentHandler` interface makes data from the body of an XML document available to your application, the `DTDHandler` interface provides information about the contents of the `<!DOCTYPE>` declaration of the document.

In the case of the XShell application, it isn't necessary that every script obey a particular DTD. Any well-formed XML document is potentially a valid XShell script, although elements that are not recognized XShell commands won't be executed. But some of the more advanced features of XML require that a document include a document type definition.

XML DTDs may contain a great deal of information about the valid structure and contents of an instance document. But keeping with the central theme of SAX (simplicity), only the minimal required subset of DTD information is provided to SAX applications. The only two types of DTD structures that are made available through the `DTDHandler` interface are unparsed external entity and notation declarations.

Unparsed Entities

The use of unparsed external entities is one of least-understood parts of the XML specification. Even XML experts frequently have differences of opinion about how (and even if) they should be used within XML documents. The basic purpose of an unparsed external entity is to allow an XML document author to include a reference to the contents of an external file that is not necessarily XML content and should not be parsed by the parser.

The most frequent example that is given in XML literature is the case where an image (like a GIF or JPEG file) needs to be referenced from an XML document. And although this can be accomplished by using external unparsed entities, many naysayers point out that the overhead required to do this (declaring a corresponding `NOTATION`, `ENTITY` declaration, special `ENTITY` attribute, and so on) outweighs the benefits.

External unparsed entities are declared using the normal XML `<!ENTITY>` declaration syntax, with the addition of the special `NDATA` keyword to associate the entity with a notation name:

```
<!NOTATION text PUBLIC "text/plain">
. . .
<!ENTITY my_msg SYSTEM "my_msg.txt" NDATA text>
```

The preceding markup declares an external entity that is stored in a file named *my_msg.txt*, which is associated with a notation that has a public ID of `text/plain`.

NOTE *We should point out that encoding the MIME type as a public ID is not an official practice that is documented by any XML standard. That being said, the true public ID mechanism is poorly documented and poorly supported by most XML processing systems. Storing the MIME type seems to have a lot more value in many cases, particularly where the content will be delivered via a type-aware channel (such as an HTTP connection).*

A Typical Application

To illustrate how notations and unparsed entities work together, we'll extend the XShell application to allow <echo> elements to dump the contents of external files using unparsed entities.

🌐 Since any script that wants to use this feature will need to have a DTD (to declare the necessary notations and entities), this feature will be available only to scripts stored in external files (scripts entered using the command-line interpreter presently can't include a <!DOCTYPE> declaration). This will also require that we modify the *XShellScript.dtd* that we first developed in Chapter 3. To allow the <echo> element to include an unparsed entity reference, we'll need to add an <!ATTLIST> declaration to the DTD:

```
<!ATTLIST echo
  src   ENTITY  #IMPLIED
>
```

This declaration instructs the XML parser to verify that the value of any src attribute of an <echo> element corresponds to a valid external unparsed entity that is declared using the <!ENTITY> syntax previously given. Depending on the XML parser to perform this type of verification allows us to greatly simplify our own application logic. If misspellings and undeclared entity references are caught by the parser, our own application can assume that the data it receives will be consistent.

The first step we need to take within our own application is registering our object instance to receive DTD event notifications. To do this, we add a call to the setDTDHandler() method of the XMLReader interface to the XShell constructor:

```
  public XShell(PrintStream ps)
  {
...
    m_xrShell.setContentHandler(this);
    m_xrShell.setErrorHandler(this);
    m_xrShell.setEntityResolver(this);
    m_xrShell.setDTDHandler(this);
```

Now we need to provide our own implementations for the notationDecl() and unparsedEntityDecl() methods of the DTDHandler interface to track the information we'll need to process entity attributes later.

Tracking NOTATION and ENTITY Declarations

The method signature for the notationDecl() method isn't very complicated:

```
public void notationDecl(String name, String publicId, String systemId)
```

The three critical pieces of information provided are the notation's name, public ID, and system ID. To keep track of this information, we'll use a HashMap object from the java.util package:

```
HashMap m_hmNotations = new HashMap();
```

Since each HashMap entry will correspond to a single NOTATION declaration, we'll need to store the publicId and systemId values in some kind of container within the HashMap object. Although we could develop an inner class to contain them, simply storing two strings can be accomplished just as well by using a regular String array:

```
public final static int PUBID_INDEX = 0;
public final static int SYSID_INDEX = 1;
. . .
public void notationDecl(String name, String publicId, String systemId)
{
  String astrIds[] = new String[2];

  astrIds[PUBID_INDEX] = publicId;
  astrIds[SYSID_INDEX] = systemId;

  m_hmNotations.put(name, astrIds);
}
```

The code that tracks entity declarations is almost identical to the notationDecl() implementation. The only difference is that unparsed entities contain one additional piece of information—the name of the notation given using the NDATA keyword:

```
public final static int NOTATION_INDEX = 2;
. . .
public void unparsedEntityDecl(String name, String publicId,
    String systemId, String notationName)
{
  String astrIds[] = new String[3];
```

```
        astrIds[PUBID_INDEX] = publicId;
        astrIds[SYSID_INDEX] = systemId;
        astrIds[NOTATION_INDEX] = notationName;

        m_hmUPEntities.put(name, astrIds);
    }
```

With these two methods, we have a complete list of all notations and unparsed entity declarations for the document being parsed. Now we can implement the function that will use this information to incorporate the contents of the external entities into the XShell output stream.

Processing Entity References

Since SAX doesn't provide information about any `<!ELEMENT>` or `<!ATTLIST>` declarations from the source document type definition, our application has to assume that the DTD has properly declared the `src` attribute of the `<echo>` element as an `ENTITY` attribute. The `doEcho()` method now checks to see if a `src` attribute is present, and if it is, it is dumped by the `dumpEntity()` method:

```
  protected void doEcho(Attributes atts, String strCharData)
  {
    String strEntity = atts.getValue("src");

    if (strEntity != null) {
      dumpEntity(strEntity);
    }
...
```

The `dumpEntity()` method basically looks for the unparsed entity information that was stored by the `unparsedEntityDecl()` method, finds the associated notation information in the `m_hmNotations HashMap`, and then decides whether to dump the contents of the file (if its base MIME type is text) or just dump the entity information without attempting to open the file (which would be more appropriate for binary files).

Moving On

So far, we have played fairly fast and loose with the contents of our XShell scripts. If our application recognizes the local part of an element name, it processes the element. If the application doesn't recognize the local part of an element name, the element is ignored. But serious XML applications should be designed with the thought that they will someday be incorporated into other XML applications, which requires that some consideration be given to namespaces. The next chapter discusses namespaces and shows how they can be incorporated into a SAX application.

6

NAMESPACE SUPPORT

If you plan for your XML application to be distributed anywhere outside of your own system, it is important to give some consideration to how it will interact with other XML applications. The Namespaces in XML standard were developed to allow multiple XML applications to coexist peacefully in the same document. SAX 2.0 is completely namespace enabled.

This chapter discusses the following topics:

- Namespace terminology.
- Checking parser capabilities.
- Recognizing namespaces at parse time.
- Tracking namespace prefixes.

Namespace Terminology

Before discussing the specific API-level namespace support included in SAX 2.0, a brief recap of XML namespaces is in order. Namespaces themselves are not particularly complex, but some of the implications of changing namespaces can lead to complications further down the road.

Namespaces were not part of the original XML 1.0 recommendation. Although the recommendation hinted at what was to come later, there were no particular restrictions on how elements and attributes could be named. Names could be composed of letters, numbers, and certain punctuation characters, including the colon (:), which has special significance to a namespace-aware parser. Figure 6-1 shows the terminology for the various parts of an XML element that incorporates namespaces.

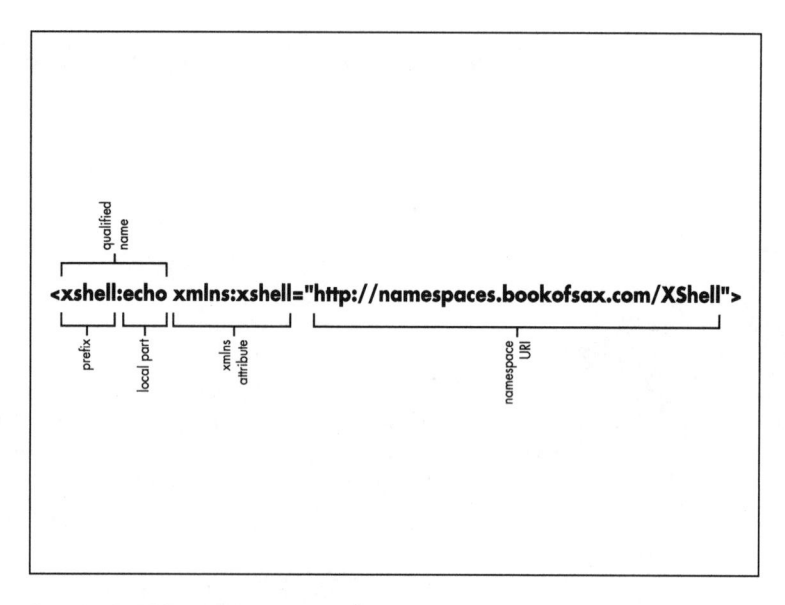

Figure 6-1: XML namespace terminology

The following list gives a brief description of each term shown in Figure 6-1:

qualified name   The entire XML name token, including the namespace prefix and the local part. Parsers that don't understand namespaces always return this name to their applications.

prefix   The namespace prefix that corresponds to a namespace URI that was declared using the special xmlns attribute. This is the portion of the qualified name to the left of the colon character.

local part   The undecorated local part of the XML tag name that uniquely identifies the tag within a particular namespace. This is the portion of the qualified name to the right of the colon character.

xmlns **attribute**	Used to map namespace URIs to namespace prefixes. Every prefix must have been declared using an xmlns attribute, either in the given element start tag, or in a parent element start tag.
namespace URI	The actual fully qualified URI for the namespace prefix being declared. When tag names are compared, the namespace URIs are used rather than a simple text comparison of the qualified tag names.

Although the figure shows an element name with a namespace prefix, attribute names may also have prefixes. If a particular element doesn't have a namespace prefix, it is considered to belong to the *default namespace*. The default namespace URI is set using an xmlns attribute alone, without a prefix name, like so:

```
<batch xmlns="http://namespaces.bookofsax.com/XShell">
. . .
```

After this declaration, any element without a prefix will belong to the given namespace URI. Oddly enough, attributes are never associated with any namespace unless they have an explicit namespace prefix. This isn't usually a problem, but if you depend on an attribute's belonging to a particular namespace, you need to make sure it is properly associated with a declared prefix.

In most cases, the namespace URI is a simple URL that points to a Web page or virtual directory on a Web server that is controlled by the author of the XML application. In this case, the well-known namespace URL for the XShell application will be:

```
http://namespaces.bookofsax.com/XShell
```

Assuming that all other XML application writers play by the rules, an XML element belonging to this namespace will always be a part of the XShell application. Since domain names are hierarchical and controlled by a central authority, as long as the authors continue to pay their registration bills, this URL will belong to them. This mechanism for assigning namespaces is as elegant as it is foolproof.

Checking Parser Capabilities

Before we modify the XShell application to recognize namespaces, we need to add some code to ensure that the underlying SAX parser will properly support them. Although it is not very common, it is conceivable that your application might be ported to a SAX parser that doesn't include namespace support. To ensure that namespaces are active and to detect whether they are supported, we will add another call to the XMLReader.setFeature() method to the XShell constructor:

```
public XShell(PrintStream ps)
{

  . . .

   try {
     m_xrShell.setFeature("http://xml.org/sax/features/namespaces", true);
     m_fUseNamespaces = true;
   } catch (SAXNotSupportedException snse) {
     System.err.println(snse);
   } catch (SAXNotRecognizedException snre) {
     System.err.println(snre);
   }
```

Note that if the `setFeature()` method doesn't throw an exception, the `m_fUseNamespaces` member is set to `true`. This value will be used later when we need to decide whether to check the namespace for a given element against the well-known namespace we have defined.

Now that we know whether or not we'll be using namespaces, we need to modify the application to only recognize commands that belong to the XShell namespace.

Recognizing Namespaces at Parse Time

The SAX parser has already been delivering namespace information to our application—we just haven't bothered to look at it. To add namespace recognition to our application, we'll start with the `endElement()` notification method. All of the real work of the application occurs when an element close tag is recognized and it matches one of the command names we've defined for the application.

Since we're already comparing the local part of the tag name to the various command names, we can further qualify a prospective command by bracketing the dispatch comparisons with another compare operation that checks to see whether the namespace matches (if namespaces are indeed available):

```
// check the namespace (if enabled)

if (!m_fUseNamespaces || namespaceURI.equals(XSHELL_NAMESPACE)) {
  // dispatch the message, based on the localName (XML tag name)
  if (localName.equals("echo")) {
    doEcho(atts, strCharData);
  } else if (localName.equals("dir")) {
    doDir(atts, strCharData);
  } else if (localName.equals("cd")) {
    doCD(atts, strCharData);
  } else if (localName.equals("shutdown")) {
    doShutdown(atts, strCharData);
  }
}
```

Now, if a tag doesn't belong to the XShell namespace, it is silently ignored, even if its name happens to match an XShell command name. Take the following test script:

```
<?xml version="1.0" encoding="UTF-8"?>
<!DOCTYPE batch SYSTEM "XShellScript.dtd">
<batch xmlns="http://namespaces.bookofsax.com/XShell"
    xmlns:other="http://namespaces.bookofsax.com/other">
  <echo>Namespace matches!</echo>
  <other:echo>This won't be displayed.</other:echo>
</batch>
```

When this script is run through the XShell application, the first message is echoed but the second message is not. The parser does complain about the presence of the `<other:echo>` element (which is not declared in the DTD), but the application doesn't interpret it as an XShell command.

Tracking Namespace Prefixes

This takes care of differentiating our application's namespaces from those of other applications, but what if we need to keep track of the different namespace prefixes that are currently in scope? There are several cases where this information is important. Many applications, such as XML schemas, dictate that prefixes be used within attribute values to distinguish one value from another.

Luckily, there is ample support within SAX to track namespace declarations as they go in and out of scope. There are two `ContentHandler` notification methods—`startPrefixMapping()` and `endPrefixMapping()`—that are called just before and just after namespace prefixes become valid. This is necessary because a namespace prefix may be used on the element name of the start tag that declares it.

One very helpful class that is provided as part of the `org.xml.sax.helpers` package is the `NamespaceSupport` class. It is intended for use by parser writers that need to track namespace declarations as they go in and out of scope (based on element nesting), but can also be used within your SAX application to track namespaces. It is based on a stack model, pushing and popping namespace contexts for each element open and close tag.

Unfortunately, the way that SAX notifies applications about namespace prefixes doesn't really correspond to the way in which the `NamespaceSupport` object tracks namespace declarations. The notification interface provides start and end notifications before and after the corresponding element begin and end tags are recognized. The `NamespaceSupport` object, however, expects a new context to be pushed when the open element tag is recognized, prefixes to be declared as the `xmlns` attributes are encountered, and then the context popped when the element is closed. Getting around this little problem requires that we make some assumptions about how notifications are sent by SAX.

Namespace Support **43**

We know that if an element open tag contains namespace prefix declarations, we will receive one or more startPrefixMapping() notifications prior to the startElement() notification. With this in mind, we can create a flag called m_fFirstNS that we initialize to true. The first method—either startPrefixMapping() or startElement()—that is called with this flag set to true will call the NamespaceSupport.pushContext() method. The endElement() method will then call the popContext() method to clean up the context stack.

⊕ The code for all of this can be found in the *XShell.java* source file, which also includes support for a new XShell command element, <dump>. This command takes a single attribute parameter, type, and is used to dump internal program structures for debugging (and illustrative) purposes. The <dump> element initially supports type="namespaces", which causes XShell to print all of the namespace prefixes and URIs that are currently in scope (in XML format).

Moving On

This chapter concludes the coverage of the core interfaces and classes that will be used by most SAX programmers. The next three chapters deal with advanced concepts, such as the XMLFilter mechanism, and the various support classes that are provided to help migrate old applications to new parsers, and vice versa.

7

ADVANCED SAX CONCEPTS

This chapter discusses the following topics:

- The XMLFilter interface.
- Extending XMLFilterImpl.
- Filter chaining.

The XMLFilter Interface

During the development of the SAX 2.0 specification, the designers noticed that one thing that SAX developers frequently needed to do was to implement filter classes that could intercept event notifications, perform some intermediate processing that might alter the data, and then pass the results on to the next event consumer in the chain. To reduce the effort involved in building these types of applications, SAX 2.0 includes an explicit mechanism for tapping into the event stream: the XMLFilter interface.

How filtering works in practice is fairly straightforward. Figure 7-1 shows the flow of notifications in an unfiltered SAX application:

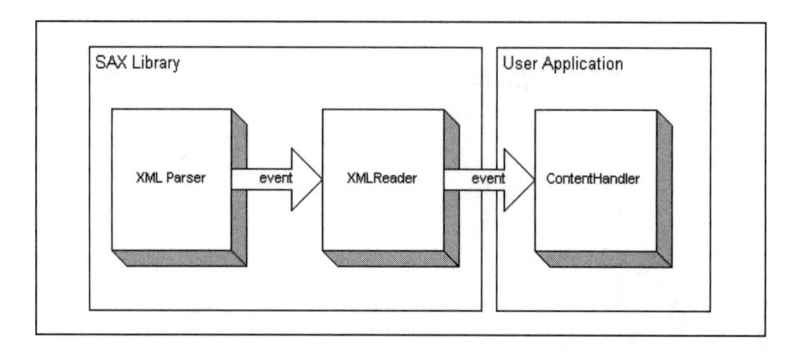

Figure 7-1: Normal SAX event notification flow

When a SAX filter is to be used, the object implementing the XMLFilter interface takes the place of the XMLReader object and intercepts notifications before they are passed to the registered ContentHandler, as shown in Figure 7-2:

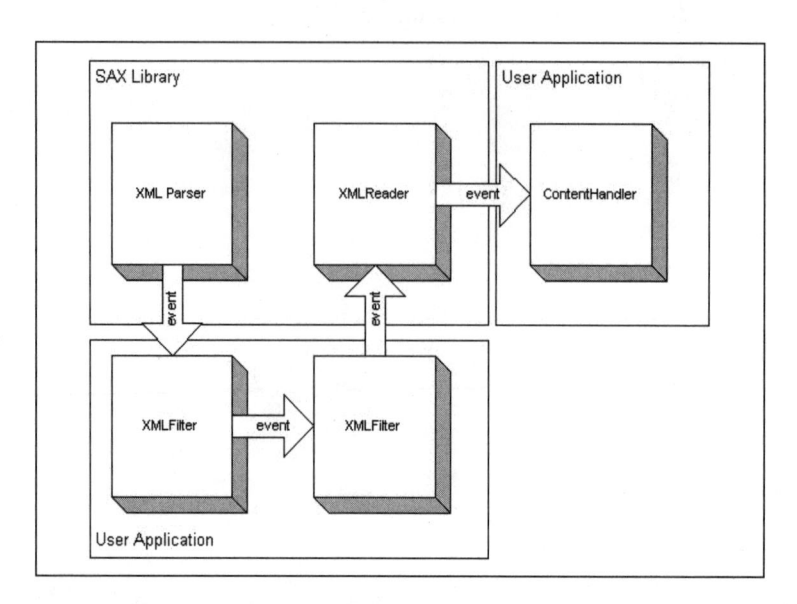

Figure 7-2: Filtered SAX event notification flow

46 Chapter 7

The `XMLFilter` interface provides access to all four of the SAX notification interfaces: `ContentHandler`, `DTDHandler`, `EntityResolver`, and `ErrorHandler`. To avoid having to write stubs for all of those notification methods, the `XMLFilterImpl` class (located in the `org.xml.sax.helpers` package) provides default implementations for all required methods. To implement your own filter, simply write your own class that extends `XMLFilterImpl` and override only the methods your application needs to process. To see how this works, we'll implement a filter that performs XML-public-ID-to-system-ID (URL) conversion.

Extending XMLFilter

There are several XML constructs (such as `<!DOCTYPE>` and `<!ENTITY>` declarations) that can accept an XML system ID (a URI), a public ID (well-known identifier), or both. In cases where a public ID is given, it would be nice to create a simple lookup mechanism that would link public IDs to their corresponding URLs. The purpose of this feature is to allow copies of well-known external entities (such as the DTD for XHTML) to be replicated across the Internet. Moving copies of these entities closer to the documents that use them not only relieves congestion on the Internet, but also speeds up parsing.

The new filter class is called `PubIDFilter`, and it extends the `XMLFilterImpl` helper class. The only SAX notification method it explicitly overrides is the `EntityResolver.resolveEntity()` method, which is shown here:

```
public InputSource resolveEntity(String publicId, String systemId)
    throws SAXException, IOException
{
  if (publicId != null && m_hmURLs.containsKey(publicId)) {
    return new InputSource((String)m_hmURLs.get(publicId));
  } else {
    return super.resolveEntity(publicId, systemId);
  }
}
```

All this filter does is check to see if a public ID was provided for this particular entity. If one was, it checks a `HashMap` object that has already been populated with a list of public-ID-to-URL mappings to see if a mapping exists for this particular public ID. If it does, it tries to open and return it. Otherwise, it passes the request to the next listener in the filter chain.

Of course, for this process to work, it's necessary to populate the hash map with a list of public-ID-to-URL mappings. And what could be more natural than to store that list in an XML document? To simplify this, `PubIDFilter` includes a simple inner class called `LoadMap`.

The `LoadMap` class instance accepts a `java.util.HashMap` object instance through its constructor. The caller then registers the `LoadMap` class instance with the `setContentHandler()` method of the an `XMLReader` instance. Then it calls the `XMLReader.parse()` method, and the `startElement()` method of the `LoadMap` class processes every <item> element in the target document that includes key and value attributes, like so:

```
<item key="-//Book of SAX//My Message//EN" value="my_msg.txt"/>
```

When a new `PubIDFilter` instance is created, the constructor loads the mapping from the XML document URL provided as the `strPath` argument:

```
PubIDFilter(String strPath)
{
  XMLReader xr = (XMLReader)new org.apache.xerces.parsers.SAXParser();

  LoadMap lm = new LoadMap(m_hmURLs);

  xr.setContentHandler(lm);
  try {
    xr.parse(strPath);
  } catch (SAXException se) {
    System.err.println(se);
  } catch (IOException ioe) {
    System.err.println(ioe);
  }
}
```

Filter Chaining

The SAX filter mechanism is designed to permit more than one filter to participate in the flow of events from a SAX parser. When chaining multiple filters together, the most important thing to consider is the impact of one filter on the operation of another. For example, the `PubIDFilter` class processes some resolveEntity() calls without passing them on to other filters in the chain. This could be a problem if another filter were expecting to receive all of the resolveEntity() notifications for a particular document.

Also, some filters modify the data that was passed to them before passing it on to other filters in the chain. Side effects caused by this behavior need to be thought about in advance before determining the order of filter registration.

Moving On

Now we have covered all of the features of SAX 2.0. The next chapter is targeted at developers who have already written SAX 1.0 applications and want to migrate them to a 2.0 parser.

8

MIGRATING SAX 1.0 APPLICATIONS

One of the most interesting decisions made by the designers of SAX 2.0 was to almost completely deprecate the interfaces and classes that made up SAX 1.0 and replace them. Then, to ease the burden on SAX 1.0 developers and parser writers, they provided a set of helper classes to adapt old applications and parsers to SAX 2.0.

This chapter discusses the following topics:

- Differences between SAX 1.0 and 2.0.
- Migration strategies.
- Using the XMLReaderAdapter class.
- Replacing deprecated code.
- Using old parsers.

Differences between SAX 1.0 and 2.0

When comparing the SAX 1.0 and SAX 2.0 APIs, the most obvious differences are a result of the inclusion of namespace support in 2.0. To add this support, the following classes and interfaces were deprecated:

- `Parser`
- `ParserFactory`
- `DocumentHandler`
- `HandlerBase`
- `AttributeList`
- `AttributeListImpl`

Since the `DocumentHandler` and `AttributeList` interfaces were two of the most important and frequently used pieces of a SAX 1.0 application, virtually every old application is affected by the introduction of SAX 2.0. To ease the transition by allowing old applications to be executed using newer parsers, the `XMLReaderAdapter` helper class is provided. This class is used to make an `XMLReader` object instance (a SAX 2.0 parser) behave like a SAX 1.0 `Parser` object.

The only other major addition to SAX 2.0 is the inclusion of the `XMLFilter` interface, which allows a SAX application author to encapsulate preprocessing functionality into self-contained filter classes that can be chained together at run time. Chapter 7, "Advanced SAX Concepts," discusses filters in depth.

Migration Strategies

If you've written or inherited an application that was developed using SAX 1.0, there are two basic approaches for migrating to SAX 2.0:

- Use the XMLReaderAdapter class to execute your 1.0 application using a newer 2.0 parser.
- Rewrite your application, replacing deprecated method, class, and interface references with the new 2.0 equivalents.

The first approach is definitely the quickest way to migrate an old application to a newer parser, but unless the application is being replaced, it is not a good long-term solution. The most obvious limitation is that the application will still not be namespace aware. Also, as newer versions of SAX are released, the temporary migration classes such as `XMLReaderAdapter` will, no doubt, themselves be deprecated.

The second approach is time consuming, but if the application will continue to be used, this approach will definitely be needed. Later in this chapter, you'll find a step-by-step procedure for making the necessary changes to a 1.0 application in order to make it 2.0 compliant.

⊕ To show how this process works, we will be working with a real SAX 1.0 application. Listing 8-1 gives partial source code for the OldSAXApp class. This application parses an XHTML document and outputs the contents of any <table> elements it encounters in a comma-separated value (CSV) format.

Listing 8-1: Listing for OldSAXApp class

```
. .
public class OldSAXApp extends HandlerBase
{
  public static void main(String[] args)
  {
    try {
      OldSAXApp osa = new OldSAXApp();

      Parser p = (Parser)new org.apache.xerces.parsers.SAXParser();

      p.setDocumentHandler(osa);

      if (args.length > 0) {
        for (int i = 0; i < args.length; i++) {
          p.parse(args[i]);
        }
      } else {
        InputSource is = new InputSource(System.in);

        p.parse(is);
      }
    } catch (Exception e) {
      System.err.println(e);
    }
  }
  StringBuffer m_sbCD = null;
  int m_cCols = 0;

  public void startElement(java.lang.String name, AttributeList atts)
  {
    if (name.equalsIgnoreCase("td")) {
      m_sbCD = new StringBuffer();
    }
  }


  public void characters(char[] ch, int start, int length)
  {
    if (m_sbCD != null) {
      m_sbCD.append(ch, start, length);
    }
```

(continued on next page)

```
      }

      public void endElement(String name)
      {
        if (name.equalsIgnoreCase("td")) {
          if (m_cCols++ > 0) {
            System.out.print(",");
          }


          System.out.print("\"" + m_sbCD + "\"");
          m_sbCD = null;
        } else if (name.equalsIgnoreCase("tr")) {
          System.out.println();
          m_cCols = 0;
        }
      }
    }
```

Next we'll see how to adapt a SAX 2.0 XMLReader parser to call our 1.0 DocumentHandler-based application.

The XMLReaderAdapter Class

Using the XMLReaderAdapter is very straightforward. The only modification that needs to be made to your application is to replace calls to the Parser interface with calls to an XMLReaderAdapter object that wraps an XMLReader instance. For the OldSAXApp class, the only method that needs to be modified to use the XMLReaderAdapter is the main() method:

```
  public static void main(String[] args)
  {
    try {
      OldSAXApp osa = new OldSAXApp();

      XMLReader xr = (XMLReader)new org.apache.xerces.parsers.SAXParser();

      XMLReaderAdapter xra = new XMLReaderAdapter(xr);

      xra.setDocumentHandler(osa);

      if (args.length > 0) {
        for (int i = 0; i < args.length; i++) {
          xra.parse(args[i]);
        }
      } else {
        InputSource is = new InputSource(System.in);
```

```
      xra.parse(is);
    }
  } catch (Exception e) {
    System.err.println(e);
  }
}
```

Now, instead of creating a SAX 1.0 `Parser` object, we create an `XMLReader` object. We then pass the reader to the constructor for the `XMLReaderAdapter` instance. Then we just need to replace all of the references to the `Parser` interface with references to the new reader adapter instance, and the application will continue to function as before.

But this is not a good long-term solution. The real answer requires that the old application be partially rewritten in order to use the SAX 2.0 objects and interfaces.

Replacing Deprecated Code

Several of the major classes and interfaces were deprecated between SAX versions 1.0 and 2.0. Table 8-1 shows the mapping between deprecated items and their replacements.

Deprecated SAX 1.0 Item	SAX 2.0 Equivalent
org.xml.sax package	
AttributeList	Attributes
DocumentHandler	ContentHandler
Parser	XMLReader
HandlerBase	DefaultHandler
org.xml.sax.helpers package	
AttributeListImpl	AttributesImpl
ParserFactory	XMLReaderFactory

To convert the `OldSAXApp` class to a SAX 2.0 application, we need to make the following changes:

- Change the class declaration to extend the `DefaultHandler` class instead of the `ContentHandler` class.
- Remove the `XMLReaderAdapter` support from the `main()` method, and call methods of the `XMLReader` class instead.
- Replace the call to `setDocumentHandler()` with `setContentHandler()`.
- Change the `startElement()` and `endElement()` notification method signatures to match the SAX 2.0 parameter lists; if parameter names change, the changes must be reflected in the code.

⊕ After making these few changes, we now have a working SAX 2.0 application. The resulting class is available at this book's Web site as *NewSAXApp.java*.

Although many of the class and interface names have changed, there are correspondences between the methods for the new classes and those for the old. For example, there is a getValue() method that accepts a single string argument for both the old AttributeList and the new Attributes interfaces. In some cases, a global search and replace may be enough to get an application running right away.

Using Old Parsers

Although this is an infrequent case, it is conceivable that at some time you will need to run a 2.0 application using a 1.0 parser. The process for doing this is almost identical to the process for using an XMLReaderAdapter to execute a 1.0 application with a 2.0 parser. For example, to run the NewSAXApp class using a Parser object, you would need to modify the main() function like so:

```java
public static void main(String[] args)
{
  try {
    NewSAXApp osa = new NewSAXApp();

    Parser p = (Parser)new org.apache.xerces.parsers.SAXParser();
    ParserAdapter pa = new ParserAdapter(p);

    pa.setContentHandler(osa);

    if (args.length > 0) {
      for (int i = 0; i < args.length; i++) {
        pa.parse(args[i]);
      }
    } else {
      InputSource is = new InputSource(System.in);

      pa.parse(is);
    }
  } catch (Exception e) {
    System.err.println(e);
  }
}
```

Moving On

The next chapter is the last chapter in the tutorial section of this book. It covers some of the issues that are important to individuals who develop SAX implementations.

9

PARSER SUPPORT

This chapter is intended for those of you who are interested in writing your own SAX parser, or just interested in knowing more about how a parser works. To better understand the problem ourselves, we wrote a complete (nonvalidating) SAX 2.0 parser, which we call picoSAX. The entire parser consists of around 1,000 lines of Java code in two classes. The compiled package is about 20K and would be suitable for use in a Java applet for client-side XML parsing. The rest of the chapter talks about picoSAX and the different issues we encountered while writing it.

This chapter discusses the following topics:

- Using the `DefaultHandler` class.
- Working with `InputSource`.
- SAX features and properties.
- Namespace tracking.
- The `LocatorImpl` class.
- Error handling.

> **A quick note about picoSAX**
>
> Although picoSAX is a complete implementation of SAX 2.0, it isn't necessarily the best possible implementation of SAX. Whenever a particular decision had to be made, the primary consideration was keeping the code as simple and clear as possible. For this reason, the overall performance of picoSAX is not bad, but it could certainly be better. Also, some shortcuts were taken with respect to the core XML 1.0 spec. For example, instead of explicitly coding all of the Unicode character classes (*BaseChar*, *CombiningChar*, and so on), it relies on the Java is `LetterOrDigit()` method. So while it seems to have correctly parsed all of the well-formed XML documents we've thrown at it (including the XML 1.0 Recommendation itself), don't be surprised if in some cases it parses something that isn't officially well-formed. Conversely, if you're parsing a Japanese language document, it might reject something that was perfectly legal. Since we're releasing the source code for the parser itself into the public domain, feel free to fix any problems you encounter and post your changes. But please send us a copy at picoSAX@bookofsax.com for our own edification.

Using the DefaultHandler Class

Just because we're writing a parser doesn't mean we can't take advantage of all of the resources provided to us by the generic SAX library. One of the issues we'll need to deal with right away is how to handle notification events that the user of the parser hasn't registered. For example, if the caller never sets a `DTDHandler` implementation, how can we make sure that a nonexistent object instance isn't called?

There are a couple of valid approaches. One is to set all of the members that keep track of registered handlers to `null` and then always check the reference before firing off any notification methods. This would work, and it would provide the best performance (unnecessary notifications are never sent), but it would complicate the code.

Another alternative is to make sure that the various handler references always contain a valid reference to an object that implements the associated interface. This approach has the benefit of allowing the parser to just call notification methods without the need to check the reference in advance. This is the approach we took, and since we needed to provide a valid object reference, we decided to use the `DefaultHandler` class to simplify our lives.

The class declaration for `picoSAX` looks like this:

```
public class picoSAX extends DefaultHandler implements XMLReader
```

Then the various handler reference members are initialized to point to the current object instance:

```
ContentHandler m_chUser = this;
DTDHandler m_dhUser = this;
EntityResolver m_erUser = this;
ErrorHandler m_ehUser = this;
```

This does require a little bit of additional logic within the various get and set handler methods, to check for references to this and translate them to null. For example, see how the getContentHandler() and setContentHandler() methods are implemented:

```
public ContentHandler getContentHandler()
{
   return m_chUser == this ? null : m_chUser;
}
...
public void setContentHandler(ContentHandler handler)
{
   m_chUser =  handler == null ? this : handler;
}
```

NOTE *For those of you who've read the SAX documentation, you're probably complaining right now that we're not complying with the documented behavior of* setContentHandler() *when it is passed a* null *pointer (according to the documentation, it is supposed to throw a* NullPointerException*). But obeying this particular rule creates an asymmetry in the API, since once you've set a particular handler, there is no way to unset it. Maybe the SAX authors will address this in their next release, or maybe they won't. If it truly bothers you, go ahead and change the code yourself!*

Now that we've allowed the user to set the various handler methods, we need to implement the parse() methods so the user will be able to actually do something.

Working with the InputSource Class

Although we covered the user's side of the InputSource class back in Chapter 4, there are some additional issues we need to be aware of as we write the low-level I/O routines for our parser. There are two different parse() methods that can be used to invoke the XMLReader on a given XML document:

```
public void parse(java.lang.String systemId)
public void parse(InputSource input)
```

Since it is possible to create a new InputSource using only a system ID, we'll implement the first method as a pass-through to the second, which will do the real work. Listing 9-1 gives the full source code for the parse() method.

Listing 9-1: Listing for the `picoSAX.parse()` method

```java
public void parse(InputSource input) throws java.io.IOException,
    org.xml.sax.SAXException
{
  try {
    m_tCur = new Tokenizer(input);

    m_chUser.setDocumentLocator(m_tCur.getLocator());

    m_chUser.startDocument();

    while (parseMarkup())
      ;

    int iChar = m_tCur.readChar();

    if (iChar != -1) {
        throw new SAXParseException("found '" + (char)iChar
            + "', expected valid markup", m_tCur.getLocator());
    }

    if (!m_fSawDocElement) {
      throw new SAXParseException("no document element found",
          m_tCur.getLocator());
    }

    m_chUser.endDocument();

    m_tCur = null;
  } catch (SAXParseException se) {
    m_ehUser.fatalError(se);
  }
}
```

The first thing this method does is create a new Tokenizer class instance using the InputSource instance given. The Tokenizer class is a helper class that handles the reading of characters from the input document, the maintenance of the current line and character position information, and the reading of lower-level lexical constructs such as XML names and quoted strings.

One of the issues that the Tokenizer class constructor has to deal with is which of the possible sources of character data available through the InputSource class should be used. Depending on how the caller configured the class, there may be a valid value for either the getCharacterStream() or getByteStream() InputSource method. It is also possible that neither one will be available, which means that the Tokenizer class constructor must try to open the document directly by using the system ID. The constructor code that handles this is shown in Listing 9-2.

Listing 9-2: The Tokenizer class constructor

```
public Tokenizer(InputSource is) throws SAXException, IOException
{
  m_isIn = is;

  if (m_isIn.getCharacterStream() != null) {
    m_brIn = new BufferedReader(m_isIn.getCharacterStream());
  } else if (m_isIn.getByteStream() != null) {
    m_brIn = new BufferedReader(new InputStreamReader(m_isIn.getByteStream()));
  } else {
    try {
      m_brIn = new BufferedReader(new java.io.FileReader(is.getSystemId()));
    } catch (FileNotFoundException fnfe) {
      try {
        URL url = new URL(is.getSystemId());

        m_brIn = new BufferedReader(new InputStreamReader(url.openStream()));
      } catch (Exception e) {
        throw new SAXException("unable to open document '"
            + is.getSystemId() + "'", e);
      }
    }
  }
  m_liCur.setLineNumber(1);
  m_liCur.setColumnNumber(0);
}
```

Notice the order of preference used to select the source of characters that will be set through the BufferedReader member (m_brIn):

- An open Reader instance.
- An open InputStream instance.
- A file found using the system ID as a file path.
- The document found at the URL given as the system ID.

Only after exhausting all of these possibilities does the Tokenizer constructor give up and throw an exception back to the picoSAX parser.

SAX Features and Properties

One of the best features of SAX is the extensibility mechanism provided by the feature and property methods of the `XMLReader` interface. In practice, the major difference between features and properties is that features can only be turned on or off, while properties may be set to contain arbitrary values including object references. Both the feature and the property interfaces accept a URL to uniquely identify the quantity to be set.

The SAX 2.0 specification provides a few recommended features and properties, but a minimal implementation only needs to support two features, both of them related to namespace support:

http://xml.org/sax/features/namespaces
Turns on and off namespace support within the parser. When this feature is set to false, namespace URIs are not reported, and only fully qualified element and attribute names are used.

http://xml.org/sax/features/namespace-prefixes
Determines whether or not the parser will report xmlns attributes to the application. This feature is ignored if the namespaces feature is set to false.

The `getFeature()` and `setFeature()` methods recognize these two feature names and throw the `SAXNotRecognized` exception for any other features that the user attempts to set. Unlike some parsers, picoSAX doesn't attempt to prevent users from modifying these features in the middle of parsing a document. But it also doesn't guarantee that the results will be correct, or even that it will continue to parse correctly.

Namespace Tracking

One of the most useful parts of the SAX 2.0 library for the aspiring parser writer is the `NamespaceSupport` class. Having this ready-made class available to parse qualified names, track namespace declarations, and resolve namespaces certainly saved us a few hours of utility-class writing.

NOTE *With this great time-saving class included as part of the base SAX 2.0 specification, we did find it interesting that there is no way to access it from the `XMLReader` interface. Apparently the authors of SAX 2.0 didn't want to dictate that SAX implementers had to use the `NamespaceSupport` class. But since resolving namespace prefixes that aren't part of element or attribute names is such a frequent occurrence, it seems that exposing the parser's own namespace state would save a lot of duplicated effort on the part of SAX application writers everywhere. Maybe SAX 3.0...*

These are the crucial methods that are needed to implement namespace support within the parser:

`pushContext()`	Pushes a new, empty namespace context onto the top of the context stack. All subsequent namespace declarations will belong to this context and can easily be removed by popping the current context. This method generally is executed for each new element start tag.
`popContext()`	Pops the current namespace context off the top of the namespace stack, exposing the previous context. This method generally is executed upon leaving a particular element scope, either due to parsing a close tag or leaving an empty element.
`declarePrefix()`	Associates a prefix with the given namespace URI. This method obscures any other declarations with the same prefix that belong to namespace contexts deeper in the namespace context stack.
`processName()`	A very useful method that parses a qualified element or attribute name using the current namespace context. This method returns the namespace URI, local part, and raw identifier for the qualified name given. It also takes into account the different default namespace behaviors between attribute and element names.
`getDeclaredPrefixes()`	Returns all of the prefixes that were declared in the current context. This is very important when it comes time to notify the application about namespaces going out of scope.

⊕ For more details on the exact usage of the `NamespaceSupport` class, see the `parseElement()` and `parseElementEnd()` methods in *picoSAX.java*.

The LocatorImpl Class

Another useful class that is part of the SAX 2.0 library is the `LocatorImpl` class. This helper class provides a concrete implementation of the SAX `Locator` interface and is an important part of a consistent error handling strategy within the parser.

In the picoSAX parser, the `Tokenizer` class owns the primary `LocatorImpl` instance used to track the parser's current position within the source document. It is a reference to this object instance that is passed to the SAX application using the `setDocumentLocator()` method. The current location is also included in any parse exceptions that are generated.

Within the `Tokenizer` class, the `readChar()` and `pushback()` methods are responsible for updating the current line and column positions. The basic approach is to increment the column position for every nonlinefeed (0x0a) character read or to reset the column position to zero and advance the current line number when a linefeed is read. One complication arises when the character that is pushed back is a linefeed character, which requires that the column position be reset to the last column position on the preceding line.

Error Handling

Handling parse-time errors for this particular parser is a simple task. The most frequent error condition occurs when the input document is not well-formed, which results in the parser's throwing a `SAXParseException`. A slightly less common scenario is when a physical problem (such as an `IOException`) occurs, in which case the parser either allows it to be thrown directly, or wraps it in a new `SAXException` class and throws it to the caller.

The only interruption in the normal Java exception handling procedure is the necessity to call the SAX `ErrorHandler` interface whenever an error occurs. Since the picoSAX parser is not a validating parser, the only type of error that can occur is a fatal error. The `try...catch` block in the `parse()` method (Listing 9-1) catches any `SAXParseExceptions` that are thrown and calls the `fatalError()` notification method of the registered `ErrorHandler` listener. Fortunately, the `fatalError()` method implementation of the `DefaultHandler` object rethrows the parse exception, which causes the exception to be thrown to the original caller of the `parse()` method.

Where to Go from Here

⊕ This concludes the tutorial portion of this book. The next part, "Part II: SAX 2.0 Reference," is a complete reference to all of the classes and interfaces that make up the SAX 2.0 core library. If you haven't done so already, you'll probably want to download a SAX implementation and start writing your own applications. If you want to get started quickly, download the picoSAX parser from this book's Web site (www.bookofsax.com/picoSAX) and try it out. Other implementations can be found by going to a good XML resource directory like the one at www.xml.com and looking for SAX parsers. The Xerces parser is a very full-featured parser that includes support for more advanced XML technologies, such as XML schemas. Xerces is located at the Apache XML Project Web site, at xml.apache.org.

10

SAX 2.0 API REFERENCE

SAX, the Simple API for XML, is a common set of interfaces and classes for parsing XML documents. Unlike the tree-based Document Object Model API, SAX is a streaming, event-based API. The two API's are complementary: the DOM is resource intensive but allows contextual access to the entire document at once; SAX, on the other hand, has a small and fairly static resource footprint but does not keep track of document content, leaving that task to the client application.

This chapter details the SAX 2.0 API. The deprecated SAX 1.0 interfaces and methods are documented in Chapter 11. The primary difference between the versions is the addition of namespace support. All new applications should be written using the SAX 2.0 interfaces and classes. If you must interface with a SAX 1.0 parser, or if you are upgrading to a SAX 2.0 parser and need to support SAX 1.0 interfaces, see the helper classes `XMLReaderAdapter` and `ParserAdapter`.

Both chapters are organized alphabetically by class or interface name. Within each class or interface, methods are organized first by constructor and then alphabetically.

Attributes Interface

By implementing the `Attributes` interface, an object may represent a list of attributes on a start tag. The most common use of an `Attributes` object is as an argument to the `ContentHandler.startElement()` event handler.

Individual attributes within the Attributes collection object may be accessed in three ways:

- By index
- By namespace URI and localname
- By qualified (prefixed) name

The order of attributes in the list is not guaranteed to match the order in the XML document.

Only attributes that have been specified or defaulted will be included in the attribute list; #IMPLIED attributes will not appear in the list.

Two features affecting the processing of attributes are http://xml.org/sax/features/namespaces and http://xml.org/sax/features/namespace-prefixes. If the namespaces feature is `false`, access by namespace-qualified names may not be available. If the feature `namespace-prefixes` is set to its default value of `false`, the ability to access an attribute by qualified name may not be available. If `namespace-prefixes` is set to `true`, attributes declaring namespace declarations (xmlns:*) will be included in the `Attributes` object.

Visual Basic Equivalent
IVBSAX Attributes

See Also
org.xml.sax.helpers.AttributesImpl
org.xml.sax.ContentHandler.startElement(java.lang.String, java.lang.String, java.lang.String, org.xml.sax.Attributes)

Example
```
import org.xml.sax.Attributes;
import org.xml.sax.SAXException;
import org.xml.sax.helpers.DefaultHandler;
public class AttributesSample extends DefaultHandler
{
    public void startElement( String namespaceURI,
                    String localName,
                    String qualifiedName,
                    Attributes atts )
                    throws SAXException
    {
. . .
        //Do stuff with the Attributes.
```

Members

getIndex Method

Java Signature
public int getIndex(String qName)

Visual Basic Signature
Public Function getIndexFromQName(ByVal strQName As String) As Long

This method returns the index of the **Attributes** collection for the attribute specified by the passed qualified name. If no corresponding attribute is found, -1 is returned.

If the feature http://xml.org/sax/features/namespace-prefixes is set to its default value of **false**, the ability to access an attribute by qualified name may not be available.

Example
```
import org.xml.sax.Attributes;
import org.xml.sax.SAXException;
import org.xml.sax.helpers.DefaultHandler;
...
    public void startElement( String namespaceURI,
                              String localName,
                              String qualifiedName,
                              Attributes atts )
                      throws SAXException
    {
        String qName, nsURI, lName, attType, value;
...
            System.out.println( "Index by Qualified Name: " +
                                atts.getIndex( qName ) );
```

Parameters

String **qName**   The attribute's qualified (prefixed) name.

Returns

int   The index of the specified attribute, or **-1** if no matching attribute is found.

getIndex Method

Java Signature
public int getIndex(String uri, String localPart)

Visual Basic Signature
Public Function getIndexFromName(ByVal strURI As String, ByVal strLocalName As String) As Long

This method returns the index into the **Attributes** collection for the attribute specified by the passed namespace URI and localname. If no corresponding attribute is found, **-1** is returned.

If the feature http://xml.org/sax/features/namespaces is **false**, access by namespace-qualified names may not be available.

Example
```
import org.xml.sax.Attributes;
import org.xml.sax.SAXException;
import org.xml.sax.helpers.DefaultHandler;
. . .
    public void startElement( String namespaceURI,
                              String localName,
                              String qualifiedName,
                              Attributes atts )
                       throws SAXException
    {
        String qName, nsURI, lName, attType, value;
. . .
            System.out.println( "Index by Namespace: " +
                                atts.getIndex( nsURI, lName ) );
```

Parameters

String **uri**   The attribute's namespace URI, or an empty string if the attribute has no namespace URI.

String **localPart**   The local name of the attribute.

Returns

int   The index of the specified attribute, or `-1` if no matching attribute is found.

getLength Method

Java Signature
```
public int getLength()
```

Visual Basic Signature
```
Public Property Get IVBSAXAttributes_length() As Long
```

This method returns the number of attributes in the **Attributes** list.

See Also
```
org.xml.sax.Attributes.getLocalName(int)
org.xml.sax.Attributes.getQName(int)
org.xml.sax.Attributes.getType(int)
org.xml.sax.Attributes.getURI(int)
org.xml.sax.Attributes.getValue(int)
```

Example
```
import org.xml.sax.Attributes;
import org.xml.sax.SAXException;
import org.xml.sax.helpers.DefaultHandler;
. . .
    public void startElement( String namespaceURI,
                              String localName,
                              String qualifiedName,
```

```
                    Attributes atts )
                    throws SAXException
    {
. . .
        //Iterate through the attributes.
        for( int i=0 ; i<atts.getLength() ; i++ )
        {
. . .
        }
```

Returns

int   The number of attributes in the list.

getLocalName Method

Java Signature
```
public String getLocalName(int index)
```

Visual Basic Signature
```
Public Function getLocalName(ByVal nIndex As Long) As String
```

The method returns a string containing the local name for the attribute specified by the passed index if namespace processing is being performed; otherwise, an empty string is returned. If the passed index is out of range, null is returned.

If the feature http://xml.org/sax/features/namespaces is set to false, disabling namespace processing, an empty string is returned.

See Also
org.xml.sax.Attributes.getLength()

Example
```
import org.xml.sax.Attributes;
import org.xml.sax.SAXException;
import org.xml.sax.helpers.DefaultHandler;
. . .
    public void startElement( String namespaceURI,
                              String localName,
                              String qualifiedName,
                              Attributes atts )
                              throws SAXException
    {
        String qName, nsURI, lName, attType, value;
        //Do stuff with the Attributes.
        //Iterate through the attributes.
        for( int i=0 ; i<atts.getLength() ; i++ )
        {
. . .
```

(continued on next page)

```
            // Get the local name by index.
            lName = atts.getLocalName(i);
...
        }
```

Parameters

int **index**   The index into the list of attributes.

Returns

String   The local name for the specified attribute, or an empty string if the local name is unavailable. If the index is out of range, the method returns null.

getQName Method

Java Signature
public String getQName(int index)

Visual Basic Signature
Public Function getQName(ByVal nIndex As Long) As String

The method returns the qualified name, if available, for the attribute specified by the passed index. If no qualified name is available, an empty string is returned. If the passed index is out of range, null is returned.

See Also
org.xml.sax.Attributes.getLength()

Example
```
import org.xml.sax.Attributes;
import org.xml.sax.SAXException;
import org.xml.sax.helpers.DefaultHandler;
...
    public void startElement( String namespaceURI,
                              String localName,
                              String qualifiedName,
                              Attributes atts )
                              throws SAXException
    {
        String qName, nsURI, lName, attType, value;
        //Do stuff with the Attributes.
        //Iterate through the attributes.
        for( int i=0 ; i<atts.getLength() ; i++ )
        {
            // Get the qualified name by index.
            qName = atts.getQName(i);
...
        }
```

Parameters

int **index**   The index into the list of attributes.

Returns

String   The qualified name for the specified attribute or an empty string if the qualified name is unavailable. If the index is out of range, the method returns null.

getType Method

Java Signature
public String getType(int index)

Visual Basic Signature
Public Function getType(ByVal nIndex As Long) As String

The method returns a string representing the type of the attribute specified by the passed index. The type is one of these strings:

- CDATA
- ID
- IDREF
- IDREFS
- NMTOKEN
- ENTITY
- ENTITIES
- NOTATION

In accordance with the XML 1.0 specification, if the parser does not report attribute types or has not parsed a declaration for the attribute, the parser must return CDATA.

If the passed index is out of range, null is returned.

See Also
org.xml.sax.Attributes.getLength()

Example
```
import org.xml.sax.Attributes;
import org.xml.sax.SAXException;
import org.xml.sax.helpers.DefaultHandler;
. . .
    public void startElement( String namespaceURI,
                    String localName,
                    String qualifiedName,
                    Attributes atts )
                    throws SAXException
    {
        String qName, nsURI, lName, attType, value;
        //Do stuff with the Attributes.
        //Iterate through the attributes.
```

(continued on next page)

```
        for( int i=0 ; i<atts.getLength() ; i++ )
        {
...
            // Get the type by index.
            attType = atts.getType(i);
...
        }
```

Parameters

int **index**   The index into the list of attributes.

Returns

String   The type of the specified attribute, or null if the passed index is out of range.

getType Method

Java Signature
```
public String getType(String qName)
```

Visual Basic Signature
```
Public Function getTypeFromQName(ByVal strQName As String) As String
```

The method returns a string representing the type of the attribute specified by the passed qualified name. The type is one of these strings:

- CDATA
- ID
- IDREF
- IDREFS
- NMTOKEN
- ENTITY
- ENTITIES
- NOTATION

In accordance with the XML 1.0 specification, if the parser does not report attribute types or has not parsed a declaration for the attribute, the parser must return CDATA.

If a corresponding attribute is not found in the list or if qualified names are not available, the function returns null.

If the feature http://xml.org/sax/features/namespace-prefixes is set to its default value of false, the ability to access an attribute by qualified name may not be available.

Example
```
import org.xml.sax.Attributes;
import org.xml.sax.SAXException;
import org.xml.sax.helpers.DefaultHandler;
...
    public void startElement( String namespaceURI,
```

```
                       String localName,
                       String qualifiedName,
                       Attributes atts )
                       throws SAXException
{
    String qName, nsURI, lName, attType, value;
...
            System.out.println( "Type by Qualified Name: " +
                                atts.getType( qName ) );
```

Parameters

String **qName**   The attribute's qualified name.

Returns

String   The type of the specified attribute, or null if no matching attribute is found or if qualified names are not available.

getType Method

Java Signature
```
public String getType(String uri, String localName)
```

Visual Basic Signature
```
Public Function getTypeFromName(ByVal strURI As String, ByVal strLocalName As String) As String
```

The method returns a string representing the type of the attribute specified by the passed namespace URI and localname. The type is one of these strings:

- CDATA
- ID
- IDREF
- IDREFS
- NMTOKEN
- ENTITY
- ENTITIES
- NOTATION

In accordance with the XML 1.0 specification, if the parser does not report attribute types or has not parsed a declaration for the attribute, the parser must return CDATA.

If a corresponding attribute is not found in the list or if namespace processing is not being performed, the function returns null.

If the feature http://xml.org/sax/features/namespaces is false, access by namespace-qualified names may not be available.

SAX 2.0 API Reference **71**

Example
```
import org.xml.sax.Attributes;
import org.xml.sax.SAXException;
import org.xml.sax.helpers.DefaultHandler;
. . .
    public void startElement( String namespaceURI,
                    String localName,
                    String qualifiedName,
                    Attributes atts )
                    throws SAXException
{
    String qName, nsURI, lName, attType, value;
. . .
        System.out.println( "Type by Namespace: " +
                    atts.getType( nsURI, lName ) );
```

Parameters

String **uri**   The namespace URI, or an empty string if the attribute has no namespace URI.

String **localName**   The local name of the attribute.

Returns

String   The type of the specified attribute, or null if no matching attribute is found or if namespace processing is not being performed.

getURI Method

Java Signature
```
public String getURI(int index)
```

Visual Basic Signature
```
Public Function getURI(ByVal nIndex As Long) As String
```

The method returns the namespace URI for the attribute specified by the passed index. If no URI is available, an empty string is returned. If the passed index is out of range, null is returned.

See Also
org.xml.sax.Attributes.getLength()

Example
```
import org.xml.sax.Attributes;
import org.xml.sax.SAXException;
import org.xml.sax.helpers.DefaultHandler;
. . .
    public void startElement( String namespaceURI,
                    String localName,
                    String qualifiedName,
                    Attributes atts )
```

```
                    throws SAXException
{
    String qName, nsURI, lName, attType, value;
    //Do stuff with the Attributes.
    //Iterate through the attributes.
    for( int i=0 ; i<atts.getLength() ; i++ )
    {
...
        // Get the namespace URI by index.
        nsURI = atts.getURI(i);
...
    }
```

Parameters

int **index**   The index into the list of attributes.

Returns

String   The namespace URI for the specified attribute or an empty string if the namespace URI is unavailable. If the index is out of range, null is returned.

getValue Method

Java Signature
public String getValue(int index)

Visual Basic Signature
Public Function getValue(ByVal nIndex As Long) As String

This method returns a string representing the value of the attribute specified by the passed index. If the attribute is of a type (ENTITIES, IDREFS, NMTOKENS) such that its value is a list of tokens, the tokens are concatenated into a single space-delimited string.

If the passed index is out of range, null is returned.

See Also
org.xml.sax.Attributes.getLength()

Example
```
import org.xml.sax.Attributes;
import org.xml.sax.SAXException;
import org.xml.sax.helpers.DefaultHandler;
...
    public void startElement( String namespaceURI,
                              String localName,
                              String qualifiedName,
                              Attributes atts )
                    throws SAXException
    {
        String qName, nsURI, lName, attType, value;
        //Do stuff with the Attributes.
```

(continued on next page)

```
            //Iterate through the attributes.
            for( int i=0 ; i<atts.getLength() ; i++ )
            {
...
                // Get the value by index.
                value = atts.getValue(i);
...
            }
```

Parameters

int index   The index into the list of attributes.

Returns

String   The value of the specified attribute, or null if the index is out of range.

getValue Method

Java Signature
```
public String getValue(String qName)
```

Visual Basic Signature
```
Public Function getValueFromQName(ByVal strQName As String) As String
```

The method returns the value of the attribute specified by the passed qualified name. If the attribute is of a type (ENTITIES, IDREFS, NMTOKENS) such that its value is a list of tokens, the tokens are concatenated into a single space-delimited string.

If a corresponding attribute is not found in the list, the function returns null.

If the feature http://xml.org/sax/features/namespace-prefixes is set to its default value of false, the ability to access an attribute by qualified name may not be available.

Example
```
import org.xml.sax.Attributes;
import org.xml.sax.SAXException;
import org.xml.sax.helpers.DefaultHandler;
...
    public void startElement( String namespaceURI,
                    String localName,
                    String qualifiedName,
                    Attributes atts )
                    throws SAXException
    {
        String qName, nsURI, lName, attType, value;
...
            System.out.println( "Value by Qualified Name: " +
                            atts.getValue( qName ) );
```

Parameters

String qName   The qualified name for the attribute.

Returns

String   The value of the specified attribute, or null if no matching attribute is found.

getValue Method

Java Signature
```
public String getValue(String uri, String localName)
```

Visual Basic Signature
```
Public Function getValueFromName(ByVal strURI As String, ByVal strLocalName As String) As String
```

The method returns a string representing the value of the attribute specified by the passed namespace URI and local name. If the attribute is of a type (ENTITIES, IDREFS, NMTOKENS) such that its value is a list of tokens, the tokens are concatenated into a single space-delimited string.

If a corresponding attribute is not found in the list, the function returns null.

If the feature http://xml.org/sax/features/namespaces is false, access by namespace-qualified names may not be available.

Example
```
import org.xml.sax.Attributes;
import org.xml.sax.SAXException;
import org.xml.sax.helpers.DefaultHandler;
...
    public void startElement( String namespaceURI,
                              String localName,
                              String qualifiedName,
                              Attributes atts )
                              throws SAXException
    {
        String qName, nsURI, lName, attType, value;
...
            System.out.println( "Value by Namespace: " +
                                atts.getValue( nsURI, lName ) );
```

Parameters

String uri   The namespace URI, or an empty string if the attribute has no namespace URI.

String localName   The local name of the attribute.

Returns

String   The value of the specified attribute, or null if no matching attribute is found.

AttributesImpl Class

The helper class `AttributesImpl` exposes two areas of functionality to the SAX application developer. First, the class provides a default implementation of the `org.xml.sax.Attributes` interface. Second, the class provides additional methods (over and above the `Attributes` interface set of methods) to create and modify a list of attributes.

The two most common uses of this class are to make a copy of an object that implements the `Attributes` interface in the `startElement()` method of a `ContentHandler` implementation, and to create and modify an object that implements the `Attributes` interface in a SAX filter or driver.

Since `AttributesImpl` contains unique methods not declared as part of the `Attributes` interface, you should never assume that a passed `Attributes` object was instantiated via the `AttributesImpl` class. Java developers should use the `instanceof` keyword to verify that an object is an instantiation of `AttributesImpl` before attempting to use any of the extended methods not declared in the `Attributes` interface.

Visual Basic Equivalent
SAXAttributes30

See Also
org.xml.sax.Attributes
org.xml.sax.ContentHandler.startElement(java.lang.String, java.lang.String, java.lang.String, org.xml.sax.Attributes)

Example
```
import org.xml.sax.Attributes;
import org.xml.sax.SAXException;
import org.xml.sax.helpers.AttributesImpl;
import org.xml.sax.helpers.DefaultHandler;
...
        AttributesImpl attsImpl = null;
```

Constructors

Java Signature
```
public  AttributesImpl()
```

Visual Basic Signature
```
dim oAttributes as new SAXAttributes30
```

This constructor method creates a new, empty instance of the `AttributesImpl` class. Parser writers will find this method useful for creating a single instance of `AttributesImpl` that can be reused throughout the processing of an XML document by resetting the list via invocation of the `clear()` method.

See Also
org.xml.sax.helpers.AttributesImpl(org.xml.sax.Attributes)
org.xml.sax.helpers.AttributesImpl.clear()

Example
```
import org.xml.sax.Attributes;
import org.xml.sax.SAXException;
import org.xml.sax.helpers.AttributesImpl;
import org.xml.sax.helpers.DefaultHandler;
. . .
    public void startElement( String namespaceURI,
                      String localName,
                      String qualifiedName,
                      Attributes atts )
                      throws SAXException
    {
        AttributesImpl attsImpl = null;
        String qName, nsURI, lName, attType, value;
        int i;
        if( useEmptyConstructor == true )
        {
            attsImpl = new AttributesImpl();
            // Copy the passed Attributes list into our local object.
            attsImpl.setAttributes( atts );
        }
        else
        {
            attsImpl = new AttributesImpl( atts );
        }
```

Java Signature
```
public  AttributesImpl(Attributes atts)
```

Visual Basic Signature
N/A.

This constructor method creates a new instance of an **AttributesImpl** object, copying the contents of the passed **Attributes** object. This constructor method is often used by application developers to make a copy of an existing attribute list.

See Also
org.xml.sax.helpers.AttributesImpl()

Example
```
import org.xml.sax.Attributes;
import org.xml.sax.SAXException;
import org.xml.sax.helpers.AttributesImpl;
import org.xml.sax.helpers.DefaultHandler;
. . .
    public void startElement( String namespaceURI,
                      String localName,
                      String qualifiedName,
```

(continued on next page)

```
                        Attributes atts )
                        throws SAXException
    {
        AttributesImpl attsImpl = null;
        String qName, nsURI, lName, attType, value;
        int i;
        if( useEmptyConstructor == true )
        {
            attsImpl = new AttributesImpl();
            // Copy the passed Attributes list into our local object.
            attsImpl.setAttributes( atts );
        }
        else
        {
            attsImpl = new AttributesImpl( atts );
        }
```

Parameters

Attributes **atts**   An object that implements the `Attributes` interface.

Members

addAttribute Method

Java Signature
```
public void addAttribute(String uri, String localName, String qName, String type, String value)
```

Visual Basic Signature
```
Public Sub addAttribute(strURI As String, strLocalName As String, strQName As String, strType As String, strValue As String)
```

This method adds an attribute to the end of the list. For performance reasons, `addAttribute()` does not check to see if the attribute already exists in the list; rather, it delegates the responsibility to the application.

Note that this method is not a member of the `Attributes` interface.

See Also
org.xml.sax.helpers.AttributesImpl.removeAttribute(int)

Example
```
import org.xml.sax.Attributes;
import org.xml.sax.SAXException;
import org.xml.sax.helpers.AttributesImpl;
import org.xml.sax.helpers.DefaultHandler;
. . .
    public void startElement( String namespaceURI,
                         String localName,
                         String qualifiedName,
                         Attributes atts )
```

```
                   throws SAXException
         {
 ...
                   // Add an attribute to the end of our list.
                   attsImpl.addAttribute( nsURI,
                                          lName,
                                          qName,
                                          attType,
                                          value );
```

Parameters

String **uri**   The namespace URI if it is available; if no URI is available or namespace processing is not being performed, an empty string.

String **localName**   The local name if namespace processing is being performed; otherwise, an empty string.

String **qName**   The qualified (prefixed) name if it is available; otherwise, an empty string.

String **type**   The attribute type as a string containing one of the following values:

- CDATA
- ID
- IDREF
- IDREFS
- NMTOKEN
- ENTITY
- ENTITIES
- NOTATION

String **value**   The attribute's value as a string.

Returns
void

N/A.

clear Method

Java Signature
`public void clear()`

Visual Basic Signature
`Public Sub clear()`

This method clears an attribute list; however, to enhance performance, it does not actually free the memory in use by the list.

Parser writers will find this method useful for clearing the attribute list in order to reuse the list between `ContentHandler.startElement()` events. It is more efficient to reuse a single instance of an `AttributesImpl` object rather than creating and destroying an `AttributesImpl` object with each encountered element.

Note that this method is not a member of the `Attributes` interface.

Example

```
import org.xml.sax.Attributes;
import org.xml.sax.SAXException;
import org.xml.sax.helpers.AttributesImpl;
import org.xml.sax.helpers.DefaultHandler;
. . .
    public void startElement( String namespaceURI,
                              String localName,
                              String qualifiedName,
                              Attributes atts )
                              throws SAXException
    {
. . .
        attsImpl.clear();
```

Returns

void

N/A.

getIndex Method

Java Signature

`public int getIndex(String qName)`

Visual Basic Signature

N/A.

This method returns the list position of the attribute specified by the passed qualified name. If no corresponding attribute is found, -1 is returned.

Note that this method is part of the implementation of the `Attributes` interface.

See Also

`org.xml.sax.Attributes.getIndex(java.lang.String)`

Example

See the `Attributes.getIndex()` method documentation for an example.

Parameters

String qName   The attribute's qualified name.

Returns

int   The position of the specified attribute in the list, or -1 if no matching attribute is found.

getIndex Method

Java Signature
public int getIndex(String uri, String localName)

Visual Basic Signature
N/A.

This method returns the list position of the attribute specified by the passed namespace URI and local name. If no corresponding attribute is found, -1 is returned.
   Note that this method is part of the implementation of the Attributes interface.

See Also
org.xml.sax.Attributes.getIndex(java.lang.String, java.lang.String)

Example
See the Attributes.getIndex() method documentation for an example.

Parameters

String uri   The attribute's namespace URI, or an empty string if the attribute has no namespace URI.

String localName   The attribute's local name.

Returns

int   The position in the list of the specified attribute, or -1 if no matching attribute is found.

getLength Method

Java Signature
public int getLength()

Visual Basic Signature
N/A.

This method returns the number of attributes in the list. Obtaining the number of attributes in the list is the first step in iterating through the attributes by index.
   Note that this method is part of the implementation of the Attributes interface.

See Also
org.xml.sax.Attributes.getLength()

Example
See the Attributes.getLength() method documentation for an example.

Returns

int   The number of attributes in the list.

getLocalName Method

Java Signature
public String getLocalName(int index)

Visual Basic Signature
N/A.

If namespace processing is being performed, this method returns the local name for the attribute specified by the passed index. If namespace processing is *not* being performed, an empty string is returned. If the passed index is out of range, null is returned.

Note that this method is part of the implementation of the Attributes interface.

See Also
org.xml.sax.Attributes.getLocalName(int)

Example
See the Attributes.getLocalName() method documentation for an example.

Parameters
int **index**   The index into the list of attributes.

Returns
String   The name of the specified attribute if namespace processing is being performed; otherwise, an empty string. If the passed index is out of range, null is returned.

getQName Method

Java Signature
public String getQName(int index)

Visual Basic Signature
N/A.

This method returns the qualified name, if available, for the attribute specified by the passed index. If no qualified name is available, an empty string is returned. If the passed index is out of range, null is returned.

Note that this method is part of the implementation of the Attributes interface.

See Also
org.xml.sax.Attributes.getQName(int)

Example
See the Attributes.getQName() method documentation for an example.

Parameters
int **index**   The index into the list of attributes.

Returns
String   The qualified name of the specified attribute, or null if the passed index is out of range.

getType Method

Java Signature
```
public String getType(int index)
```

Visual Basic Signature
N/A.

This method returns a string representing the type for the attribute specified by the passed index. The type is one of these strings:

- CDATA
- ID
- IDREF
- IDREFS
- NMTOKEN
- ENTITY
- ENTITIES
- NOTATION

In accordance with the XML 1.0 specification, if the parser does not report attribute types or has not parsed a declaration for the attribute, the parser must return CDATA.

If the passed index is out of range, null is returned.

Note that this method is part of the implementation of the Attributes interface.

See Also
org.xml.sax.Attributes.getType(int)

Example
See the Attributes.getType() method documentation for an example.

Parameters
int **index**   The index into the list of attributes.

Returns
String   The type of the specified attribute, or null if the passed index is out of range.

getType Method

Java Signature
```
public String getType(String qName)
```

Visual Basic Signature
N/A.

The method returns a string representing the type for the attribute specified by the passed qualified name. The type is one of these strings:

- CDATA
- ID
- IDREF
- IDREFS
- NMTOKEN
- ENTITY
- ENTITIES
- NOTATION

In accordance with the XML 1.0 specification, if the parser does not report attribute types or has not parsed a declaration for the attribute, the parser must return CDATA.

If a corresponding attribute is not found in the list or if qualified names are not available, the method returns null.

Note that this method is part of the implementation of the Attributes interface.

See Also

org.xml.sax.Attributes.getType(java.lang.String)

Example

See the Attributes.getType() method documentation for an example.

Parameters

String qName   The attribute's qualified name.

Returns

String   The type of the specified attribute, or null if no matching attribute is found in the list.

getType Method

Java Signature
public String getType(String uri, String localName)

Visual Basic Signature
N/A.

The method returns a string representing the type for the attribute specified by the passed namespace URI and local name. The type is one of these strings:

- CDATA
- ID
- IDREF
- IDREFS
- NMTOKEN
- ENTITY

- ENTITIES
- NOTATION

In accordance with the XML 1.0 specification, if the parser does not report attribute types or has not parsed a declaration for the attribute, the parser must return CDATA.

If a corresponding attribute is not found in the list or if namespace processing is not being performed, the method returns null.

Note that this method is part of the implementation of the Attributes interface.

See Also
org.xml.sax.Attributes.getType(int)

Example
See the Attributes.getType() method documentation for an example.

Parameters

String **uri**   The namespace URI, or an empty string if the attribute has no namespace URI.

String **localName**   The local name of the attribute.

Returns

String   The type of the specified attribute, or null if no matching attribute is found.

getURI Method

Java Signature
public String getURI(int index)

Visual Basic Signature
N/A.

This method returns the namespace URI for the attribute specified by the passed index. If no URI is available, an empty string is returned. If the passed index is out of range, null is returned.

Note that this method is part of the implementation of the Attributes interface.

See Also
org.xml.sax.Attributes.getURI(int)

Example
See the Attributes.getURI() method documentation for an example.

Parameters

int **index**   The index into the list of attributes.

Returns

String   The namespace URI for the specified attribute, or null if the passed index is out of range.

getValue Method

Java Signature
public String getValue(int index)

Visual Basic Signature
N/A.

This method returns the value of the attribute specified by the passed index. If the attribute is of a type (ENTITIES, IDREFS, NMTOKENS) such that its value is a list of tokens, the tokens are concatenated into a single space-delimited string.

If the passed index is out of range, null is returned.

Note that this method is part of the implementation of the Attributes interface.

See Also
org.xml.sax.Attributes.getValue(int)

Example
See the Attributes.getValue() method documentation for an example.

Parameters
int **index**   The index into the list of attributes.

Returns
String   The value of the specified attribute, or null if the passed index is out of range.

getValue Method

Java Signature
public String getValue(String qName)

Visual Basic Signature
N/A.

This method returns the value of the attribute specified by the passed qualified name. If the attribute is of a type (ENTITIES, IDREFS, NMTOKENS) such that its value is a list of tokens, the tokens are concatenated into a single space-delimited string. If a corresponding attribute is not found in the list, the method returns null.

Note that this method is part of the implementation of the Attributes interface.

See Also
org.xml.sax.Attributes.getValue(java.lang.String)

Example
See the Attributes.getValue() method documentation for an example.

Parameters
String **qName**   The attribute's qualified name.

Returns
String   The value of the specified attribute, or null if no matching attribute is found in the list.

getValue Method

Java Signature
```
public String getValue(String uri, String localName)
```

Visual Basic Signature
N/A.

The method returns the value of the attribute specified by the passed namespace URI and local name. If the attribute is of a type (ENTITIES, IDREFS, NMTOKENS) such that its value is a list of tokens, the tokens are concatenated into a single space-delimited string. If a corresponding attribute is not found in the list, the function returns null.

Note that this method is part of the implementation of the Attributes interface.

See Also
org.xml.sax.Attributes.getValue(int)

Example
See the Attributes.getValue() method documentation for an example.

Parameters

String uri   The namespace URI, or an empty string if the attribute has no namespace URI.

String localName   The local name of the attribute.

Returns

String   The value of the specified attribute, or null if no matching attribute is found in the list.

removeAttribute Method

Java Signature
```
public void removeAttribute(int index)
```

Visual Basic Signature
```
Public Sub removeAttribute(nIndex As Long)
```

The method removes the attribute at the specified index from the list, thereby changing the length of the list and possibly the position of other attributes in the list.

If the specified index is out of range, the java.lang.ArrayIndexOutOfBoundsException is thrown.

This method is *not* a member of the Attributes interface.

See Also
org.xml.sax.Attributes.getLength()
org.xml.sax.helpers.AttributesImpl.addAttribute(java.lang.String, java.lang.String, java.lang.String, java.lang.String, java.lang.String)

Example
```
import org.xml.sax.Attributes;
import org.xml.sax.SAXException;
import org.xml.sax.helpers.AttributesImpl;
import org.xml.sax.helpers.DefaultHandler;
...
    public void startElement( String namespaceURI,
                              String localName,
                              String qualifiedName,
                              Attributes atts )
                              throws SAXException
    {
...
        // Now let's remove all the attributes from our list.
        // Note that we delete from the end so we don't have any
        // worries with respect to the changing length of the list.
        while( attsImpl.getLength() > 0 )
            attsImpl.removeAttribute( attsImpl.getLength() );
```

Parameters
int **index**   The position in the list of the attribute to be removed.

Returns
void   N/A.

setAttribute Method

Java Signature
```
public void setAttribute(int index, String uri, String localName, String qName, String type, String value)
```

Visual Basic Signature
```
Public Sub setAttribute(nIndex As Long, strURI As String, strLocalName As String, strQName As String, strType As String, strValue As String)
```

The method modifies the properties of the attribute specified by the passed index. For performance reasons, the method does not perform any checking for name conflicts or well-formedness; instead, such checks are the responsibility of the calling application.

If the specified index is out of range, a `java.lang.ArrayIndexOutOfBoundsException` is thrown.

Note that this method is *not* a member of the `Attributes` interface.

See Also
org.xml.sax.Attributes.getIndex(java.lang.String)
org.xml.sax.Attributes.getIndex(java.lang.String, java.lang.String)

Example

```
import org.xml.sax.Attributes;
import org.xml.sax.SAXException;
import org.xml.sax.helpers.AttributesImpl;
import org.xml.sax.helpers.DefaultHandler;
...
    public void startElement( String namespaceURI,
                              String localName,
                              String qualifiedName,
                              Attributes atts )
                    throws SAXException
    {
...
            attsImpl.setAttribute(  i,
                                    nsURI,
                                    lName,
                                    qName,
                                    attType,
                                    value );
```

Parameters

int **index**   The index of the attribute.

String **uri**   The attribute's namespace URI, or an empty string if no namespace URI is available or namespace processing is not being performed.

String **localName**   The attribute's local name, or an empty string if namespace processing is not being performed.

String **qName**   The attribute's qualified name, or the empty string if the qualified name is not available.

String **type**   The attribute's type as a string containing one of the following values:

- CDATA
- ID
- IDREF
- IDREFS
- NMTOKEN
- ENTITY
- ENTITIES
- NOTATION
- String **value**

The attribute's value as a string.

Returns

void   N/A.

setAttributes Method

Java Signature
public void setAttributes(Attributes atts)

Visual Basic Signature
Public Sub setAttributes(varAtts as Variant)

The method copies all of the attribute elements from an object that implements the Attributes interface into this AttributesImpl object. The same functionality may be achieved by either iterating the elements of an object that implements the Attributes interface and calling AttributesImpl.addAttribute() method for each iteration, or creating an instance of this class using the AttributesImpl(Attributes) constructor method.

Note that this method is not a member of the Attributes interface.

Example
```
import org.xml.sax.Attributes;
import org.xml.sax.SAXException;
import org.xml.sax.helpers.AttributesImpl;
import org.xml.sax.helpers.DefaultHandler;
. . .
    public void startElement( String namespaceURI,
                    String localName,
                    String qualifiedName,
                    Attributes atts )
                    throws SAXException
    {
        AttributesImpl attsImpl = null;
        String qName, nsURI, lName, attType, value;
        int i;
        if( useEmptyConstructor == true )
        {
            attsImpl = new AttributesImpl();
            // Copy the passed Attributes list into our local object.
            attsImpl.setAttributes( atts );
        }
        else
        {
            attsImpl = new AttributesImpl( atts );
        }
```

Parameters

Attributes **atts**   An instance of the object that implements the Attributes interface that you want to copy.

Returns

void   N/A.

setLocalName Method

Java Signature
public void setLocalName(int index, String localName)

Visual Basic Signature
Public Sub setLocalName(nIndex As Long, strLocalName As String)

This method sets the local name of an attribute specified by the passed index. The method does not perform checks for name conflicts; instead, such checks are the responsibility of the calling application.

If the specified index is out of range, a java.lang.ArrayIndexOutOfBoundsException is thrown.

Note that this method is not a member of the Attributes interface.

Example
```
import org.xml.sax.Attributes;
import org.xml.sax.SAXException;
import org.xml.sax.helpers.AttributesImpl;
import org.xml.sax.helpers.DefaultHandler;
. . .
    public void startElement( String namespaceURI,
                              String localName,
                              String qualifiedName,
                              Attributes atts )
                              throws SAXException
    {
. . .
         attsImpl.setLocalName( i, lName );
```

Parameters

int **index**   The index of the attribute.

String **localName**   The attribute's local name, or an empty string for none.

Returns

void   N/A.

setQName Method

Java Signature
public void setQName(int index, String qName)

Visual Basic Signature
Public Sub setQName(nIndex As Long, strQName As String)

This method sets the qualified name for the attribute specified by the passed index. It is the responsibility of the calling application to perform any necessary name conflict checks.

If the specified index is out of range, a `java.lang.ArrayIndexOutOfBoundsException` is thrown.

Note that this method is not a member of the `Attributes` interface.

Example
```
import org.xml.sax.Attributes;
import org.xml.sax.SAXException;
import org.xml.sax.helpers.AttributesImpl;
import org.xml.sax.helpers.DefaultHandler;
. . .
    public void startElement( String namespaceURI,
                              String localName,
                              String qualifiedName,
                              Attributes atts )
                              throws SAXException
    {
. . .
        attsImpl.setQName( i, qName );
```

Parameters

int **index**   The index of the attribute.

String **qName**   The attribute's qualified name, or an empty string if no qualified name is available.

Returns

void   N/A.

setType Method

Java Signature
```
public void setType(int index, String type)
```

Visual Basic Signature
```
Public Sub setType(nIndex As Long, strType As String)
```

This method sets the type for the attribute specified by the passed index.

The type is one of these strings:

- CDATA
- ID
- IDREF
- IDREFS
- NMTOKEN
- ENTITY
- ENTITIES
- NOTATION

If the specified index is out of range, a
`java.lang.ArrayIndexOutOfBoundsException` is thrown.

Note that this method is not a member of the `Attributes` interface.

Example
```
import org.xml.sax.Attributes;
import org.xml.sax.SAXException;
import org.xml.sax.helpers.AttributesImpl;
import org.xml.sax.helpers.DefaultHandler;
. . .
    public void startElement( String namespaceURI,
                    String localName,
                    String qualifiedName,
                    Attributes atts )
                    throws SAXException
    {
. . .
        attsImpl.setType( i, attType );
```

Parameters

int **index**   The index of the attribute.

String **type**   The attribute's type as a string.

Returns

void   N/A.

setURI Method

Java Signature
```
public void setURI(int index, String uri)
```

Visual Basic Signature
```
Public Sub setURI(nIndex As Long, strURI As String)
```

This method sets the namespace URI for the attribute specified by the passed index. The method does not perform any checks for name conflicts, but rather leaves that as a responsibility of the calling application.

If the specified index is out of range, a
`java.lang.ArrayIndexOutOfBoundsException` is thrown.

Note that this method is not a member of the `Attributes` interface.

Example
```
import org.xml.sax.Attributes;
import org.xml.sax.SAXException;
import org.xml.sax.helpers.AttributesImpl;
import org.xml.sax.helpers.DefaultHandler;
. . .
    public void startElement( String namespaceURI,
```

(continued on next page)

```
                        String localName,
                        String qualifiedName,
                        Attributes atts )
                        throws SAXException
    {
...
            attsImpl.setURI( i, nsURI );
```

Parameters

int **index**   The index of the attribute.

String **uri**   The attribute's namespace URI, or an empty string if no namespace is available.

Returns

void   N/A.

setValue Method

Java Signature
```
public void setValue(int index, String value)
```

Visual Basic Signature
```
Public Sub setValue(nIndex As Long, strValue As String)
```

This method sets the value, as a string, for the attribute specified by the passed index.
    If the specified index is out of range, a java.lang.ArrayIndexOutOfBoundsException is thrown.
    Note that this method is not a member of the **Attributes** interface.

Example
```
import org.xml.sax.Attributes;
import org.xml.sax.SAXException;
import org.xml.sax.helpers.AttributesImpl;
import org.xml.sax.helpers.DefaultHandler;
...
    public void startElement( String namespaceURI,
                        String localName,
                        String qualifiedName,
                        Attributes atts )
                        throws SAXException
    {
...
            attsImpl.setValue( i, value );
```

Parameters

int **index**   The index of the attribute.

String **value**   The attribute's value as a string.

Returns

void   N/A.

ContentHandler Interface

The ContentHandler interface is the heart of SAX; almost all SAX applications implement this callback interface so as to receive notification of parsing events. The application registers an instance of an object that implements the ContentHandler interface with the parser by using the setContentHandler() method of XMLReader. As the XML document is processed, the parser calls methods in the registered ContentHandler, thereby triggering events in the application.

Applications that do not want to implement the entire ContentHandler interface, can derive a class from DefaultHandler. DefaultHandler provides a default implementation of the ContentHandler interface. Applications can then override desired event methods for custom processing.

Visual Basic Equivalent
IVBSAXContentHandler

See Also
org.xml.sax.DTDHandler
org.xml.sax.ErrorHandler
org.xml.sax.helpers.DefaultHandler
org.xml.sax.Locator
org.xml.sax.XMLReader
org.xml.sax.XMLReader.getContentHandler()
org.xml.sax.XMLReader.setContentHandler(org.xml.sax.ContentHandler)

Example
```
import org.xml.sax.Attributes;
import org.xml.sax.ContentHandler;
import org.xml.sax.Locator;
import org.xml.sax.SAXException;
public class ContentHandlerSample implements ContentHandler
{
. . .
}
```

Members

characters Method

Java Signature
public void characters(char[] ch, int start, int length)

Visual Basic Signature
Public Sub characters(strChars as String)

The parser calls this method as it finds character data. The character data may be passed to this method in one contiguous chunk, or the parser may split the data into several chunks using multiple notifications.

Validating parsers will report whitespace that is not significant using the ignorableWhitespace() method instead of the characters() method.

Thrown Exceptions
org.xml.sax.SAXException

See Also
org.xml.sax.Locator
org.xml.sax.ContentHandler.ignorableWhitespace(char[], int, int)

Example
```
import org.xml.sax.Attributes;
import org.xml.sax.ContentHandler;
import org.xml.sax.Locator;
import org.xml.sax.SAXException;
. . .
    public void characters( char[] text, int start, int length )
                     throws SAXException
    {
        String data = "";
        System.out.println("characters event fired.  " +
                         "Number of chars: " + length);
        data = String.copyValueOf( text, start, length);
        System.out.println( "\t" + data );
    }
```

Parameters

char[] **ch**   The characters from the XML document.

int **start**   The start position in the array.

int **length**   The number of characters to read from the array.

Returns

void   N/A.

endDocument Method

Java Signature
```
public void endDocument()
```

Visual Basic Signature
```
Public Sub endDocument()
```

This method is the last notification received from the parser during the processing of a document. The method is called when the end of the XML document is reached, or when the parser abandons parsing due to a fatal error.

This method is the logical place for the application to perform any needed document post-processing such as the clean up of resources.

Thrown Exceptions
org.xml.sax.SAXException

See Also
org.xml.sax.ContentHandler.startDocument()

Example

```
import org.xml.sax.Attributes;
import org.xml.sax.ContentHandler;
import org.xml.sax.Locator;
import org.xml.sax.SAXException;
. . .
    public void endDocument() throws SAXException
    {
        System.out.println( "endDocument event fired." );
    }
```

Returns

void   N/A.

endElement Method

Java Signature

```
public void endElement(String namespaceURI, String localName, String qName)
```

Visual Basic Signature

```
Public Sub endElement(ByVal strNamespaceURI As String, ByVal strLocalName As String, ByVal strQName As String)
```

The parser invokes this method for every element end tag encountered in an XML document. Obviously, a corresponding startElement() notification should have already been received.

For *all* elements, including empty elements, the application will receive both startElement() and endElement() notifications.

The value of the parameters passed to this method vary depending on the values of the SAX features http://xml.org/sax/features/namespaces and http://xml.org/sax/features/namespace-prefixes. If the namespaces feature is set to its default value of true, the namespace URI and local name are both required and the qualified name is optional. However, if the namespace-prefixes feature is true (the default is false), a qualified name is required, and the namespace URI and local name are optional. Note that the two features are mutually exclusive and, in fact, setting the namespaces feature to false will automatically set the namespace-prefixes feature to true.

Thrown Exceptions

org.xml.sax.SAXException

Example

```
import org.xml.sax.Attributes;
import org.xml.sax.ContentHandler;
import org.xml.sax.Locator;
import org.xml.sax.SAXException;
. . .
    public void endElement( String namespaceURI,
                            String localName,
```

(continued on next page)

```
                            String qualifiedName )
                            throws SAXException
    {
        System.out.println( "End element event fired.\n\t" +
                            "namespaceURI: " + namespaceURI + "\n\t" +
                            "localName: " + localName + "\n\t" +
                            "qualifiedName: " + qualifiedName );
    }
```

Parameters

String **namespaceURI**   The namespace URI of the element, or an empty string if namespace processing is not being performed.

String **localName**   The local name of the element, or an empty string if namespace processing is not being performed.

String **qName**   The qualified name of the element, or an empty string if qualified names are not available.

Returns

void   N/A.

endPrefixMapping Method

Java Signature
```
public void endPrefixMapping(String prefix)
```

Visual Basic Signature
```
Public Sub endPrefixMapping(strPrefix As String)
```

This method is called when a prefix-URI mapping goes out of scope. This event always occurs after a corresponding endElement() event, but the order of events is not otherwise guaranteed.

Normally, prefix-URI mapping is not needed for namespace resolution because the SAX reader provides namespace URIs for names when the http://xml.org/sax/feature/namespaces feature is set to its default value of true. However, circumstances may require an application to use prefixes in attribute values or character data where they cannot be expanded. The prefix-URI mapping event methods —startPrefixMapping() and endPrefixMapping()— provide an application with the information necessary to expand prefixes in those circumstances.

Since the xml prefix is predeclared and immutable, an application should never receive a prefix mapping event for it.

Thrown Exceptions
org.xml.sax.SAXException

See Also
org.xml.sax.ContentHandler.endElement(java.lang.String, java.lang.String, java.lang.String)
org.xml.sax.ContentHandler.startPrefixMapping(java.lang.String, java.lang.String)

Example
```
import org.xml.sax.Attributes;
import org.xml.sax.ContentHandler;
import org.xml.sax.Locator;
import org.xml.sax.SAXException;
...
    public void endPrefixMapping( String prefix )
                                  throws SAXException
    {
        System.out.println( "endPrefixMapping fired.\n\t" +
                            "prefix: " + prefix );
    }
```

Parameters
String **prefix**   The namespace prefix that went out of scope.

Returns
void   N/A.

ignorableWhitespace Method

Java Signature
`public void ignorableWhitespace(char[] ch, int start, int length)`

Visual Basic Signature
`Public Sub ignorableWhitespace(strChars as String)`

The parser calls this method when it finds ignorable whitespace data. The whitespace data may be passed to this method in one contiguous chunk, or the parser may split the data into several chunks using multiple notifications.

Validating parsers *must* use this method to report ignorable whitespace encountered during parsing. The event is optional for other parsers.

Thrown Exceptions
org.xml.sax.SAXException

See Also
org.xml.sax.ContentHandler.characters(char[], int, int)

Example
```
import org.xml.sax.Attributes;
import org.xml.sax.ContentHandler;
import org.xml.sax.Locator;
import org.xml.sax.SAXException;
...
    public void ignorableWhitespace(    char[] text,
                                        int start,
                                        int length )
                                        throws SAXException
```

(continued on next page)

```
{
    System.out.println( "ignorableWhitespace event fired." +
                        "\t" + length +
                        " whitespace chars ignored." );
}
```

Parameters

char[] **ch**   The whitespace character data from the XML document.

int **start**   The start position in the array.

int **length**   The number of characters to read from the array.

Returns

void   N/A.

processingInstruction Method

Java Signature
```
public void processingInstruction(String target, String data)
```

Visual Basic Signature
```
Public Sub processingInstruction(strTarget As String, strData As String)
```

This method is invoked when the parser finds a processing instruction in the XML document. Note that processing instructions may occur before and/or after the startElement() and endElement() events for the root element.
    According to the W3C XML specification, a parser must never report a text or XML declaration.

Thrown Exceptions
org.xml.sax.SAXException

Example
```
import org.xml.sax.Attributes;
import org.xml.sax.ContentHandler;
import org.xml.sax.Locator;
import org.xml.sax.SAXException;
. . .
    public void processingInstruction( String target, String data ) throws SAXException
    {
        System.out.println( "processingInstruction event fired.\n\t" +
                            "target: " + target + "\n\t" +
                            "data: " + data );
    }
```

Parameters

String **target**   The processing instruction target.

String **data**   The processing instruction data, or null if none was supplied. The data does not include any whitespace separating the data from the target.

Returns

void   N/A.

setDocumentLocator Method

Java Signature
```
public void setDocumentLocator(Locator locator)
```

Visual Basic Signature
```
Public Property documentLocator as IVBSAXLocator
```

This method supplies the application with a `Locator` object reference; a `Locator` object allows the application to determine the document location of any event. If a SAX parser supplies `Locator` objects, this method will be invoked at the start of XML document parsing, before any other events. Parsers are strongly encouraged, but not required, to supply `Locator` objects to applications.

See Also
org.xml.sax.Locator

Example
```
import org.xml.sax.Attributes;
import org.xml.sax.ContentHandler;
import org.xml.sax.Locator;
import org.xml.sax.SAXException;
. . .
    public void setDocumentLocator( Locator locator )
    {
        System.out.println( "setDocumentLocator event fired.\n\t" +
                            "Parser Locator support = " +
                            (locator != null) );
        myLocator = locator;
    }
```

Parameters

Locator **locator**   A Locator object capable of returning the location of any document-related event.

Returns

void   N/A.

skippedEntity Method

Java Signature
```
public void skippedEntity(String name)
```

Visual Basic Signature
```
Public Sub skippedEntity(strName As String)
```

The parser invokes this method for each skipped entity.

Parsers may skip external entities depending on the values for the three SAX features http://xml.org/sax/features/external-general-entities, http://xml.org/sax/features/external-parameter-entities, and http://xml.org/sax/features/validation. When the feature external-general-entities is set to false (the default is true), the parser will not attempt to resolve external parsed general entities. When the feature external-parameter-entities is false (the default is true), the parser will not attempt to resolve external parameter entities. When the validation feature is true (the default is false), the parser is required to resolve all entities, effectively setting the previous two features to true. To summarize, for a parser to skip entities, all three of the above-mentioned features must be set to false.

Thrown Exceptions
org.xml.sax.SAXException

Example
```
import org.xml.sax.Attributes;
import org.xml.sax.ContentHandler;
import org.xml.sax.Locator;
import org.xml.sax.SAXException;
. . .
    public void skippedEntity( String name ) throws SAXException
    {
        System.out.println( "skippedEntity fired.\n\t" +
                            "name: " + name );
    }
```

Parameters
String **name**   The name of the skipped entity. If the entity is a parameter, the name will begin with %. If the entity is an external DTD subset, it will be the string [dtd].

Returns
void   N/A.

startDocument Method

Java Signature
public void startDocument()

Visual Basic Signature
Public Sub startDocument()

This event is invoked by the parser at the beginning of an XML document. With the possible exception of setDocumentLocator(), this method will be the first event fired by the parser. However, unlike setDocumentLocator(), the startDocument() method will *always* be invoked. Thus, this method is the logical location for any initialization or resource allocation code that the application may need.

Thrown Exceptions
org.xml.sax.SAXException

See Also

org.xml.sax.ContentHandler.endDocument()

Example
```
import org.xml.sax.Attributes;
import org.xml.sax.ContentHandler;
import org.xml.sax.Locator;
import org.xml.sax.SAXException;
. . .
    public void startDocument() throws SAXException
    {
        System.out.println( "startDocument event fired." );
    }
```

Returns

void   N/A.

startElement Method

Java Signature
```
public void startElement(String namespaceURI, String localName, String qName, Attributes atts)
```

Visual Basic Signature
```
Public Sub startElement(strNamespaceURI As String, strLocalName As String, strQName As String, oAttributes As IVBSAXAttributes)
```

The parser invokes this method for every element start tag encountered in an XML document. Every startElement() event will be matched by an endElement() event, even for empty elements.

The value of the parameters passed to this method vary depending on the values of the SAX features http://xml.org/sax/features/namespaces and http://xml.org/sax/features/namespace-prefixes. If the namespaces feature is set to its default value of true, the namespace URI and local name are both required and the qualified name is optional. However, if the namespace-prefixes feature is true (the default is false), a qualified name is required, and the namespace URI and local name are optional. Note that the two features are mutually exclusive and, in fact, setting the namespaces feature to false will automatically set the namespace-prefixes feature to true.

Thrown Exceptions

org.xml.sax.SAXException

See Also

org.xml.sax.Attributes
org.xml.sax.ContentHandler.endElement(java.lang.String, java.lang.String, java.lang.String)

Example
```
import org.xml.sax.Attributes;
import org.xml.sax.ContentHandler;
import org.xml.sax.Locator;
import org.xml.sax.SAXException;
. . .
    public void startElement( String namespaceURI,
                              String localName,
                              String qualifiedName,
                              Attributes atts )
                              throws SAXException
    {
        System.out.println( "Start element event fired.\n\t" +
                            "namespaceURI: " + namespaceURI + "\n\t" +
                            "localName: " + localName + "\n\t" +
                            "qualifiedName: " + qualifiedName );
    }
```

Parameters

String **namespaceURI**   The element's namespace URI, or an empty string if namespace processing is not being performed or if no namespace was provided.

String **localName**   The local name of the element, or an empty string if namespace processing is not being performed.

String **qName**   The element's qualified name, or an empty string if qualified names are not available.

Attributes **atts**   An instance of an object that implements the Attributes interface containing a list of the attributes attached to the element.

Returns
void   N/A.

startPrefixMapping Method

Java Signature
`public void startPrefixMapping(String prefix, String uri)`

Visual Basic Signature
`Public Sub startPrefixMapping(strPrefix As String, strURI As String)`

This method is called when a prefix-URI mapping comes into scope. This event always occurs before a corresponding startElement() event, but the order of events is not otherwise guaranteed.

   Normally, prefix-URI mapping is not needed for namespace resolution because the SAX reader provides namespace URIs for names when the http://xml.org/sax/feature/namespaces feature is set to its default value of true. However, circumstances may require an application to use prefixes in attribute values or character data where they cannot be expanded. The prefix-URI mapping event methods —startPrefixMapping() and endPrefixMapping()— provide an application with the information necessary to expand prefixes in those circumstances.

Since the xml prefix is predeclared and immutable, an application should never receive a prefix mapping event for it.

Thrown Exceptions

org.xml.sax.SAXException

See Also

org.xml.sax.ContentHandler.endPrefixMapping(java.lang.String)
org.xml.sax.ContentHandler.startElement(java.lang.String, java.lang.String, java.lang.String, org.xml.sax.Attributes)

Example

```
import org.xml.sax.Attributes;
import org.xml.sax.ContentHandler;
import org.xml.sax.Locator;
import org.xml.sax.SAXException;
. . .
    public void startPrefixMapping( String prefix,
                                    String uri )
                                    throws SAXException
    {
        System.out.println( "startPrefixMapping fired.\n\t" +
                            "prefix: " + prefix + "\n\t" +
                            "uri: " + uri );
    }
```

Parameters

String **prefix**   The namespace prefix coming into scope.

String **uri**   The namespace URI to which the prefix is mapped.

Returns

void   N/A.

DefaultHandler Class

The helper class, DefaultHandler, provides default implementations of the base SAX event handler interfaces in the org.xml.sax package. These interfaces are ContentHandler, DTDHandler, EntityResolver, and ErrorHandler.

The default event methods provided by the DefaultHandler class are, for the most part, empty methods, meaning that they do not perform any processing. This makes DefaultHandler extremely useful to application developers as SAX applications may inherit from this class and override only the event methods for which the application needs to perform custom processing, leaving the parent DefaultHandler class to handle any events that the application does not care about.

Parsers will also use this class to assign default event handlers. This allows the parser to perform its processing even if applications do not implement and assign event handlers.

Visual Basic Equivalent
N/A.

See Also
org.xml.sax.ContentHandler
org.xml.sax.DTDHandler
org.xml.sax.EntityResolver
org.xml.sax.ErrorHandler

Example
```
import org.xml.sax.Attributes;
import org.xml.sax.SAXException;
import org.xml.sax.helpers.DefaultHandler;
public class DefaultHandlerSample extends DefaultHandler
{
    //Override the ContentHandler.startElement method.
    public void startElement( String namespaceURI,
                              String localName,
                              String qualifiedName,
                              Attributes atts )
                              throws SAXException
    {
        System.out.println( "Start element event fired.\n\t" +
                            "Do some custom processing here." );
    }
}
```

Constructors

Java Signature
```
public DefaultHandler()
```

Visual Basic Signature
N/A.

This constructor method creates a `DefaultHandler` object. The `DefaultHandler` class is extremely useful in that it provides default implementations of the `ContentHandler`, `DTDHandler`, `EntityResolver`, and `ErrorHandler` interfaces.

Application writers should use the `DefaultHandler` class by extending the class; therefore, they will not have much use for this constructor method. However, parser writers will find this method useful for creating a default event handler so that it will function properly even if client application does not provide its own event handler class.

Example
```
DefaultHandler defHandler = new DefaultHandler();
```

Members

characters Method

Java Signature
```
public void characters(char[] ch, int start, int length)
```

Visual Basic Signature
N/A.

This method is an implementation of the `characters()` method of the `ContentHandler` interface. This default implementation does nothing. Applications may override this method to perform custom processing. See `ContentHandler.characters()` for further details.

Thrown Exceptions
org.xml.sax.SAXException

See Also
org.xml.sax.ContentHandler.characters(char[], int, int)

Example
See the `ContentHandler.characters()` method documentation for an example.

Parameters

char[] **ch**   The characters from the XML document.

int **start**   The start position in the character array.

int **length**   The number of characters to read from the array.

Returns
void   N/A.

endDocument Method

Java Signature
```
public void endDocument()
```

Visual Basic Signature
N/A.

This method is an implementation of the `endDocument()` method of the `ContentHandler` interface. This default implementation does nothing. Applications may override this method to perform custom processing. See `ContentHandler.endDocument()` for details.

Thrown Exceptions
org.xml.sax.SAXException

See Also
org.xml.sax.ContentHandler.endDocument()

Example
See the `ContentHandler.endDocument()` method documentation for an example.

Returns
void   N/A.

endElement Method

Java Signature
public void endElement(String uri, String localName, String qName)

Visual Basic Signature
N/A.

This method is an implementation of the endElement() method of the ContentHandler interface. This default implementation does nothing. Applications may override this method to perform custom processing.
　　See ContentHandler.endElement() for further details.

Thrown Exceptions
org.xml.sax.SAXException

See Also
org.xml.sax.ContentHandler.endElement(java.lang.String, java.lang.String, java.lang.String)

Example
See the ContentHandler.endElement() method documentation for an example.

Parameters
String uri　　The namespace URI of the element, or an empty string if namespace processing is not being performed.

String localName　　The local name of the element, or an empty string if namespace processing is not being performed.

String qName　　The qualified name of the element, or an empty string if qualified names are not available.

Returns
void　　N/A.

endPrefixMapping Method

Java Signature
public void endPrefixMapping(String prefix)

Visual Basic Signature
N/A.

This method is an implementation of the endPrefixMapping() method of the ContentHandler interface. This default implementation does nothing. Applications may override this method to perform custom processing.
　　See ContentHandler.endPrefixMapping() for details.

Thrown Exceptions
org.xml.sax.SAXException

See Also
org.xml.sax.ContentHandler.endPrefixMapping(java.lang.String)

Example

See the `ContentHandler.endPrefixMapping()` method documentation for an example.

Parameters

`String` **prefix**   The namespace prefix that went out of scope.

Returns

`void`   N/A.

error Method

Java Signature
```
public void error(SAXParseException e)
```

Visual Basic Signature
N/A.

This method is an implementation of the `error()` method of the `ErrorHandler` interface. This default implementation does nothing. Applications may override this method to perform custom processing. See `ErrorHandler.error()` for details.

Thrown Exceptions
`org.xml.sax.SAXException`

See Also
`org.xml.sax.SAXParseException`
`org.xml.sax.ErrorHandler.error(org.xml.sax.SAXParseException)`

Example

See the `ErrorHandler.error()` method documentation for an example.

Parameters

`SAXParseException` **e**   An instance of a SAX parse exception that encapsulates the details of the error.

Returns

`void`   N/A.

fatalError Method

Java Signature
```
public void fatalError(SAXParseException e)
```

Visual Basic Signature
N/A.

This method is an implementation of the `fatalError()` method of the `ErrorHandler` interface. This default implementation throws a `SAXParseException` error. Applications may override this method to perform custom processing. See `ErrorHandler.fatalError()` for details.

Thrown Exceptions
org.xml.sax.SAXException

See Also
org.xml.sax.SAXParseException
org.xml.sax.ErrorHandler.fatalError(org.xml.sax.SAXParseException)

Example
See the `ErrorHandler.fatalError()` method documentation for an example.

Parameters
SAXParseException **e**   An instance of a SAX parse exception that encapsulates the details of the error.

Returns
void   N/A.

ignorableWhitespace Method

Java Signature
public void ignorableWhitespace(char[] ch, int start, int length)

Visual Basic Signature
N/A.

This method is an implementation of the `ignorableWhitespace()` method of the `ContentHandler` interface. This default does nothing. Applications may override this method to perform custom processing. See `ContentHandler.ignorableWhitespace()` for details.

Thrown Exceptions
org.xml.sax.SAXException

See Also
org.xml.sax.ContentHandler.ignorableWhitespace(char[], int, int)

Example
See the `ContentHandler.ignorableWhitespace()` method documentation for an example.

Parameters
char[] **ch**   The whitespace character data from the XML document.

int **start**   The start position in the character array.

int **length**   The number of characters to read from the array.

Returns
void   N/A.

notationDecl Method

Java Signature
public void notationDecl(String name, String publicId, String systemId)

Visual Basic Signature
N/A.

This method is an implementation of the notationDecl() method of the DTDHandler interface. This default does nothing. Applications may override this method to perform custom processing. See DTDHandler.notationDecl() for details.

Thrown Exceptions
org.xml.sax.SAXException

See Also
org.xml.sax.DTDHandler.notationDecl(java.lang.String, java.lang.String, java.lang.String)

Example
See the DTDHandler.notationDecl() method documentation for an example.

Parameters
String **name**   The notation name.

String **publicId**   The public identifier of the notation, or null if no public identifier is available.

String **systemId**   The system identifier of the notation, or null if no system identifier is available. If this parameter is a URL, the parser must fully resolve it before calling the notationDecl() method in the application.

Returns
void   N/A.

processingInstruction Method

Java Signature
public void processingInstruction(String target, String data)

Visual Basic Signature
N/A.

This method is an implementation of the processingInstruction() method of the ContentHandler interface. This default does nothing. Applications may override this method to perform custom processing. See ContentHandler.processingInstruction() for details.

Thrown Exceptions
org.xml.sax.SAXException

See Also
org.xml.sax.ContentHandler.processingInstruction(java.lang.String, java.lang.String)

Example

See the ContentHandler.processingInstruction() method documentation for an example.

Parameters

String **target**   The processing instruction target.

String **data**   The processing instruction data, or null if no data was supplied. The data does not include any whitespace separating the data from the target.

Returns

void   N/A.

resolveEntity Method

Java Signature
public InputSource resolveEntity(String publicId, String systemId)

Visual Basic Signature
N/A.

This method is an implementation of the resolveEntity() method of the EntityResolver interface. This default implementation always returns null, forcing the parser to use the system identifier in the XML document. Applications may override this method to perform custom processing. See EntityResolver.resolveEntity() for details.

Thrown Exceptions
org.xml.sax.SAXException

See Also
org.xml.sax.EntityResolver.resolveEntity(java.lang.String, java.lang.String)

Example

See the EntityResolver.resolveEntity() method documentation for an example.

Parameters

String **publicId**   The public identifier of the external entity being referenced, or null if no public identifier was supplied.

String **systemId**   The system identifier of the external entity being referenced. If the system identifier is a URL, the parser must fully resolve the reference before triggering this event.

Returns

InputSource   An InputSource for the resolved entity. This default implementation always returns null.

setDocumentLocator Method

Java Signature
public void setDocumentLocator(Locator locator)

Visual Basic Signature
N/A.

This method is an implementation of the setDocumentLocator() method of the ContentHandler interface. This default implementation does nothing. Applications may override this method to perform custom processing. See ContentHandler.setDocumentLocator() for details.

See Also
org.xml.sax.Locator
org.xml.sax.ContentHandler.setDocumentLocator(org.xml.sax.Locator)

Example
See the ContentHandler.setDocumentLocator() method documentation for an example.

Parameters
Locator **locator**   A Locator object capable of returning the location of any document-related event.

Returns
void   N/A.

skippedEntity Method

Java Signature
public void skippedEntity(String name)

Visual Basic Signature
N/A.

This method is an implementation of the skippedEntity() method of the ContentHandler interface. This default implementation does nothing. Applications may override this method to perform custom processing. See ContentHandler.skippedEntity() for details.

Thrown Exceptions
org.xml.sax.SAXException

See Also
org.xml.sax.ContentHandler.processingInstruction(java.lang.String, java.lang.String)

Example
See the ContentHandler.skippedEntity() method documentation for an example.

Parameters
String **name**   The name of the skipped entity. If it is a parameter entity, the name will begin with %. If the entity is an external DTD subset, it will be the string [dtd].

Returns

void   N/A.

startDocument Method

Java Signature
public void startDocument()

Visual Basic Signature
N/A.

This method is an implementation of the startDocument() method of the ContentHandler interface. This default implementation does nothing. Applications may override this method to perform custom processing. See ContentHandler.startDocument() for details.

Thrown Exceptions
org.xml.sax.SAXException

See Also
org.xml.sax.ContentHandler.startDocument()

Example
See the ContentHandler.startDocument() method documentation for an example.

Returns

void   N/A.

startElement Method

Java Signature
public void startElement(String uri, String localName, String qName, Attributes attributes)

Visual Basic Signature
N/A.

This method is an implementation of the startElement() method of the ContentHandler interface. This default implementation does nothing. Applications may override this method to perform custom processing. See ContentHandler.startElement() for details.

Thrown Exceptions
org.xml.sax.SAXException

See Also
org.xml.sax.ContentHandler.startElement(java.lang.String, java.lang.String, java.lang.String, org.xml.sax.Attributes)

Example
See the ContentHandler.startElement() method documentation for an example.

Parameters

String **uri**   The element's namespace URI, or an empty string if namespace processing is not being performed.

String **localName**   The local name of the element, or an empty string if namespace processing is not being performed.

String **qName**   The element's qualified name, or an empty string if the qualified name is not available.

Attributes **attributes**   An instance of an object that implements the Attributes interface that represents the list of attributes attached to the element.

Returns

void   N/A.

startPrefixMapping Method

Java Signature
public void startPrefixMapping(String prefix, String uri)

Visual Basic Signature
N/A.

This method is an implementation of the startPrefixMapping() method of the ContentHandler interface. This default implementation does nothing. Applications may override this method to perform custom processing.
    See ContentHandler.startPrefixMapping() for details.

Thrown Exceptions
org.xml.sax.SAXException

See Also
org.xml.sax.ContentHandler.startPrefixMapping(java.lang.String, java.lang.String)

Example

See the ContentHandler.startPrefixMapping() method documentation for an example.

Parameters

String **prefix**   The namespace prefix coming into scope.

String **uri**   The namespace URI to which the prefix is mapped.

Returns

void   N/A.

unparsedEntityDecl Method

Java Signature
public void unparsedEntityDecl(String name, String publicId, String systemId, String notationName)

Visual Basic Signature
N/A.

This method is an implementation of the `unparsedEntityDecl()` method of the `DTDHandler` interface. This default implementation does nothing. Applications may override this method to perform custom processing.

See `DTDHandler.unparsedEntityDecl()` for details.

Thrown Exceptions
org.xml.sax.SAXException

See Also
org.xml.sax.DTDHandler.unparsedEntityDecl(java.lang.String, java.lang.String, java.lang.String, java.lang.String)

Example
See the `DTDHandler.unparsedEntityDecl()` method documentation for an example.

Parameters
String **name**   The unparsed entity's name.

String **publicId**   The public identifier of the entity, or `null` if no public identifier was given.

String **systemId**   The system identifier of the entity, or `null` if no system identifier was given. If this parameter is a URL, the parser must fully resolve it before calling the `unparsedEntityDecl()` method in the application.

String **notationName**   The name of the notation corresponding to a `notationDecl()` event.

Returns
void   N/A.

warning Method

Java Signature
public void warning(SAXParseException e)

Visual Basic Signature
N/A.

This method is an implementation of the `warning()` method of the `ErrorHandler` interface. This default implementation does nothing. Applications may override this method to perform custom processing.

See `ErrorHandler.warning()` for details.

Thrown Exceptions
org.xml.sax.SAXException

See Also

org.xml.sax.SAXParseException
org.xml.sax.ErrorHandler.warning(org.xml.sax.SAXParseException)

Example

See the `ErrorHandler.warning()` method documentation for an example.

Parameters

SAXParseException **e**   An instance of a SAX parse exception that encapsulates the details of the warning.

Returns

void   N/A.

DTDHandler Interface

The `DTDHandler` interface provides visibility for DTD-related events to applications implementing this callback interface. The application registers an instance of an object that implements the `DTDHandler` interface with the parser using the `setDTDHandler()` method of `XMLReader`. As the XML document is processed, the parser calls methods in the registered `DTDHandler` each time it encounters a notation or unparsed entity, thereby triggering events in the application.

It is the application's responsibility to retain DTD information so that the information can later be retrieved about unparsed entities encountered while reading the XML document.

Visual Basic Equivalent

IVBSAXDTDHandler

See Also

org.xml.sax.ContentHandler
org.xml.sax.ErrorHandler
org.xml.sax.helpers.DefaultHandler
org.xml.sax.XMLReader.getDTDHandler()
org.xml.sax.XMLReader.setDTDHandler(org.xml.sax.DTDHandler)

Example

```
import org.xml.sax.DTDHandler;
import org.xml.sax.SAXException;
public class DTDHandlerSample implements DTDHandler
{
. . .
}
```

Members

notationDecl Method

Java Signature
```
public void notationDecl(String name, String publicId, String systemId)
```

Visual Basic Signature
Public Sub notationDecl(StrName As String, strPublicId As String, strSystemId As String)

This method is invoked when the parser finds a notation declaration in the XML document; however, there is no guarantee that the declaration will be reported before any unparsed entities that use it.

At least one of the two parameters, publicId and systemId, must be non-null. If the parameter systemId is a URL, the parser must fully resolve the URL before triggering this event method in the application.

Thrown Exceptions
org.xml.sax.SAXException

See Also
org.xml.sax.AttributeList
org.xml.sax.DTDHandler.unparsedEntityDecl(java.lang.String, java.lang.String, java.lang.String, java.lang.String)

Example
```
import org.xml.sax.DTDHandler;
import org.xml.sax.SAXException;
. . .
    public void notationDecl(   String name,
                                String publicID,
                                String systemID ) throws SAXException
    {
        System.out.println("notationDecl event fired.\n\t" +
                            "name: " + name + "\n\t" +
                            "publicID: " + publicID + "\n\t" +
                            "systemID: " + systemID );
    }
```

Parameters

String name   The notation name.

String publicId   The public identifier of the notation, or null if none was given.

String systemId   The system identifier of the notation, or null if none was given. If this parameter is a URL, the parser must fully resolve it before calling the notationDecl() method in the application.

Returns
void   N/A.

unparsedEntityDecl Method

Java Signature
public void unparsedEntityDecl(String name, String publicId, String systemId, String notationName)

Visual Basic Signature
Public Sub unparsedEntityDecl(strName As String, strPublicId As String, strSystemId As String, strNotationName As String)

This method is invoked when the parser finds an unparsed entity declaration in the XML document.

At least one of the two parameters, publicId and systemId, must be non-null. If the parameter systemId is a URL, the parser must fully resolve the URL before triggering this event method in the application.

The parameter notationName corresponds to a notation declaration reported by a notationDecl() event.

Thrown Exceptions
org.xml.sax.SAXException

See Also
org.xml.sax.AttributeList
org.xml.sax.DTDHandler.notationDecl(java.lang.String, java.lang.String, java.lang.String)

Example
```
import org.xml.sax.DTDHandler;
import org.xml.sax.SAXException;
. . .
    public void unparsedEntityDecl( String name,
                                    String publicID,
                                    String systemID,
                                    String notationName )
                          throws SAXException
    {
        System.out.println( "unparsedEntityDecl event fired.\n\t" +
                            "name: " + name + "\n\t" +
                            "publicID: " + publicID + "\n\t" +
                            "systemID: " + systemID + "\n\t" +
                            "notationName: " + notationName );
    }
```

Parameters

String **name**   The unparsed entity's name.

String **publicId**   The public identifier of the entity, or null if none was given.

String **systemId**   The system identifier of the entity, or null if none was given. If this parameter is a URL, the parser must fully resolve it before calling the unparsedEntityDecl() method in the application.

String **notationName**   The name of the notation corresponding to a notationDecl() event.

Returns
void   N/A.

EntityResolver Interface

By implementing the `EntityResolver` interface, a SAX application may intercept parser requests for resolution of external entities, allowing the application to provide support for custom entities. The application registers an instance of an object that implements the `EntityResolver` interface with the parser by using the `setEntityResolver()` method of `XMLReader`.

Most applications do not need to implement this interface; however, implementing the `EntityResolver` interface provides a very powerful and flexible technique to application writers. By intercepting external entity resolution requests, the application can provide the resolution for the entity itself. In this case, the application may perform tasks as simple as substituting a local DTD for an external DTD —a useful technique when the parser is trapped behind a corporate firewall. Another possible and more exotic technique is the use of an implementation of `EntityResolver` to support a custom URL protocol, such as one involving database links or environment variables. This technique is illustrated in Chapter 4.

Visual Basic Equivalent
IVBSAXEntityResolver

See Also
org.xml.sax.InputSource
org.xml.sax.XMLReader.getEntityResolver()
org.xml.sax.XMLReader.setEntityResolver(org.xml.sax.EntityResolver)

Example
```
import java.io.IOException;
import org.xml.sax.EntityResolver;
import org.xml.sax.InputSource;
import org.xml.sax.SAXException;
public class EntityResolverSample implements EntityResolver
{
. . .
}
```

Members

resolveEntity Method

Java Signature
```
public InputSource resolveEntity(String publicId, String systemId)
```

Visual Basic Signature
```
Public Function resolveEntity(strPublicId As String, strSystemId As String) As Variant
```

The parser invokes this method to request resolution of an external entity reference. The parser requests resolution for *all* external entities except top-level document entities.

By intercepting external entity requests, an application may either resolve the requests itself or request that the parser resolve the entity by returning `null`.

Thrown Exceptions
java.io.IOException
org.xml.sax.SAXException

See Also

org.xml.sax.InputSource

Example
```
import java.io.IOException;
import org.xml.sax.EntityResolver;
import org.xml.sax.InputSource;
import org.xml.sax.SAXException;
...
    public InputSource resolveEntity(   String publicID,
                                        String systemID )
                                        throws SAXException,
                                        IOException
    {
        InputSource inSource;
        System.out.println( "resolveEntity event fired.\n\t" +
                            "publicID: " + publicID + "\n\t" +
                            "systemID: " + systemID );
        inSource = new InputSource( systemID );
        return( inSource );
    }
```

Parameters

String **publicId**   The public identifier of the external entity being referenced, or null if none was supplied.

String **systemId**   The system identifier of the external entity being referenced. If the system identifier is a URL, the parser must fully resolve the reference before triggering this event.

Returns

InputSource   An InputSource for the external entity or null.

ErrorHandler Interface

The ErrorHandler interface allows an application to receive notification of error events by implementing this callback interface. The application registers an instance of an object that implements the ErrorHandler interface with the parser by using the setErrorHandler() method of the XMLReader. If an application does not register an instance of an object that implements the ErrorHandler interface with the parser, parsing errors will go unreported with unpredictable results.

By receiving notification of error events, an application may implement custom error handling for particular error classes. The SAXParseException passed to each of the methods in this interface provides detailed information about the cause and location of the error.

The definitions of *fatal error*, *error*, and *warning* conform to the W3C XML 1.0 recommendation.

Visual Basic Equivalent

IVBSAXErrorHandler

See Also

org.xml.sax.helpers.DefaultHandler
org.xml.sax.SAXParseException
org.xml.sax.XMLReader.getErrorHandler()
org.xml.sax.XMLReader.setErrorHandler(org.xml.sax.ErrorHandler)

Example

```
import org.xml.sax.ErrorHandler;
import org.xml.sax.SAXException;
import org.xml.sax.SAXParseException;
public class ErrorHandlerSample implements ErrorHandler
{
. . .
}
```

Members

error Method

Java Signature

```
public void error(SAXParseException exception)
```

Visual Basic Signature

```
Public Sub error(ByVal oLocator As IVBSAXLocator, strErrorMessage As String, ByVal nErrorCode As Long)
```

This method is invoked by the parser whenever the parser encounters a recoverable error as defined in the W3C XML 1.0 recommendation. For example, a recoverable error event occurs when a validating parser encounters an element that does not conform to the document's DTD. Since, according to the definition of *recoverable error*, the parser should be able to continue processing the XML document, the parser must continue to provide normal parsing events after invoking this method.

Thrown Exceptions

org.xml.sax.SAXException

See Also

org.xml.sax.SAXParseException

Example

```
import org.xml.sax.ErrorHandler;
import org.xml.sax.SAXException;
import org.xml.sax.SAXParseException;
. . .
    public void error( SAXParseException exception )
                throws SAXException
    {
        System.err.println( "error event fired\n\t" +
            "Line: " + exception.getLineNumber() + "\n\t" +
```

```
                "Column: " + exception.getColumnNumber() + "\n\t" +
                "PublicID: " + exception.getPublicId() + "\n\t" +
                "SystemID: " + exception.getSystemId() + "\n\t" +
                "Message: " + exception.getMessage() );
    }
```

Parameters

SAXParseException **exception**   An instance of a SAX parse exception that encapsulates the details of the error.

Returns

void   N/A.

fatalError Method

Java Signature
```
public void fatalError(SAXParseException exception)
```

Visual Basic Signature
```
Public Sub fatalError(ByVal oLocator As IVBSAXLocator, strErrorMessage As String, ByVal nErrorCode As Long)
```

This method is invoked by the parser whenever the parser encounters a fatal error as defined in the W3C XML 1.0 recommendation. Non-recoverable errors are generally violations of XML well-formedness rules such as a missing end element tag. Since, according to the definition of *fatal error*, the parser should not be able to continue processing the XML document, the parser is free to abort processing of the XML document after invoking this method.

Thrown Exceptions
org.xml.sax.SAXException

See Also
org.xml.sax.SAXParseException

Example
```
import org.xml.sax.ErrorHandler;
import org.xml.sax.SAXException;
import org.xml.sax.SAXParseException;
. . .
    public void fatalError( SAXParseException exception )
                    throws SAXException
    {
        System.err.println( "fatal error event fired\n\t" +
                "Line: " + exception.getLineNumber() + "\n\t" +
                "Column: " + exception.getColumnNumber() + "\n\t" +
                "PublicID: " + exception.getPublicId() + "\n\t" +
                "SystemID: " + exception.getSystemId() + "\n\t" +
                "Message: " + exception.getMessage() );
    }
```

Parameters

SAXParseException **exception**   An instance of a SAX parse exception that encapsulates the details of the error.

Returns

void   N/A.

warning Method

Java Signature
```
public void warning(SAXParseException exception)
```

Visual Basic Signature
```
Public Sub ignorableWarning(ByVal oLocator As IVBSAXLocator, strErrorMessage As String, ByVal nErrorCode As Long)
```

This method is invoked by the parser whenever the parser encounters a warning as defined in the W3C XML 1.0 recommendation. For example, the parser may issue a warning event if it encounters duplicate declarations of an external parsed entity. Since, according to the definition of *warning*, the parser should be able to continue processing the XML document, the parser must continue to provide normal parsing events after invoking this method.

Thrown Exceptions
org.xml.sax.SAXException

See Also
org.xml.sax.SAXParseException

Example
```java
import org.xml.sax.ErrorHandler;
import org.xml.sax.SAXException;
import org.xml.sax.SAXParseException;
. . .
    public void warning( SAXParseException exception ) throws SAXException
    {
        System.err.println( "warning event fired\n\t" +
                "Line: " + exception.getLineNumber() + "\n\t" +
                "Column: " + exception.getColumnNumber() + "\n\t" +
                "PublicID: " + exception.getPublicId() + "\n\t" +
                "SystemID: " + exception.getSystemId() + "\n\t" +
                "Message: " + exception.getMessage() );
    }
```

Parameters

SAXParseException **exception**   An instance of a SAX parse exception that encapsulates the details of the warning.

Returns

void   N/A.

InputSource Class

The InputSource class is an abstraction of an XML data source, allowing a SAX application to encapsulate information about the input source such as the public identifier, system identifier, byte stream, and character stream. The application may specify an InputSource object to the parser as an argument to the XMLReader.parse() (or Parser.parse() if using SAX 1.0) method or as the return value of the EntityResolver.resolveEntity() method.

The parser uses the specified InputSource object to determine the method of reading the XML document. If the InputSource object supplies a character stream, the parser will use it. If no character stream is available and the InputSource object supplies a byte stream, the parser will use the supplied byte stream. If no stream is available, the parser will attempt to use the URI specified by the system identifier in the InputSource object.

Visual Basic Equivalent
N/A.

See Also
java.io.InputStream
java.io.Reader
org.xml.sax.EntityResolver.resolveEntity(java.lang.String, java.lang.String)
org.xml.sax.Parser.parse(org.xml.sax.InputSource)

Example
```
import org.xml.sax.InputSource;
import java.io.InputStream;
import java.io.FileInputStream;
import java.io.Reader;
import java.io.FileReader;
import java.io.FileNotFoundException;
. . .
    private InputSource myInputSource;
    public InputSourceSample( Object source )
    {
        if( source == null )
            myInputSource = new InputSource();
        else if( source instanceof String )
            myInputSource = new InputSource( (String)source );
        else if( source instanceof InputStream )
            myInputSource = new InputSource( (InputStream)source );
        else if( source instanceof Reader )
            myInputSource = new InputSource( (Reader)source );
    }
```

Constructors

Java Signature
```
public  InputSource()
```

Visual Basic Signature
N/A.

This constructor method creates a new, empty instance of InputSource. The class's set*() methods must be used to configure the object.

See Also
org.xml.sax.InputSource.setByteStream(java.io.InputStream)
org.xml.sax.InputSource.setCharacterStream(java.io.Reader)
org.xml.sax.InputSource.setEncoding(java.lang.String)
org.xml.sax.InputSource.setPublicId(java.lang.String)
org.xml.sax.InputSource.setSystemId(java.lang.String)

Example
```java
import org.xml.sax.InputSource;
import java.io.InputStream;
import java.io.FileInputStream;
import java.io.Reader;
import java.io.FileReader;
import java.io.FileNotFoundException;
. . .
    private InputSource myInputSource;
    public InputSourceSample( Object source )
    {
        if( source == null )
            myInputSource = new InputSource();
        else if( source instanceof String )
            myInputSource = new InputSource( (String)source );
        else if( source instanceof InputStream )
            myInputSource = new InputSource( (InputStream)source );
        else if( source instanceof Reader )
            myInputSource = new InputSource( (Reader)source );
    }
```

Java Signature
public InputSource(InputStream byteStream)

Visual Basic Signature
N/A.

This constructor method creates a new instance of InputSource with the passed byte stream. Applications may invoke the InputSource.setEncoding() method to specify the resulting stream's encoding. See the InputSource.setEncoding() method documentation for more information on character encoding.

See Also
org.xml.sax.InputSource.setByteStream(java.io.InputStream)
org.xml.sax.InputSource.setCharacterStream(java.io.Reader)
org.xml.sax.InputSource.setEncoding(java.lang.String)
org.xml.sax.InputSource.setPublicId(java.lang.String)
org.xml.sax.InputSource.setSystemId(java.lang.String)

Example
```
import org.xml.sax.InputSource;
import java.io.InputStream;
import java.io.FileInputStream;
import java.io.Reader;
import java.io.FileReader;
import java.io.FileNotFoundException;
. . .
    private InputSource myInputSource;
    public InputSourceSample( Object source )
    {
        if( source == null )
            myInputSource = new InputSource();
        else if( source instanceof String )
            myInputSource = new InputSource( (String)source );
        else if( source instanceof InputStream )
            myInputSource = new InputSource( (InputStream)source );
        else if( source instanceof Reader )
            myInputSource = new InputSource( (Reader)source );
    }
```

Parameters

InputStream **byteStream**   A raw byte stream from which the XML document may be read.

Java Signature
```
public  InputSource(Reader characterStream)
```

Visual Basic Signature
N/A.

This constructor method creates a new InputSource encapsulating the passed character stream.

See Also
org.xml.sax.InputSource.setByteStream(java.io.InputStream)
org.xml.sax.InputSource.setCharacterStream(java.io.Reader)
org.xml.sax.InputSource.setPublicId(java.lang.String)
org.xml.sax.InputSource.setSystemId(java.lang.String)

Example
```
import org.xml.sax.InputSource;
import java.io.InputStream;
import java.io.FileInputStream;
import java.io.Reader;
import java.io.FileReader;
import java.io.FileNotFoundException;
. . .
    private InputSource myInputSource;
```

(continued on next page)

```
    public InputSourceSample( Object source )
    {
        if( source == null )
            myInputSource = new InputSource();
        else if( source instanceof String )
            myInputSource = new InputSource( (String)source );
        else if( source instanceof InputStream )
            myInputSource = new InputSource( (InputStream)source );
        else if( source instanceof Reader )
            myInputSource = new InputSource( (Reader)source );
    }
```

Parameters

Reader **characterStream**   A character stream from which the XML document may be read.

Java Signature
```
public  InputSource(String systemId)
```

Visual Basic Signature
N/A.

This constructor method creates a new instance of InputSource with the specified system identifier (URI). If the passed system identifier is a URL, it must be fully resolved.

See Also
```
org.xml.sax.InputSource.setByteStream(java.io.InputStream)
org.xml.sax.InputSource.setCharacterStream(java.io.Reader)
org.xml.sax.InputSource.setEncoding(java.lang.String)
org.xml.sax.InputSource.setPublicId(java.lang.String)
org.xml.sax.InputSource.setSystemId(java.lang.String)
```

Example
```
import org.xml.sax.InputSource;
import java.io.InputStream;
import java.io.FileInputStream;
import java.io.Reader;
import java.io.FileReader;
import java.io.FileNotFoundException;
. . .
    private InputSource myInputSource;
    public InputSourceSample( Object source )
    {
        if( source == null )
            myInputSource = new InputSource();
        else if( source instanceof String )
            myInputSource = new InputSource( (String)source );
        else if( source instanceof InputStream )
```

```
            myInputSource = new InputSource( (InputStream)source );
        else if( source instanceof Reader )
            myInputSource = new InputSource( (Reader)source );
    }
```

Parameters

String `systemId`   A fully resolved system identifier.

Members

getByteStream Method

Java Signature
```
public InputStream getByteStream()
```

Visual Basic Signature
N/A.

This method returns the byte stream for an instance of an InputSource. If no byte stream has been supplied for the InputSource object, null is returned. Applications may discover the character encoding scheme by invoking the InputSource.getEncoding() method.

See Also
org.xml.sax.InputSource.getEncoding()
org.xml.sax.InputSource.setByteStream(java.io.InputStream)

Example
```
import org.xml.sax.InputSource;
import java.io.InputStream;
import java.io.FileInputStream;
import java.io.Reader;
import java.io.FileReader;
import java.io.FileNotFoundException;
. . .
        InputStream myStream;
        myStream = myInputSource.getByteStream();
```

Returns

InputStream   The encapsulated byte stream, or null if the InputSource is not using a byte stream.

getCharacterStream Method

Java Signature
```
public Reader getCharacterStream()
```

Visual Basic Signature
N/A.

This method returns the character stream for an instance of an InputSource. If no character stream has been supplied for the InputSource object, null is returned.

See Also
org.xml.sax.InputSource.setCharacterStream(java.io.Reader)

Example
```
import org.xml.sax.InputSource;
import java.io.InputStream;
import java.io.FileInputStream;
import java.io.Reader;
import java.io.FileReader;
import java.io.FileNotFoundException;
. . .
      Reader myReader;
      myReader = myInputSource.getCharacterStream();
```

Returns

Reader   The encapsulated character stream, or null if the InputSource is not using a character stream.

getEncoding Method

Java Signature
```
public String getEncoding()
```

Visual Basic Signature
N/A.

This method returns the character encoding scheme in use by an instance of InputSource. If no character encoding scheme was supplied for the InputSource object, null is returned. Character encoding schemes are meaningful only when InputSource is encapsulating a byte stream.

See Also
org.xml.sax.InputSource.getByteStream()
org.xml.sax.InputSource.getSystemId()
org.xml.sax.InputSource.setByteStream(java.io.InputStream)

Example
```
import org.xml.sax.InputSource;
import java.io.InputStream;
import java.io.FileInputStream;
import java.io.Reader;
import java.io.FileReader;
import java.io.FileNotFoundException;
. . .
      System.out.println( "Encoding: " +
                      myInputSource.getEncoding() );
```

Returns

String   The character encoding scheme for InputSource.

getPublicId Method

Java Signature
public String getPublicId()

Visual Basic Signature
N/A.

This method returns the public identifier for an instance of an InputSource class. If no public identifier was supplied for the InputSource object, null is returned.

See Also
org.xml.sax.InputSource.setPublicId(java.lang.String)

Example
```
import org.xml.sax.InputSource;
import java.io.InputStream;
import java.io.FileInputStream;
import java.io.Reader;
import java.io.FileReader;
import java.io.FileNotFoundException;
. . .
        System.out.println( "Public ID: " +
                        myInputSource.getPublicId() );
```

Returns
String   The public identifier for InputSource.

getSystemId Method

Java Signature
public String getSystemId()

Visual Basic Signature
N/A.

This method returns the system identifier (URI) for an instance of the InputSource class. If the system identifier is a URL, it will be fully resolved.

See Also
org.xml.sax.InputSource.getEncoding()
org.xml.sax.InputSource.setSystemId(java.lang.String)

Example
```
import org.xml.sax.InputSource;
import java.io.InputStream;
import java.io.FileInputStream;
import java.io.Reader;
import java.io.FileReader;
import java.io.FileNotFoundException;
. . .
        System.out.println( "System ID: " +
                        myInputSource.getSystemId() );
```

Returns

String   The system identifier (URI) for InputSource, or null if none is available.

setByteStream Method

Java Signature
public void setByteStream(InputStream byteStream)

Visual Basic Signature
N/A.

This method provides an instance of the InputSource class with an input byte stream. The character encoding for the byte stream should be supplied to the InputSource object by invoking the InputSource.setEncoding() method.

If a character stream is supplied for the InputSource, the parser will use the character stream in preference to any supplied byte streams. If no character or byte stream is supplied for the InputSource, the parser will open a URI connection to the system identifier.

See Also
java.io.InputStream
org.xml.sax.InputSource.getByteStream()
org.xml.sax.InputSource.getEncoding()
org.xml.sax.InputSource.setEncoding(java.lang.String)

Example
```
import org.xml.sax.InputSource;
import java.io.InputStream;
import java.io.FileInputStream;
import java.io.Reader;
import java.io.FileReader;
import java.io.FileNotFoundException;
. . .
        FileInputStream myInputStream = null;
        try
        {
           myInputStream =
               new FileInputStream( "c:\\temp\\someFile.xml" );
        }
        catch( FileNotFoundException e )
        {
           System.out.println( "ERROR: " + e.toString() );
        }
        myInputSource.setByteStream( myInputStream );
```

Parameters
InputStream **byteStream**   An input byte stream containing an XML document.

Returns
void   N/A.

setCharacterStream Method

Java Signature
```
public void setCharacterStream(Reader characterStream)
```

Visual Basic Signature
N/A.

This method provides an instance of the InputSource class with an input character stream.

If a character stream is supplied for the InputSource, the parser will ignore any supplied byte streams and will not open any URI connections to the system identifier.

See Also
java.io.Reader
org.xml.sax.InputSource.getCharacterStream()

Example
```
import org.xml.sax.InputSource;
import java.io.InputStream;
import java.io.FileInputStream;
import java.io.Reader;
import java.io.FileReader;
import java.io.FileNotFoundException;
. . .
        FileReader myReader = null;
        try
        {
            myReader = new FileReader( "c:\\temp\\someFile.xml" );
        }
        catch( FileNotFoundException e )
        {
            System.out.println( "ERROR: " + e.toString() );
        }
        myInputSource.setCharacterStream( myReader );
```

Parameters
Reader **characterStream**   A character stream containing an XML document.

Returns
void   N/A.

setEncoding Method

Java Signature
```
public void setEncoding(String encoding)
```

Visual Basic Signature
N/A.

This method sets the character encoding for an instance of the `InputSource` class. Character encoding defines the mapping of binary numbers to human-readable characters. Therefore, this method is meaningful only for instances of `InputSource` that encapsulate a byte stream; if a character stream has been supplied for the `InputSource`, this method is meaningless and has no effect. If the `InputSource` is encapsulating a byte stream, then, as a matter of good practice, the character encoding scheme should be set.

All `XMLReader` implementations are required to support the character sets UTF-8 and UTF-16. These character encodings are Unicode 8-bit and 16-bit respectively. A list of character encodings supported by Java can be found at http://java.sun.com/j2se/1.3/docs/guide/intl/encoding.doc.html.

See Also
org.xml.sax.InputSource.getEncoding()
org.xml.sax.InputSource.setByteStream(java.io.InputStream)
org.xml.sax.InputSource.setSystemId(java.lang.String)

Example
```
import org.xml.sax.InputSource;
import java.io.InputStream;
import java.io.FileInputStream;
import java.io.Reader;
import java.io.FileReader;
import java.io.FileNotFoundException;
. . .
        myInputSource.setEncoding( "utf-8" );
```

Parameters
String encoding   A string meeting the W3C requirements for an XML encoding declaration (http://www.w3.org/TR/REC-xml#charencoding).

Returns
void   N/A.

setPublicId Method

Java Signature
`public void setPublicId(String publicId)`

Visual Basic Signature
N/A.

This method supplies the public identifier for an instance of the `InputSource` class. The public identifier is always optional; however, if one is supplied, it will be provided as part of the location information.

See Also
org.xml.sax.InputSource.getPublicId()
org.xml.sax.Locator.getPublicId()
org.xml.sax.SAXParseException.getPublicId()

Example
```
import org.xml.sax.InputSource;
import java.io.InputStream;
import java.io.FileInputStream;
import java.io.Reader;
import java.io.FileReader;
import java.io.FileNotFoundException;
. . .
        String publicID =   "-//Netscape Communications" +
                            "//DTD RSS 0.91//EN";
        myInputSource.setPublicId( publicID );
```

Parameters

String publicId   The public identifier for the InputSource.

Returns

void   N/A.

setSystemId Method

Java Signature
`public void setSystemId(String systemId)`

Visual Basic Signature
N/A.

This method supplies the system identifier (URI) to an instance of the InputSource class. If no character stream or byte stream has been associated with the InputSource, a system identifier is mandatory. Conversely, if the InputSource encapsulates a character stream or a byte stream, the system identifier is optional. In either case, if the system identifier is supplied, the information is available for error messages, and it may also be used to resolve relative URIs; therefore, it is recommended that the application always supply a system identifier to the InputSource.

If the system identifier is a URL, it must be fully resolved.

See Also
org.xml.sax.InputSource.getSystemId()
org.xml.sax.InputSource.setEncoding(java.lang.String)
org.xml.sax.Locator.getSystemId()
org.xml.sax.SAXParseException.getSystemId()

Example
```
import org.xml.sax.InputSource;
import java.io.InputStream;
import java.io.FileInputStream;
```

(continued on next page)

```
import java.io.Reader;
import java.io.FileReader;
import java.io.FileNotFoundException;
. . .
        String systemID =   "http://my.netscape.com/" +
                            "public/formats/rss-0.91.dtd";
        myInputSource.setSystemId( systemID );
```

Parameters

String **systemId**   A string containing the system identifier (URI). If the string contains a URL, it must be fully resolved.

Returns

void   N/A.

Locator Interface

The Locator interface differs from most other SAX interfaces in that the client application does not provide an implementation of the Locator interface. Instead, the parser *may* provide an implementation of this interface; if a SAX parser supplies Locator objects, the parser will invoke the client application's ContentHandler.setDocumentLocator() method at the start of XML document parsing, before any other events.

Once a client application has a reference to the parser's Locator, it may be used to determine the XML document, line, and column generating any document event.

Parsers are strongly encouraged, but not required, to supply Locator objects to applications; therefore, client applications must ensure that the parser has supplied a Locator object before attempting to use its methods.

Visual Basic Equivalent

IVBSAXLocator

See Also

org.xml.sax.ContentHandler.setDocumentLocator(org.xml.sax.Locator)

Example

```
import org.xml.sax.Attributes;
import org.xml.sax.Locator;
import org.xml.sax.SAXException;
import org.xml.sax.helpers.DefaultHandler;
. . .
public class LocatorSample extends DefaultHandler
{
    private Locator myLocator;
    public void setDocumentLocator( Locator locator )
    {
        myLocator = locator;
    }
. . .
}
```

Members

getColumnNumber Method

Java Signature
```
public int getColumnNumber()
```

Visual Basic Signature
```
Public Property columnNumber As Long
```

This method returns the column number for the end of the XML content generating the current document event. The column number is an approximation intended for use by error reporting and is not sufficiently accurate to be used for content editing of the XML document.

If no column number is available, -1 is returned.

See Also
org.xml.sax.Locator.getLineNumber()

Example
```
import org.xml.sax.Attributes;
import org.xml.sax.Locator;
import org.xml.sax.SAXException;
import org.xml.sax.helpers.DefaultHandler;
. . .
        System.out.println( "Column: " +
                        myLocator.getColumnNumber() );
```

Returns

int   The column number of the entity generating the event, or -1 if no column number is available.

getLineNumber Method

Java Signature
```
public int getLineNumber()
```

Visual Basic Signature
```
Public Property lineNumber As Long
```

This method returns the line number for the end of the XML content generating the current document event. The line number is an approximation intended for use by error reporting and is not sufficiently accurate to be used for content editing of the XML document.

If no line number is available, -1 is returned.

See Also
org.xml.sax.Locator.getColumnNumber()

Example

```
import org.xml.sax.Attributes;
import org.xml.sax.Locator;
import org.xml.sax.SAXException;
import org.xml.sax.helpers.DefaultHandler;
...
      System.out.println( "Line: " +
                         myLocator.getLineNumber() );
```

Returns

`int`   The line number of the entity generating the event, or -1 if no line number is available.

getPublicId Method

Java Signature
`public String getPublicId()`

Visual Basic Signature
`Public Property publicId As String`

This method returns the public identifier of the `InputSource` object triggering the current SAX event. If no public identifier is available, an empty string is returned.

See Also
`org.xml.sax.Locator.getSystemId()`

Example

```
import org.xml.sax.Attributes;
import org.xml.sax.Locator;
import org.xml.sax.SAXException;
import org.xml.sax.helpers.DefaultHandler;
...
      System.out.println( "PublicID: " +
                         myLocator.getPublicId() );
```

Returns

`String`   The public identifier of the `InputSource` object generating the event, or an empty string if no public identifier is available.

getSystemId Method

Java Signature
`public String getSystemId()`

Visual Basic Signature
`Public Property systemId As String`

This method returns the system identifier (URI) of the `InputSource` triggering the current SAX event. If the system identifier is a URL, the parser will fully resolve it before returning it to the application. If no system identifier is available, an empty string is returned.

See Also
org.xml.sax.Locator.getPublicId()

Example
```
import org.xml.sax.Attributes;
import org.xml.sax.Locator;
import org.xml.sax.SAXException;
import org.xml.sax.helpers.DefaultHandler;
. . .
        System.out.println( "SystemID: " +
                        myLocator.getSystemId() );
```

Returns
String   The system identifier of the InputSource generating the event, or an empty string if none is available.

LocatorImpl Class

The LocatorImpl class is a default implementation of the Locator interface found in the org.xml.sax package. The class serves two purposes. First, it provides a default implementation of the Locator interface for the convenience of parser writers. Secondly, application writers may use this class to create a copy of a Locator object, preserving its current state.

In addition to the get*() methods of the Locator interface, this class offers manipulator methods for setting the values of the system identifier, public identifier, line number, and column number.

Since LocatorImpl contains unique methods not declared as part of the Locator interface, you should never assume a passed Locator object was instantiated via the LocatorImpl class. Java developers should use the instanceof keyword to verify that an object is an instantiation of LocatorImpl before attempting to use any of the extended methods not declared in the Locator interface.

Visual Basic Equivalent
N/A.

See Also
org.xml.sax.Locator
org.xml.sax.ContentHandler.setDocumentLocator(org.xml.sax.Locator)

Example
```
import org.xml.sax.Attributes;
import org.xml.sax.Locator;
import org.xml.sax.SAXException;
import org.xml.sax.helpers.DefaultHandler;
import org.xml.sax.helpers.LocatorImpl;
. . .
        LocatorImpl locImpl = null;
```

Constructors

Java Signature
```
public LocatorImpl()
```

Visual Basic Signature
N/A.

This constructor method creates a new, empty instance of the `LocatorImpl` class. This method will not normally be useful to application writers, but it may be used by parser writers to create a single, reusable instance of `LocatorImpl`.

Example
```
import org.xml.sax.Attributes;
import org.xml.sax.Locator;
import org.xml.sax.SAXException;
import org.xml.sax.helpers.DefaultHandler;
import org.xml.sax.helpers.LocatorImpl;
. . .
        LocatorImpl locImpl = null;
. . .
        locImpl = new LocatorImpl();
```

Java Signature
```
public LocatorImpl(Locator locator)
```

Visual Basic Signature
N/A.

This constructor method creates an instance of the `LocatorImpl` class, copying the current state of the passed `Locator` object. This method is useful to applications that need to make a snapshot of a `Locator` object.

Example
```
import org.xml.sax.Attributes;
import org.xml.sax.Locator;
import org.xml.sax.SAXException;
import org.xml.sax.helpers.DefaultHandler;
import org.xml.sax.helpers.LocatorImpl;
. . .
        LocatorImpl locImpl = null;
. . .
        locImpl = new LocatorImpl( myLocator );
```

Parameters

`Locator` **locator**   An instance of an object that implements the `Locator` interface.

Members

getColumnNumber Method

Java Signature
public int getColumnNumber()

Visual Basic Signature
N/A.

This method is an implementation of the getColumnNumber() method of the Locator interface.
See Locator.getColumnNumber() for details.

See Also
org.xml.sax.helpers.LocatorImpl.setColumnNumber(int)
org.xml.sax.Locator.getColumnNumber()

Example
See the Locator.getColumnNumber() method documentation for an example.

Returns
int   The column number, within the XML document, of the element triggering the current event, or -1 if no column number is available.

getLineNumber Method

Java Signature
public int getLineNumber()

Visual Basic Signature
N/A.

This method is an implementation of the getLineNumber() method of the Locator interface.
See Locator.getLineNumber() for details.

See Also
org.xml.sax.helpers.LocatorImpl.setLineNumber(int)
org.xml.sax.Locator.getLineNumber()

Example
See the Locator.getLineNumber() method documentation for an example.

Returns
int   The line number, in the XML document, of the element triggering the current event, or -1 if no line number is available.

getPublicId Method

Java Signature
public String getPublicId()

Visual Basic Signature
N/A.

This method is an implementation of the `getpublicId()` method of the `Locator` interface.
　See `Locator.getpublicId()` for details.

See Also
org.xml.sax.InputSource
org.xml.sax.helpers.LocatorImpl.setPublicId(java.lang.String)
org.xml.sax.Locator.getPublicId()

Example
See the `Locator.getPublicID()` method documentation for an example.

Returns
String　The public identifier of the `InputSource` object associated with the current event.

getSystemId Method

Java Signature
public String getSystemId()

Visual Basic Signature
N/A.

This method is an implementation of the `getSystemID()` method of the `Locator` interface.
　See `Locator.getSystemID()` for details.

See Also
org.xml.sax.InputSource
org.xml.sax.helpers.LocatorImpl.setSystemId(java.lang.String)
org.xml.sax.Locator.getSystemId()

Example
See the `Locator.getSystemID()` method documentation for an example.

Returns
String　The system identifier of the XML `InputSource` object associated with the current event.

setColumnNumber Method

Java Signature
public void setColumnNumber(int columnNumber)

Visual Basic Signature
N/A.

This method sets the current XML document column number for the `LocatorImpl` object. Parser writers must use this method to set the column number before triggering a document event.

See Also
org.xml.sax.helpers.LocatorImpl.getColumnNumber()

Example
```
import org.xml.sax.Attributes;
import org.xml.sax.Locator;
import org.xml.sax.SAXException;
import org.xml.sax.helpers.DefaultHandler;
import org.xml.sax.helpers.LocatorImpl;
. . .
        LocatorImpl locImpl = null;
. . .
            locImpl.setColumnNumber( myLocator.getColumnNumber() );
```

Parameters

int **columnNumber**   The column number, or -1 if no column number is available.

Returns

void   N/A.

setLineNumber Method

Java Signature
```
public void setLineNumber(int lineNumber)
```

Visual Basic Signature
N/A.

This method sets the current XML document line number for the `LocatorImpl` object. Parser writers must use this method to set the line number before triggering a document event.

See Also
org.xml.sax.helpers.LocatorImpl.getLineNumber()

Example
```
import org.xml.sax.Attributes;
import org.xml.sax.Locator;
import org.xml.sax.SAXException;
import org.xml.sax.helpers.DefaultHandler;
import org.xml.sax.helpers.LocatorImpl;
. . .
        LocatorImpl locImpl = null;
. . .
            locImpl.setLineNumber( myLocator.getLineNumber() );
```

Parameters

int **lineNumber**   The line number, or -1 if no line number is available.

Returns

void   N/A.

setPublicId Method

Java Signature
```
public void setPublicId(String publicId)
```

Visual Basic Signature
N/A.

This method sets the current XML document public identifier for the LocatorImpl object. Parser writers must use this method to set the public identifier before triggering a document event.

See Also
org.xml.sax.helpers.LocatorImpl.getPublicId()

Example
```
import org.xml.sax.Attributes;
import org.xml.sax.Locator;
import org.xml.sax.SAXException;
import org.xml.sax.helpers.DefaultHandler;
import org.xml.sax.helpers.LocatorImpl;
. . .
        LocatorImpl locImpl = null;
. . .
            locImpl.setPublicId( myLocator.getPublicId() );
```

Parameters

String **publicId**   The public identifier, or null if no public identifier is available.

Returns

void   N/A.

setSystemId Method

Java Signature
```
public void setSystemId(String systemId)
```

Visual Basic Signature
N/A.

This method sets the current XML document system identifier for the LocatorImpl object. Parser writers must use this method to set the system identifier before triggering a document event. If the system identifier is not known, it should be set to null.

See Also

org.xml.sax.helpers.LocatorImpl.getSystemId()

Example
```
import org.xml.sax.Attributes;
import org.xml.sax.Locator;
import org.xml.sax.SAXException;
import org.xml.sax.helpers.DefaultHandler;
import org.xml.sax.helpers.LocatorImpl;
. . .
        LocatorImpl locImpl = null;
. . .
            locImpl.setSystemId( myLocator.getSystemId() );
```

Parameters

String **systemId**   The system identifier, or null if no system identifier is available.

Returns

void   N/A.

NamespaceSupport Class

The NamespaceSupport class encapsulates namespace processing logic by parsing qualified names into their namespace parts and keeping track of declarations for each context (scope).

An instance of the NamespaceSupport class may be reused, but its reset() method must be called between each session.

See Chapter 6 for a detailed discussion of the NamespaceSupport class.

Visual Basic Equivalent

N/A.

See Also

org.xml.sax.ContentHandler.endPrefixMapping(java.lang.String)
org.xml.sax.ContentHandler.startPrefixMapping(java.lang.String, java.lang.String)

Example
```
import org.xml.sax.Attributes;
import org.xml.sax.SAXException;
import org.xml.sax.helpers.DefaultHandler;
import org.xml.sax.helpers.NamespaceSupport;
import java.util.Enumeration;
. . .
    private NamespaceSupport supportNS = null;
```

Constructors

Java Signature
```
public NamespaceSupport()
```

Visual Basic Signature
N/A.

This constructor method creates a new, empty instance of the `NamespaceSupport` class.

Example
```
import org.xml.sax.Attributes;
import org.xml.sax.SAXException;
import org.xml.sax.helpers.DefaultHandler;
import org.xml.sax.helpers.NamespaceSupport;
import java.util.Enumeration;
. . .
    private NamespaceSupport supportNS = null;
. . .
        supportNS = new NamespaceSupport();
```

Members

declarePrefix Method

Java Signature
```
public boolean declarePrefix(String prefix, String uri)
```

Visual Basic Signature
N/A.

This method declares a prefix in the current namespace context, returning `true` if the specified prefix is legal, and `false` otherwise. The prefix will remain in effect until the context is popped — most likely at the end of an element.

To declare a default namespace, use an empty string (""). The prefix may not begin with xml per the XML 1.0 and Namespaces in XML Recommendations.

See Also
org.xml.sax.helpers.NamespaceSupport.getPrefix(java.lang.String)
org.xml.sax.helpers.NamespaceSupport.getURI(java.lang.String)
org.xml.sax.helpers.NamespaceSupport.popContext()
org.xml.sax.helpers.NamespaceSupport.processName(java.lang.String, java.lang.String[], boolean)
org.xml.sax.helpers.NamespaceSupport.pushContext()

Example
```
import org.xml.sax.Attributes;
import org.xml.sax.SAXException;
import org.xml.sax.helpers.DefaultHandler;
import org.xml.sax.helpers.NamespaceSupport;
import java.util.Enumeration;
. . .
    private boolean firstNamespaceFlag = true;
. . .
    //Override the DefaultHandler.startPrefixMapping method.
    public void startPrefixMapping( String prefix,
```

```
                            String uri )
                        throws SAXException
{
    if( firstNamespaceFlag == true )
    {
        // This is the first namespace, so we need to push
        // a new context.
        supportNS.pushContext();
        firstNamespaceFlag = false;
    }
    // Now declare the prefix.
    if( supportNS.declarePrefix( prefix, uri ) == false )
    {
        SAXException e = new SAXException( "Prefix: " +
                    prefix + " is not valid!" );
        throw e;
    }
}
```

Parameters

String prefix   A string containing the prefix to be declared. If declaring the default namespace, use an empty string.

String uri   A string containing the prefix's namespace URI.

Returns

boolean   If the specified prefix is legal, the method returns true; otherwise, it returns false.

getDeclaredPrefixes Method

Java Signature
```
public Enumeration getDeclaredPrefixes()
```

Visual Basic Signature
N/A.

This method returns an enumeration containing all the prefixes in the current namespace context. The default prefix will be included in the enumeration.

See Also
org.xml.sax.helpers.NamespaceSupport.getPrefixes()
org.xml.sax.helpers.NamespaceSupport.getURI(java.lang.String)

Example
```
import org.xml.sax.Attributes;
import org.xml.sax.SAXException;
import org.xml.sax.helpers.DefaultHandler;
import org.xml.sax.helpers.NamespaceSupport;
```

(continued on next page)

```
import java.util.Enumeration;
. . .
    Enumeration list;
    String nameSpace = null;
    String prefix = null;
    //Get list of currently declared prefixes.
    list = supportNS.getDeclaredPrefixes();
    System.out.println( "Declared prefixes: " );
    while( list.hasMoreElements() )
    {
        prefix = list.nextElement().toString();
        System.out.println( "\tNS: " + supportNS.getURI(prefix) +
                            "\tPrefix: " + prefix );
    }
```

Returns

Enumeration   An enumeration containing all the prefixes in the current context.

getPrefix Method

Java Signature
```
public String getPrefix(String uri)
```

Visual Basic Signature
N/A.

This method returns one of the prefixes associated with the specified namespace URI, or null if no prefixes are mapped to the URI or if the URI is assigned to the default namespace. If multiple prefixes are associated with the specified URI, the method will arbitrarily pick a prefix to return. To retrieve all of the prefixes associated with the URI, invoke the getPrefixes() method instead.

See Also
org.xml.sax.helpers.NamespaceSupport.getPrefixes(java.lang.String)
org.xml.sax.helpers.NamespaceSupport.getURI(java.lang.String)

Example
```
import org.xml.sax.Attributes;
import org.xml.sax.SAXException;
import org.xml.sax.helpers.DefaultHandler;
import org.xml.sax.helpers.NamespaceSupport;
import java.util.Enumeration;
. . .
    //Fetch one prefix for nameSpace.
    System.out.println( "NS: " + nameSpace +
        " has the prefix: " + supportNS.getPrefix( nameSpace ) );
```

Parameters

String uri   A string containing the namespace URI for which you want to find a prefix.

Returns

String   A prefix associated with the specified namespace URI, or null if no prefix exists.

getPrefixes Method

Java Signature
```
public Enumeration getPrefixes()
```

Visual Basic Signature
N/A.

This method returns an enumeration of *all* declared prefixes. The default (empty) prefix will not be included in the enumeration.

See Also
org.xml.sax.helpers.NamespaceSupport.getDeclaredPrefixes()
org.xml.sax.helpers.NamespaceSupport.getURI(java.lang.String)

Example
```java
import org.xml.sax.Attributes;
import org.xml.sax.SAXException;
import org.xml.sax.helpers.DefaultHandler;
import org.xml.sax.helpers.NamespaceSupport;
import java.util.Enumeration;
...
    Enumeration list;
    String nameSpace = null;
    String prefix = null;
...
    //Get list of current prefixes, except for the default prefix.
    list = supportNS.getPrefixes();
    System.out.println( "Declared prefixes (no default): " );
    while( list.hasMoreElements() )
    {
        prefix = list.nextElement().toString();
        nameSpace = supportNS.getURI( prefix );
        System.out.println( "\tNS: " + nameSpace +
                            "\tPrefix: " + prefix );
    }
```

Returns

Enumeration   An enumeration of *all* declared prefixes.

getPrefixes Method

Java Signature
```
public Enumeration getPrefixes(String uri)
```

Visual Basic Signature
N/A.

This method returns an enumeration of all prefixes currently declared for a namespace URI. The enumeration will include the xml: prefix but will not include the default (empty) prefix.

See Also
org.xml.sax.helpers.NamespaceSupport.getDeclaredPrefixes()
org.xml.sax.helpers.NamespaceSupport.getPrefix(java.lang.String)
org.xml.sax.helpers.NamespaceSupport.getURI(java.lang.String)

Example
```
import org.xml.sax.Attributes;
import org.xml.sax.SAXException;
import org.xml.sax.helpers.DefaultHandler;
import org.xml.sax.helpers.NamespaceSupport;
import java.util.Enumeration;
. . .
    Enumeration list;
    String nameSpace = null;
    String prefix = null;
. . .
    //Get list of prefixes for nameSpace.
    list = supportNS.getPrefixes( nameSpace );
    System.out.println( "Prefixes for NS (" + nameSpace + "): " );
    while( list.hasMoreElements() )
    {
        prefix = list.nextElement().toString();
        System.out.println( "\tNS: " + supportNS.getURI(prefix) +
                            "\tPrefix: " + prefix );
    }
```

Parameters

String uri   A string containing the namespace URI for which you want to obtain a list of prefixes.

Returns

Enumeration   An enumeration of all prefixes associated with the specified namespace URI.

getURI Method

Java Signature
```
public String getURI(String prefix)
```

Visual Basic Signature
N/A.

This method returns the current namespace URI from the passed prefix, or null if the prefix is not declared in the current context. An empty string ("") may be used to obtain the default namespace.

See Also
org.xml.sax.helpers.NamespaceSupport.getPrefix(java.lang.String)
org.xml.sax.helpers.NamespaceSupport.getPrefixes()

Example
```
import org.xml.sax.Attributes;
import org.xml.sax.SAXException;
import org.xml.sax.helpers.DefaultHandler;
import org.xml.sax.helpers.NamespaceSupport;
import java.util.Enumeration;
. . .
          nameSpace = supportNS.getURI( prefix );
```

Parameters
String prefix   The prefix to look up.

Returns
String   The URI for the specified prefix.

popContext Method

Java Signature
```
public void popContext()
```

Visual Basic Signature
N/A.

This method causes the current namespace context to go out of scope and restores the previous (most recent) namespace context into scope. This method is usually called at the end of each XML element.

Although you can (and should) declare prefixes after pushing a context, the reverse is not true; you cannot declare additional prefixes after popping a context.

See Also
org.xml.sax.helpers.NamespaceSupport.pushContext()

Example
```
import org.xml.sax.Attributes;
import org.xml.sax.SAXException;
import org.xml.sax.helpers.DefaultHandler;
import org.xml.sax.helpers.NamespaceSupport;
import java.util.Enumeration;
. . .
    //Override the DefaultHandler.endElement method.
    public void endElement( String namespaceURI,
                   String localName,
                   String qualifiedName )
                   throws SAXException
  {
    // ALWAYS pop the namespace context.
    supportNS.popContext();
  }
```

Returns

void   N/A.

processName Method

Java Signature
public String[] processName(String qName, String[] parts, boolean isAttribute)

Visual Basic Signature
N/A.

This method processes a raw name in the current context into its component namespace parts, returning the components in an array of three interned strings representing the namespace URI (or empty string), the local name, and the raw name.

The isAttributeflag is used to determine whether the tag specified by the passed name is an attribute or element. Unprefixed elements and unprefixed attributes are processed differently. An unprefixed element will be associated with the default namespace; unprefixed attributes will not be associated with the default namespace.

See Also
org.xml.sax.helpers.NamespaceSupport.declarePrefix(java.lang.String, java.lang.String)

Example
```
import org.xml.sax.Attributes;
import org.xml.sax.SAXException;
import org.xml.sax.helpers.DefaultHandler;
import org.xml.sax.helpers.NamespaceSupport;
import java.util.Enumeration;
. . .
    public void showProcessedName( String qName, boolean isAttribute )
    {
        String[] parts = null;
        String msg = "";
        parts = supportNS.processName( qName, parts, isAttribute );
        if( isAttribute )
            msg = "Attribute ";
        else
            msg = "Element ";
        msg += qName + " processes into: \n";
        msg += "\tNamespace URI: " + parts[0] + "\n";
        msg += "\tLocal Name: " + parts[1] + "\n";
        msg += "\tRaw Name: " + parts[2];
        System.out.println( msg );
    }
```

Parameters

String **qName**   The qualified name to be processed.

String[] **parts**   An array supplied by the caller, capable of holding at least three elements.

boolean isAttribute   A flag indicating whether this is an attribute name (true) or an element name (false).

Returns

String[]   An array of three interned strings representing the namespace URI, the local name, and the raw name.

pushContext Method

Java Signature
public void pushContext()

Visual Basic Signature
N/A.

This method creates a new namespace context. Contexts are pushed onto a stack when coming into scope and popped off the stack when going out of scope. This method is usually called at the start of each XML element. All current declarations will be automatically inherited, but not copied, by the new context.

A base context is automatically created by the NamespaceSupport object with the xml: prefix declared.

See Also
org.xml.sax.helpers.NamespaceSupport.popContext()

Example
```
import org.xml.sax.Attributes;
import org.xml.sax.SAXException;
import org.xml.sax.helpers.DefaultHandler;
import org.xml.sax.helpers.NamespaceSupport;
import java.util.Enumeration;
...
    private boolean firstNamespaceFlag = true;
...
    //Override the DefaultHandler.startElement method.
    public void startElement( String namespaceURI,
                    String localName,
                    String qualifiedName,
                    Attributes atts )
                    throws SAXException
    {
        if( firstNamespaceFlag == true )
        {
            // This element didn't have any namespace declarations,
            // but we still need to push a new context to keep the
            // stack right.
            supportNS.pushContext();
        }
```

(continued on next page)

```
        else
        {
            firstNamespaceFlag = true;
        }
    }
```

Returns

void   N/A.

reset Method

Java Signature
```
public void reset()
```

Visual Basic Signature
N/A.

This method clears this instance of the `NamespaceSupport` object, rendering it safe for reuse.

Example
```
import org.xml.sax.Attributes;
import org.xml.sax.SAXException;
import org.xml.sax.helpers.DefaultHandler;
import org.xml.sax.helpers.NamespaceSupport;
import java.util.Enumeration;
. . .
    //Override the DefaultHandler.endDocument method.
    public void endDocument()
    {
        supportNS.reset();
    }
```

Returns

void   N/A.

ParserAdapter Class

The helper class `ParserAdapter` wraps a SAX 1.0 `Parser` object, using the Adapter design pattern, making it appear to be a SAX 2.0 `XMLReader` object. It does this by implementing both the SAX 1.0 `DocumentHandler` interface and the SAX 2.0 `XMLReader` interface. A SAX 2.0 client application uses the SAX 2.0 `XMLReader` interface to communicate with the `ParserAdapter` object. The `ParserAdapter` object implements the SAX 1.0 `DocumentHandler` interface so that it can register itself with the SAX 1.0 `Parser` object, causing the SAX 1.0 `Parser` object to fire events to the `ParserAdapter`, which, in turn, fires SAX 2.0 `ContentHandler` events to the `ContentHandler` object registered by the application.

Since the application communicates with the `ParserAdapter` using the `XMLReader` interface, the application should never concern itself with the `DocumentHandler` interface implementation by `ParserAdapter`. In an ideal world, the `DocumentHandler` implementation would be hidden from the application; however, since the SAX 1.0 `Parser` object must be able to access the `DocumentHandler` interface, its methods must be declared public and are, therefore, visible to the client application.

Some SAX 2.0 features are not available from an adapted SAX 1.0 `Parser` object. An emulator cannot report `skippedEntity` events as SAX 1.0 parsers do not make that information available. Also, the `ParserAdapter` does not support SAX 2.0 properties and supports only two SAX 2.0 features. The two supported features are the core features http://xml.org/sax/features/namespaces and http://xml.org/sax/features/namespace-prefixes.

As SAX 2.0 becomes ubiquitous, the `ParserAdapter` class will eventually become obsolete.

Visual Basic Equivalent
N/A.

See Also
org.xml.sax.DocumentHandler
org.xml.sax.helpers.XMLReaderAdapter
org.xml.sax.Parser
org.xml.sax.XMLReader

Example
```
import org.xml.sax.ContentHandler;
import org.xml.sax.DTDHandler;
import org.xml.sax.EntityResolver;
import org.xml.sax.ErrorHandler;
import org.xml.sax.Parser;
import org.xml.sax.SAXException;
import org.xml.sax.SAXParseException;
import org.xml.sax.XMLReader;
import org.xml.sax.helpers.DefaultHandler;
import org.xml.sax.helpers.ParserAdapter;
import org.xml.sax.helpers.ParserFactory;
import java.io.IOException;
public class ParserAdapterSample
{
    // Sample constructor method.  Receives an instance of SAX1
    // Parser and the XML file path.
    public ParserAdapterSample( Parser SAX1xmlParser,
                                String xmlFile)
    {
        ParserAdapter SAX2xmlReader = null;
        DefaultHandler docHandler;
        if( SAX1xmlParser == null )
        {
            System.setProperty( "org.xml.sax.parser",
                        "org.apache.xerces.parsers.SAXParser" );
            try
            {
```

(continued on next page)

```java
                SAX2xmlReader = new ParserAdapter();
            }
            catch( SAXException e )
            {
                System.out.println( "ERROR: " + e.getMessage() );
            }
        }
        else
        {
            SAX2xmlReader = new ParserAdapter( SAX1xmlParser );
        }
        // Use an instance of DefaultHandler to provide default
        // implementations of event handler interfaces.
        docHandler = new DefaultHandler();
        SAX2xmlReader.setContentHandler( docHandler );
        SAX2xmlReader.setDTDHandler( docHandler );
        SAX2xmlReader.setEntityResolver( docHandler );
        SAX2xmlReader.setErrorHandler( docHandler );
        try
        {
            SAX2xmlReader.parse( xmlFile );
        }
        catch( SAXParseException e )
        {
            System.out.println( xmlFile + " is not well formed." );
            System.out.println( e.getMessage() +
                                " at line " +
                                e.getLineNumber() +
                                ", column " +
                                e.getColumnNumber() );
        }
        catch( SAXException e )
        {
            System.out.println( e.getMessage() );
        }
        catch( IOException e )
        {
            System.out.println( "Could not report on " + xmlFile +
                                " because of the IOException " + e );
        }
    }
}
```

Constructors

Java Signature
```java
public  ParserAdapter()
```

Visual Basic Signature
N/A.

This constructor method creates a new instance of the `ParserAdapter` class. The `org.xml.sax.parser` system property is used to specify the SAX 1.0 `Parser` object to embed within this object.

If the `org.xml.sax.parser` property is not set, or if the specified `Parser` object cannot be instantiated, a SAXException is thrown.

Example
```
import org.xml.sax.SAXException;
import org.xml.sax.SAXParseException;
import org.xml.sax.XMLReader;
import org.xml.sax.helpers.DefaultHandler;
import org.xml.sax.helpers.ParserAdapter;
import org.xml.sax.helpers.ParserFactory;
import java.io.IOException;
. . .
        ParserAdapter SAX2xmlReader = null;
. . .
        System.setProperty( "org.xml.sax.parser",
                       "org.apache.xerces.parsers.SAXParser" );
        try
        {
            SAX2xmlReader = new ParserAdapter();
        }
        catch( SAXException e )
        {
            System.out.println( "ERROR: " + e.getMessage() );
        }
```

Java Signature
`public ParserAdapter(Parser parser)`

Visual Basic Signature
N/A.

This method creates a new instance of the `ParserAdapter` class, wrapping the passed SAX 1.0 `Parser` object. The `Parser` object may not be changed once the `ParserAdapter` has been created. The passed `Parser` object may not be null; if it is, a `java.lang.NullPointerException` is thrown.

Example
```
import org.xml.sax.SAXException;
import org.xml.sax.SAXParseException;
import org.xml.sax.XMLReader;
import org.xml.sax.helpers.DefaultHandler;
import org.xml.sax.helpers.ParserAdapter;
import org.xml.sax.helpers.ParserFactory;
```

(continued on next page)

```
import java.io.IOException;
...
        ParserAdapter SAX2xmlReader = null;
...
            SAX2xmlReader = new ParserAdapter( SAX1xmlParser );
```

Parameters

Parser **parser**   The SAX 1.0 Parser object to adapt as a SAX 2.0 XMLReader object.

Members

characters Method

Java Signature
```
public void characters(char[] ch, int start, int length)
```

Visual Basic Signature
N/A.

This method is part of the `ParserAdapter` implementation of the SAX 1.0 `DocumentHandler` interface. SAX 2.0 application writers should not concern themselves with the `DocumentHandler` functions; in an ideal world, these functions would be encapsulated and invisible to SAX 2.0 applications. However, the `ParserAdapter` must declare the `DocumentHandler` interface as public so that the SAX 1.0 `Parser` object has access to the `DocumentHandler` event methods.

Thrown Exceptions
org.xml.sax.SAXException

See Also
org.xml.sax.DocumentHandler.characters(char[], int, int)

Example
Not applicable.

Parameters

char[] **ch**   An array of characters.

int **start**   The starting position in the array.

int **length**   The number of characters to use.

Returns
void   N/A.

endDocument Method

Java Signature
```
public void endDocument()
```

Visual Basic Signature
N/A.

This method is part of the `ParserAdapter` implementation of the SAX 1.0 `DocumentHandler` interface. SAX 2.0 application writers should not concern themselves with the `DocumentHandler` methods; in an ideal world, these functions would be encapsulated and invisible to SAX 2.0 applications. However, the `ParserAdapter` must declare the `DocumentHandler` interface as public so that the SAX 1.0 `Parser` object has access to the `DocumentHandler` event methods.

Thrown Exceptions
org.xml.sax.SAXException

See Also
org.xml.sax.DocumentHandler.endDocument()

Example
Not applicable.

Returns
void   N/A.

endElement Method

Java Signature
public void endElement(String qName)

Visual Basic Signature
N/A.

This method is part of the `ParserAdapter` implementation of the SAX 1.0 `DocumentHandler` interface. SAX 2.0 application writers should not concern themselves with the `DocumentHandler` methods; in an ideal world, these functions would be encapsulated and invisible to SAX 2.0 applications. However, the `ParserAdapter` must declare the `DocumentHandler` interface as public so that the SAX 1.0 `Parser` object has access to the `DocumentHandler` event methods.

Thrown Exceptions
org.xml.sax.SAXException

See Also
org.xml.sax.DocumentHandler.endElement(java.lang.String)

Example
Not applicable.

Parameters
String qName   The qualified (prefixed) name.

Returns
void   N/A.

getContentHandler Method

Java Signature
public ContentHandler getContentHandler()

Visual Basic Signature
N/A.

This method is part of the ParserAdapter implementation of the XMLReader interface. See the XMLReader.getContentHandler() documentation for details.

See Also
org.xml.sax.XMLReader.getContentHandler()

Example
See the XMLReader.getContentHandler() method documentation for an example.

Returns
ContentHandler   The currently registered ContentHandler.

getDTDHandler Method

Java Signature
public DTDHandler getDTDHandler()

Visual Basic Signature
N/A.

This method is part of the ParserAdapter implementation of the XMLReader interface. See the XMLReader.getDTDHandler() method documentation for details.

See Also
org.xml.sax.XMLReader.getDTDHandler()

Example
See the XMLReader.getDTDHandler() method documentation for an example.

Returns
DTDHandler   The currently registered DTDHandler.

getEntityResolver Method

Java Signature
public EntityResolver getEntityResolver()

Visual Basic Signature
N/A.

This method is part of the ParserAdapter implementation of the XMLReader interface. See the XMLReader.getEntityResolver() method documentation for details.

See Also
org.xml.sax.XMLReader.getEntityResolver()

Example

See the XMLReader.getEntityResolver() method documentation for an example.

Returns

EntityResolver   The current EntityResolver object.

getErrorHandler Method

Java Signature
public ErrorHandler getErrorHandler()

Visual Basic Signature
N/A.

This method is part of the ParserAdapter implementation of the XMLReader interface. See the XMLReader.getErrorHandler() method documentation for details.

See Also
org.xml.sax.XMLReader.getErrorHandler()

Example

See the XMLReader.getErrorHandler() method documentation for an example.

Returns

ErrorHandler   The current ErrorHandler object.

getFeature Method

Java Signature
public boolean getFeature(String name)

Visual Basic Signature
N/A.

This method is part of the ParserAdapter implementation of the XMLReader interface. See the XMLReader.getFeature() method documentation for details.

The only features supported by the ParserAdapter class are the core features http://xml.org/sax/features/namespaces and http://xml.org/sax/features/namespace-prefixes. The features http://xml.org/sax/features/validation, http://xml.org/sax/features/external-general-entities, and http://xml.org/sax/features/external-parameter-entities will cause a SAXNotSupportedException error to be thrown. All other features will cause a SAXNotRecognizedException error to be thrown.

Thrown Exceptions
org.xml.sax.SAXNotRecognizedException
org.xml.sax.SAXNotSupportedException

See Also
org.xml.sax.XMLReader.getFeature(java.lang.String)
org.xml.sax.XMLReader.setFeature(java.lang.String, boolean)

Example

See the XMLReader.getFeature() method documentation for an example.

Parameters

String **name**   The feature name, as a complete URI.

Returns

boolean   The Boolean value of the specified feature.

getProperty Method

Java Signature
public Object getProperty(String name)

Visual Basic Signature
N/A.

This method is part of the ParserAdapter implementation of the XMLReader interface. See the XMLReader.getProperty() method documentation for details.

The ParserAdapter class does not support any SAX 2.0 properties. Any attempt to set or retrieve a property value will cause a SAXNotRecognizedException error to be thrown.

Thrown Exceptions
org.xml.sax.SAXNotRecognizedException
org.xml.sax.SAXNotSupportedException

See Also
org.xml.sax.XMLReader.getProperty(java.lang.String)
org.xml.sax.XMLReader.setProperty(java.lang.String, java.lang.Object)

Example

See the XMLReader.getProperty() method documentation for an example.

Parameters

String **name**   The property name.

Returns

Object   The value of the specified property as an Object.

ignorableWhitespace Method

Java Signature
public void ignorableWhitespace(char[] ch, int start, int length)

Visual Basic Signature
N/A.

This method is part of the ParserAdapter implementation of the SAX 1.0 DocumentHandler interface. SAX 2.0 application writers should not concern themselves with the DocumentHandler methods; in an ideal world, these functions would be encapsulated and invisible to SAX 2.0 applications. However, the `ParserAdapter` must declare the `DocumentHandler` interface as public so that the SAX 1.0 `Parser` object has access to the `DocumentHandler` event methods.

Thrown Exceptions
org.xml.sax.SAXException

See Also
org.xml.sax.DocumentHandler.ignorableWhitespace(char[], int, int)

Example
Not applicable.

Parameters

char[] **ch**   An array of characters.

int **start**   The starting position in the array.

int **length**   The number of characters to use.

Returns
void   N/A.

parse Method

Java Signature
public void parse(String systemId)

Visual Basic Signature
N/A.

This method is part of the `ParserAdapter` implementation of the `XMLReader` interface. See the `XMLReader.parse()` documentation for details.

Thrown Exceptions
java.io.IOException
org.xml.sax.SAXException

See Also
org.xml.sax.helpers.ParserAdapter.parse(org.xml.sax.InputSource)
org.xml.sax.XMLReader.parse(java.lang.String)

Example
See the `XMLReader.parse()` method documentation for an example.

Parameters
String **systemId**   The absolute URL of the document.

Returns
void   N/A.

parse Method

Java Signature
public void parse(InputSource input)

Visual Basic Signature
N/A.

This method is part of the ParserAdapter implementation of the XMLReader interface. See the XMLReader.parse() documentation for details.

Thrown Exceptions
java.io.IOException
org.xml.sax.SAXException

See Also
org.xml.sax.helpers.ParserAdapter.parse(java.lang.String)
org.xml.sax.XMLReader.parse(org.xml.sax.InputSource)

Example
See the XMLReader.parse() method documentation for an example.

Parameters
InputSource **input**   An input source for the document.

Returns
void   N/A.

processingInstruction Method

Java Signature
public void processingInstruction(String target, String data)

Visual Basic Signature
N/A.

This method is part of the ParserAdapter implementation of the SAX 1.0 DocumentHandler interface. SAX 2.0 application writers should not concern themselves with the DocumentHandler methods; in an ideal world, these functions would be encapsulated and invisible to SAX 2.0 applications. However, the ParserAdapter must declare the DocumentHandler interface as public so that the SAX 1.0 Parser object has access to the DocumentHandler event methods.

Thrown Exceptions
org.xml.sax.SAXException

See Also
org.xml.sax.DocumentHandler.processingInstruction(java.lang.String, java.lang.String)

Example
Not applicable.

Parameters

String **target**   The processing instruction target.

String **data**   The remainder of the processing instruction body.

Returns

void   N/A.

setContentHandler Method

Java Signature
public void setContentHandler(ContentHandler handler)

Visual Basic Signature
N/A.

This method is part of the `ParserAdapter` implementation of the `XMLReader` interface. See the `XMLReader.setContentHandler()` documentation for details.

See Also
org.xml.sax.XMLReader.getContentHandler()
org.xml.sax.XMLReader.setContentHandler(org.xml.sax.ContentHandler)

Example
See the `XMLReader.setContentHandler()` method documentation for an example.

Parameters

ContentHandler **handler**   An instance of an object that implements the ContentHandler interface.

Returns

void   N/A.

setDocumentLocator Method

Java Signature
public void setDocumentLocator(Locator locator)

Visual Basic Signature
N/A.

This method is part of the `ParserAdapter` implementation of the SAX 1.0 `DocumentHandler` interface. SAX 2.0 application writers should not concern themselves with the `DocumentHandler` methods; in an ideal world, these functions would be encapsulated and invisible to SAX 2.0 applications. However, the `ParserAdapter` must declare the `DocumentHandler` interface as public so that the SAX 1.0 `Parser` object has access to the `DocumentHandler` event methods.

See Also
org.xml.sax.DocumentHandler.setDocumentLocator(org.xml.sax.Locator)

Example

Not applicable.

Parameters

Locator **locator**   An instance of an object that implements the Locator interface and capable of returning the location of any document-related event.

Returns

void   N/A.

setDTDHandler Method

Java Signature
public void setDTDHandler(DTDHandler handler)

Visual Basic Signature
N/A.

This method is part of the ParserAdapter implementation of the XMLReader interface. See the XMLReader.setDTDHandler() method documentation for details.

See Also
org.xml.sax.XMLReader.getDTDHandler()
org.xml.sax.XMLReader.setDTDHandler(org.xml.sax.DTDHandler)

Example

See the XMLReader.setDTDHandler() method documentation for an example.

Parameters

DTDHandler **handler**   An instance of an object that implements the DTDHandler interface.

Returns

void   N/A.

setEntityResolver Method

Java Signature
public void setEntityResolver(EntityResolver resolver)

Visual Basic Signature
N/A.

This method is part of the ParserAdapter implementation of the XMLReader interface. See the XMLReader.setEntityResolver() method documentation for details.

See Also
org.xml.sax.XMLReader.getEntityResolver()
org.xml.sax.XMLReader.setEntityResolver(org.xml.sax.EntityResolver)

Example

See the `XMLReader.setEntityResolver()` method documentation for an example.

Parameters

`EntityResolver` **resolver**   An instance of an object that implements the `EntityResolver` interface.

Returns

void   N/A.

setErrorHandler Method

Java Signature
`public void setErrorHandler(ErrorHandler handler)`

Visual Basic Signature
N/A.

This method is part of the `ParserAdapter` implementation of the `XMLReader` interface. See the `XMLReader.setErrorHandler()` method documentation for details.

See Also
`org.xml.sax.XMLReader.getErrorHandler()`
`org.xml.sax.XMLReader.setErrorHandler(org.xml.sax.ErrorHandler)`

Example

See the `XMLReader.setErrorHandler()` method documentation for an example.

Parameters

`ErrorHandler` **handler**   An instance of an object that implements the `ErrorHandler` interface.

Returns

void   N/A.

setFeature Method

Java Signature
`public void setFeature(String name, boolean state)`

Visual Basic Signature
N/A.

This method is part of the `ParserAdapter` implementation of the `XMLReader` interface. See the `XMLReader.setFeature()` method documentation for details.

The only features supported by the ParserAdapter class are the core features http://xml.org/sax/features/namespaces and http://xml.org/sax/features/namespace-prefixes. The features http://xml.org/sax/features/validation, http://xml.org/sax/features/external-general-entities, and http://xml.org/sax/features/external-parameter-entities will cause a `SAXNotSupportedException` error to be thrown. All other features will cause a `SAXNotRecognizedException` error to be thrown.

Thrown Exceptions

org.xml.sax.SAXNotRecognizedException
org.xml.sax.SAXNotSupportedException

See Also

org.xml.sax.XMLReader.getFeature(java.lang.String)
org.xml.sax.XMLReader.setFeature(java.lang.String, boolean)

Example

See the XMLReader.setFeature method documentation for an example.

Parameters

String **name**   The feature name, as a complete URI.

boolean **state**   The new Boolean state for the feature.

Returns

void   N/A.

setProperty Method

Java Signature
public void setProperty(String name, Object value)

Visual Basic Signature
N/A.

This method is part of the ParserAdapter implementation of the XMLReader interface. See the XMLReader.setProperty() method documentation for details.

The ParserAdapter class does not support any SAX 2.0 properties. Any attempt to set or retrieve a property value will cause a SAXNotRecognizedException error to be thrown.

Thrown Exceptions

org.xml.sax.SAXNotRecognizedException
org.xml.sax.SAXNotSupportedException

See Also

org.xml.sax.XMLReader.getProperty(java.lang.String)
org.xml.sax.XMLReader.setProperty(java.lang.String, java.lang.Object)

Example

See the XMLReader.setProperty() method documentation for an example.

Parameters

String **name**   The property name.

Object **value**   The property value.

Returns

void   N/A.

startDocument Method

Java Signature
public void startDocument()

Visual Basic Signature
N/A.

This method is part of the `ParserAdapter` implementation of the SAX 1.0 `DocumentHandler` interface. SAX 2.0 application writers should not concern themselves with the `DocumentHandler` methods; in an ideal world, these methods would be encapsulated and invisible to SAX 2.0 applications. However, the `ParserAdapter` must declare the `DocumentHandler` interface as public so that the SAX 1.0 `Parser` object has access to the `DocumentHandler` event methods.

Thrown Exceptions
org.xml.sax.SAXException

See Also
org.xml.sax.DocumentHandler.startDocument()

Example
Not applicable.

Returns
void   N/A.

startElement Method

Java Signature
public void startElement(String qName, AttributeList qAtts)

Visual Basic Signature
N/A.

This method is part of the `ParserAdapter` implementation of the SAX 1.0 `DocumentHandler` interface. SAX 2.0 application writers should not concern themselves with the `DocumentHandler` methods; in an ideal world, these methods would be encapsulated and invisible to SAX 2.0 applications. However, the `ParserAdapter` must declare the `DocumentHandler` interface as public so that the SAX 1.0 `Parser` object has access to the `DocumentHandler` event methods.

Thrown Exceptions
org.xml.sax.SAXException

See Also
org.xml.sax.DocumentHandler.startElement(java.lang.String, org.xml.sax.AttributeList)

Example
Not applicable.

Parameters

String **qName**   The qualified name of the element.

AttributeList **qAtts**   An AttributeList object containing the XML attributes associated with the element.

Returns

void   N/A.

SAXException Exception

This SAXException class encapsulates basic warning or error information from SAX parsers and applications.

All SAX methods throw a SAXException, or one of its subclasses, whenever an error occurs. The sole exception is XMLReader.parse(), which may throw a java.io.IOException for a purely I/O-related error.

Visual Basic Equivalent
N/A.

See Also
org.xml.sax.SAXParseException

Example
```
import org.xml.sax.SAXException;
import java.lang.Exception;
. . .
        SAXException eSAX;
```

Constructors

Java Signature
```
public  SAXException(Exception e)
```

Visual Basic Signature
N/A.

This constructor method creates a new instance of the SAXException class from an existing exception. The new instance of SAXException will embed the passed exception and the embedded exception's message will become the message for the SAXException. The embedded exception may be retrieved by invoking the SAXException.getException() method.

Example
```
import org.xml.sax.SAXException;
import java.lang.Exception;
. . .
        SAXException eSAX;
. . .
            Exception e;
            e = new Exception( "embedded error msg." );
```

```
        . . .
                        eSAX = new SAXException( e );
        . . .
                //Throw the exception.
                throw eSAX;
```

Parameters

Exception **e**   The exception to be embedded in a SAXException.

Java Signature
```
public  SAXException(String message)
```

Visual Basic Signature
N/A.

This constructor method creates a new instance of the SAXException class, setting its message to the passed error message.

See Also
org.xml.sax.Parser.setLocale(java.util.Locale)

Example
```
import org.xml.sax.SAXException;
import java.lang.Exception;
. . .
        SAXException eSAX;
        String errMsg;
        errMsg = "Usage: java myProgram URL1 URL2 ...";
. . .
            eSAX = new SAXException( errMsg );
. . .
        //Throw the exception.
        throw eSAX;
```

Parameters

- String **message**

A string containing a detailed error or warning message.

Java Signature
```
public  SAXException(String message, Exception e)
```

Visual Basic Signature
N/A.

This constructor method creates a new instance of the SAXException class with its own error message from an existing exception. The new instance of SAXException will embed the passed exception; however, the new exception will have its own message. The embedded exception may be retrieved by invoking the SAXException.getException() method.

See Also
org.xml.sax.Parser.setLocale(java.util.Locale)

Example
```
import org.xml.sax.SAXException;
import java.lang.Exception;
. . .
        SAXException eSAX;
        String errMsg;
        errMsg = "Usage: java myProgram URL1 URL2 ...";
. . .
        Exception e;
        e = new Exception( "embedded error msg." );
. . .
            eSAX = new SAXException( errMsg, e );
. . .
        //Throw the exception.
        throw eSAX;
```

Parameters

String **message** A string containing a detailed error message.

Exception **e** The exception to be embedded in a SAXException.

Members

getException Method

Java Signature
```
public Exception getException()
```

Visual Basic Signature
N/A.

If this instance of SAXException contains an embedded exception, this method returns the embedded exception. Otherwise, the method returns null.

Example
```
import org.xml.sax.SAXException;
import java.lang.Exception;
. . .
    public void printError( SAXException e )
    {
        String errMsg;
        Exception ee;
        errMsg =   "SAX ERROR:\n\t" +
                   "Message: " + e.getMessage() +
                   "toString: " + e.toString();
        //Is there an embedded exception?
        if( (ee=e.getException()) != null )
        {
```

```
            //Print the embedded exception also.
            errMsg =    errMsg + "\n\t" +
                        "Embedded Msg: " + ee.getMessage();
        }
        System.err.println( errMsg );
    }
```

Returns

Exception   The embedded exception object, or null if there is no embedded exception.

getMessage Method

Java Signature
```
public String getMessage()
```

Visual Basic Signature
N/A.

This method returns the error or warning message for an instance of the SAXException class. If the SAXException does not contain its own detailed message but does have an embedded exception, the embedded exception's detail message is returned.

See Also
org.xml.sax.Parser.setLocale(java.util.Locale)

Example
```
import org.xml.sax.SAXException;
import java.lang.Exception;
 . . .
    public void printError( SAXException e )
    {
        String errMsg;
        Exception ee;
        errMsg =    "SAX ERROR:\n\t" +
                    "Message: " + e.getMessage() +
                    "toString: " + e.toString();
        //Is there an embedded exception?
        if( (ee=e.getException()) != null )
        {
            //Print the embedded exception also.
            errMsg =    errMsg + "\n\t" +
                        "Embedded Msg: " + ee.getMessage();
        }
        System.err.println( errMsg );
    }
```

Returns

String   The error or warning message for the SAXException.

toString Method

Java Signature
```
public String toString()
```

Visual Basic Signature
N/A.

This method converts the data contained in an instance of the SAXException class, including any embedded exception, into a string and returns the string.

Example
```
import org.xml.sax.SAXException;
import java.lang.Exception;
. . .
    public void printError( SAXException e )
    {
        String errMsg;
        Exception ee;
        errMsg =    "SAX ERROR:\n\t" +
                    "Message: " + e.getMessage() +
                    "toString: " + e.toString();
        //Is there an embedded exception?
        if( (ee=e.getException()) != null )
        {
            //Print the embedded exception also.
            errMsg =    errMsg + "\n\t" +
                        "Embedded Msg: " + ee.getMessage();
        }
        System.err.println( errMsg );
    }
```

Returns

String   The error information contained in the SAXException converted into a string.

SAXNotRecognizedException Exception

The parser throws a SAXNotRecognizedException whenever it encounters an unrecognized feature or property identifier.
    The SAXNotRecognizedException class is a subclass of SAXException.

Visual Basic Equivalent
N/A.

See Also
org.xml.sax.SAXNotSupportedException

Example
```
import org.xml.sax.XMLReader;
import org.xml.sax.SAXException;
import org.xml.sax.SAXNotRecognizedException;
. . .
        SAXNotRecognizedException myException = null;
```

Constructors

Java Signature
```
public  SAXNotRecognizedException(String message)
```

Visual Basic Signature
N/A.

This constructor method creates a new instance of the SAXNotRecognizedException class, setting the exception's message to the passed detailed error message.

Example
```
import org.xml.sax.XMLReader;
import org.xml.sax.SAXException;
import org.xml.sax.SAXNotRecognizedException;
. . .
        errMsg = name + " is not a recognized feature.";
        myException = new SAXNotRecognizedException(errMsg);
```

Parameters
String **message**   A string containing a detailed error message for the exception.

SAXNotSupportedException Exception

A parser throws a SAXNotSupportedException whenever it encounters a recognized but unsupported property or feature.

The SAXNotSupportedException class is a subclass of SAXException.

Visual Basic Equivalent
N/A.

See Also
org.xml.sax.SAXNotRecognizedException

Example
```
import org.xml.sax.XMLReader;
import org.xml.sax.SAXException;
import org.xml.sax.SAXNotSupportedException;
import org.xml.sax.ContentHandler;
import org.xml.sax.DTDHandler;
import org.xml.sax.ErrorHandler;
import org.xml.sax.EntityResolver;
import org.xml.sax.InputSource;
```

(continued on next page)

```
public class SAXNotSupportedExceptionSample implements XMLReader
{
    public SAXNotSupportedExceptionSample(){};
    public boolean getFeature( String name )
            throws SAXNotSupportedException
    {
        SAXNotSupportedException myException = null;
        String errMsg;
        errMsg = name + " is not a supported feature.";
        myException = new SAXNotSupportedException(errMsg);
        if( myException != null )
            throw myException;
        else
            return( false );
    }
}
```

Constructors

Java Signature
```
public  SAXNotSupportedException(String message)
```

Visual Basic Signature
N/A.

This constructor method creates a new instance of the `SAXNotSupportedException` class with the passed detailed error message.

Example
```
import org.xml.sax.XMLReader;
import org.xml.sax.SAXException;
import org.xml.sax.SAXNotSupportedException;
. . .
        myException = new SAXNotSupportedException(errMsg);
```

Parameters
String **message**   A string containing a detailed error message.

SAXParseException Exception

If a document is not well-formed, the parser will throw a `SAXParseException`. Instances of SAXParseException are also passed as parameters to `ErrorHandler` methods. Since SAXParseException is a subclass of SAXException, it not only inherits from its parent class but also adds methods to obtain error location information such as the document, line number, and column number.

Visual Basic Equivalent
N/A.

See Also
org.xml.sax.ErrorHandler
org.xml.sax.Locator
org.xml.sax.SAXException

Example
```
import org.xml.sax.EntityResolver;
import org.xml.sax.InputSource;
import org.xml.sax.Locator;
import org.xml.sax.SAXParseException;
import org.xml.sax.SAXException;
import java.lang.Exception;
import java.io.InputStream;
import java.io.IOException;
import java.net.URL;
import java.net.MalformedURLException;
public class SAXParseExceptionSample implements EntityResolver
{
    private Locator myLocator;
    // Number of constructor parms must be 2 - 6 inclusive.
    private static final int numConstructorParms = 2;
    public InputSource resolveEntity(   String publicID,
                                        String systemID )
                                        throws SAXException,
                                        IOException
    {
        InputSource inSource = null;
        InputStream inStream = null;
        URL entityURL = null;
        try
        {
            entityURL = new URL( systemID );
        }
        catch( MalformedURLException mue )
        {
            SAXParseException myException;
```

Constructors

Java Signature
```
public  SAXParseException(String message, String publicId, String systemId, int lineNumber, int columnNumber)
```

Visual Basic Signature
N/A.

This constructor method creates a new instance of the SAXParseException class using the passed identifier and location information.

See Also
org.xml.sax.Parser.setLocale(java.util.Locale)

Example
```
import org.xml.sax.EntityResolver;
import org.xml.sax.InputSource;
import org.xml.sax.Locator;
import org.xml.sax.SAXParseException;
import org.xml.sax.SAXException;
...
            myException = new SAXParseException( errMsg,
                                    publicID,
                                    systemID,
                                    myLocator.getLineNumber(),
                                    myLocator.getColumnNumber() );
...
      throw myException;
   }
```

Parameters

String **message**   A string containing a detailed error message.

String **publicId**   The public identifier of the XML markup or document content causing the error.

String **systemId**   The system identifier of the XML markup or document content causing the error. If the system identifier is a URL, it will be fully resolved by the parser before the exception is created.

int **lineNumber**   The line number of the end of the XML markup or document content causing the error.

int **columnNumber**   The column number of the end of the XML markup or document content causing the error.

Java Signature
```
public  SAXParseException(String message, String publicId, String systemId, int lineNumber, int columnNumber, Exception e)
```

Visual Basic Signature
N/A.

This constructor method creates a new instance of the SAXParseException class with an existing exception. The existing exception is embedded in the newly created SAXParseException. This method is useful for wrapping a non-SAX exception: that is, an exception that is not a subclass of SAXException.

See Also
org.xml.sax.Parser.setLocale(java.util.Locale)

Example
```
import org.xml.sax.EntityResolver;
import org.xml.sax.InputSource;
import org.xml.sax.Locator;
```

```
import org.xml.sax.SAXParseException;
import org.xml.sax.SAXException;
import java.lang.Exception;
...
    try
    {
...
    }
    catch( MalformedURLException mue )
    {
...
            myException = new SAXParseException( errMsg,
                              publicID,
                              systemID,
                              myLocator.getLineNumber(),
                              myLocator.getColumnNumber(),
                              mue );
...
        throw myException;
    }
```

Parameters

String **message**   A string containing a detailed error message, or null to use the embedded exception's error message.

String **publicId**   The public identifier of the XML markup or document content causing the error.

String **systemId**   The system identifier of the XML markup or document content causing the error.

int **lineNumber**   The line number of the end of the XML markup or document content causing the error.

int **columnNumber**   The column number of the end of the XML markup or document content causing the error.

Exception **e**   An exception to be embedded into the newly created SAXParseException.

Java Signature
```
public SAXParseException(String message, Locator locator)
```

Visual Basic Signature
N/A.

This constructor method creates a new instance of the SAXParseException class using the passed error message and location information. The passed Locator object is used to obtain and set the location information for the error.

This constructor is useful for an application that implements the ContentHandler interface and needs to generate its own exception within one of the event functions.

See Also

org.xml.sax.Locator

org.xml.sax.Parser.setLocale(java.util.Locale)

Example

```
import org.xml.sax.EntityResolver;
import org.xml.sax.InputSource;
import org.xml.sax.Locator;
import org.xml.sax.SAXParseException;
import org.xml.sax.SAXException;
. . .
            myException = new SAXParseException( errMsg,
                                                 myLocator );
. . .
      throw myException;
   }
```

Parameters

String **message**   A string containing a detailed error message.

Locator **locator**   A Locator object associated with the ContentHandler, or null if a Locator object was not provided by the parser.

Java Signature

```
public SAXParseException(String message, Locator locator, Exception e)
```

Visual Basic Signature

N/A.

This constructor method creates a new instance of the SAXParseException class, embedding an existing exception. The passed Locator object is used to obtain and set the location information for the error.

This constructor is useful for applications that need to create a SAX exception from within an event method of the ContentHandler interface, and need to wrap an existing exception that is not a subclass of SAXException.

See Also

org.xml.sax.Locator

org.xml.sax.Parser.setLocale(java.util.Locale)

Example

```
import org.xml.sax.EntityResolver;
import org.xml.sax.InputSource;
import org.xml.sax.Locator;
import org.xml.sax.SAXParseException;
import org.xml.sax.SAXException;
import java.lang.Exception;
. . .
      try
      {
```

```
        . . .
            }
            catch( MalformedURLException mue )
            {
        . . .
                    myException = new SAXParseException( errMsg,
                                                         myLocator,
                                                         mue );
        . . .
                throw myException;
            }
```

Parameters

String **message**   A string containing a detailed error message, or null to use the embedded exception's error message.

Locator **locator**   A Locator object associated with the error, or null if a Locator object was not supplied by the parser.

Exception **e**   The exception to be embedded in the SAXParseException.

Members

getColumnNumber Method

Java Signature
public int getColumnNumber()

Visual Basic Signature
N/A.

This method returns the column number of the XML document being parsed where the exception occurred.

See Also
org.xml.sax.Locator.getColumnNumber()

Example
```
import org.xml.sax.SAXParseException;
import org.xml.sax.SAXException;
import java.lang.Exception;
. . .
        System.err.println( e.getColumnNumber() );
```

Returns

int   The column number, in the XML document, of the entity causing the thrown exception.

getLineNumber Method

Java Signature
public int getLineNumber()

Visual Basic Signature
N/A.

This method returns the line number of the XML document being parsed where the exception occurred.

See Also
org.xml.sax.Locator.getLineNumber()

Example
```
import org.xml.sax.SAXParseException;
import org.xml.sax.SAXException;
import java.lang.Exception;
. . .
      System.err.println( e.getLineNumber() );
```

Returns

int   The line number, in the XML document, of the entity causing the thrown exception.

getPublicId Method

Java Signature
```
public String getPublicId()
```

Visual Basic Signature
N/A.

This method returns the public identifier, if available, for the XML markup or document content causing the parsing exception. If no public identifier is available, the method returns null.

See Also
org.xml.sax.Locator.getPublicId()

Example
```
import org.xml.sax.SAXParseException;
import org.xml.sax.SAXException;
import java.lang.Exception;
. . .
      System.err.println( e.getPublicId() );
```

Returns

String   The public identifier of the entity causing the thrown exception, or null if a public identifier is not available.

getSystemId Method

Java Signature
```
public String getSystemId()
```

Visual Basic Signature
N/A.

This method returns the system identifier (URI) of the XML markup or document content where an exception occurred while parsing the XML document. If the system identifier is a URL, it will be fully resolved.

See Also
org.xml.sax.Locator.getSystemId()

Example
```
import org.xml.sax.SAXParseException;
import org.xml.sax.SAXException;
import java.lang.Exception;
. . .
        System.err.println( e.getSystemId() );
```

Returns
String   The system identifier of the entity causing the exception, or null if the system identifier is unavailable.

XMLFilter Interface

The XMLFilter interface is used to declare an XMLReader that obtains its events from another XMLReader, instead of an InputStream. As the name implies, an implementation of XMLFilter filters, and possibly modifies, the stream of events between an original XML source and an application.

The best and easiest way to create an XML filter is by inheriting from the org.xml.sax.helpers.XMLFilterImpl class.

Visual Basic Equivalent
IVBSAXXMLFilter

See Also
org.xml.sax.helpers.XMLFilterImpl

Example
```
import org.xml.sax.XMLReader;
import org.xml.sax.helpers.XMLFilterImpl;
public class XMLFilterSample
    extends XMLFilterImpl
{
    public void setParent( XMLReader parent )
    {
        //Actually we'll just call our base class method.
        super.setParent( parent );
    }
    public XMLReader getParent()
    {
        return super.getParent();
    }
}
```

Members

getParent Method

Java Signature
```
public XMLReader getParent()
```

Visual Basic Signature
```
Public Property parent As SAXXMLReader
```

This method returns a reference to the parent XMLReader object for XMLFilter. This parent object may, in turn, be another XMLFilter. Operations should not be performed directly on the parent reader object, but rather pass through this filter.

Example
```
import org.xml.sax.XMLReader;
import org.xml.sax.helpers.XMLFilterImpl;
public class XMLFilterSample
    extends XMLFilterImpl
{
. . .
    public XMLReader getParent()
    {
        return super.getParent();
    }
```

Returns

XMLReader   The parent XMLReader object.

setParent Method

Java Signature
```
public void setParent(XMLReader parent)
```

Visual Basic Signature
```
Public Property parent As SAXXMLReader
```

This method sets the parent XMLReader object for the XMLFilter object, allowing an application to link the filter to a parent reader. The parent XMLReader object may, in turn, be another XMLFilter object.
   The passed parent XMLReader object may not be null.

Example
```
import org.xml.sax.XMLReader;
import org.xml.sax.helpers.XMLFilterImpl;
public class XMLFilterSample
    extends XMLFilterImpl
{
```

Parameters

XMLReader **parent**   A non-null reference to the parent XMLReader object.

Returns

void   N/A.

XMLFilterImpl Class

The `XMLFilterImpl` class is a convenience class that application developers can use to inherit functionality to assist in the development of XML filters. The `XMLFilterImpl` class implements the interfaces `XMLFilter`, `EntityResolver`, `DTDHandler`, `ContentHandler`, and `ErrorHandler`. With these interfaces implemented, an instance of `XMLFilterImpl` can sit between an instance of `XMLReader` and a client SAX application, acting as a pass-through for all events generated by the reader.

A filter application can inherit from `XMLFilterImpl` and override methods to perform custom processing on certain events before the client SAX application receives the event.

Filters can be tied to an instance of `XMLReader` by passing the `XMLReader` object as an argument to the filter's constructor method. The filter's `parse()` method is then invoked, not the reader's `parse()` method.

Visual Basic Equivalent
N/A.

See Also
org.xml.sax.ContentHandler
org.xml.sax.DTDHandler
org.xml.sax.EntityResolver
org.xml.sax.ErrorHandler
org.xml.sax.XMLFilter
org.xml.sax.XMLReader

Example
```
import org.xml.sax.helpers.XMLFilterImpl;
import org.xml.sax.XMLReader;
public class XMLFilterImplSample extends XMLFilterImpl
{
    public XMLFilterImplSample()
    {
        // System.out.println("Creating empty XML Filter.");
        super();
    }
    public XMLFilterImplSample( XMLReader parent )
    {
        // System.out.println("Creating XML Filter with parent.");
        super( parent );
    }
}
```

Constructors

Java Signature
public   XMLFilterImpl()

Visual Basic Signature
N/A.

This method creates a new, empty instance of the `XMLFilterImpl` class. The newly created filter will have no parent `XMLReader` object. A parent object must be assigned before any of the methods `setFeature()`, `setProperty()`, or `parse()` are invoked.

See Also
org.xml.sax.helpers.XMLFilterImpl(org.xml.sax.XMLReader)
org.xml.sax.XMLReader.setFeature(java.lang.String, boolean)
org.xml.sax.XMLReader.setProperty(java.lang.String, java.lang.Object)

Example
```
import org.xml.sax.helpers.XMLFilterImpl;
import org.xml.sax.XMLReader;
public class XMLFilterImplSample extends XMLFilterImpl
{
    public XMLFilterImplSample()
    {
        // System.out.println("Creating empty XML Filter.");
        super();
    }
    public XMLFilterImplSample( XMLReader parent )
    {
        // System.out.println("Creating XML Filter with parent.");
        super( parent );
    }
}
```

Java Signature
`public  XMLFilterImpl(XMLReader parent)`

Visual Basic Signature
N/A.

This constructor method creates a new instance of the `XMLFilterImpl` class using the specified `XMLReader` parent object. Since `XMLFilterImpl` implements the `XMLReader` interface, it is possible (and common) for `XMLFilterImpl` to be the parent of another instance of `XMLFilterImpl`, thereby creating a chain of filters.

See Also
org.xml.sax.helpers.XMLFilterImpl.getParent()
org.xml.sax.helpers.XMLFilterImpl.setParent(org.xml.sax.XMLReader)

Example
```
import org.xml.sax.helpers.XMLFilterImpl;
import org.xml.sax.XMLReader;
public class XMLFilterImplSample extends XMLFilterImpl
{
    public XMLFilterImplSample()
    {
```

```
            // System.out.println("Creating empty XML Filter.");
            super();
        }
        public XMLFilterImplSample( XMLReader parent )
        {
            // System.out.println("Creating XML Filter with parent.");
            super( parent );
        }
    }
```

Parameters

XMLReader **parent**   An object that implements the XMLReader interface.

Members

characters Method

Java Signature
```
public void characters(char[] ch, int start, int length)
```

Visual Basic Signature
N/A.

This method is an implementation of the ContentHandler.characters() event method. Override this method to perform custom processing for this event before the client application is notified.
    See ContentHandler.characters() for details.

Thrown Exceptions
org.xml.sax.SAXException

See Also
org.xml.sax.ContentHandler.characters(char[], int, int)

Example
See the ContentHandler.characters() method documentation for an example.

Parameters

char[] **ch**   An array of characters from the XML document.

int **start**   The starting position in the array.

int **length**   The number of characters to use from the array.

Returns
void   N/A.

endDocument Method

Java Signature
```
public void endDocument()
```

Visual Basic Signature
N/A.

This method is an implementation of the `ContentHandler.endDocument()` event method. Override this method to perform custom processing for this event before the client application is notified.
　See `ContentHandler.endDocument()` for details.

Thrown Exceptions
`org.xml.sax.SAXException`

See Also
`org.xml.sax.ContentHandler.endDocument()`

Example
See the `ContentHandler.endDocument()` method documentation for an example.

Returns
void　N/A.

endElement Method

Java Signature
`public void endElement(String uri, String localName, String qName)`

Visual Basic Signature
N/A.

This method is an implementation of the `ContentHandler.endElement()` event method. Override this method to perform custom processing for this event before the client application is notified.
　See `ContentHandler.endElement()` for details.

Thrown Exceptions
`org.xml.sax.SAXException`

See Also
`org.xml.sax.ContentHandler.endElement(java.lang.String, java.lang.String, java.lang.String)`

Example
See the `ContentHandler.endElement()` method documentation for an example.

Parameters
`String uri`　The namespace URI of the element, or an empty string if namespace processing is not being performed.

`String localName`　The local name of the element, or an empty string if namespace processing is not being performed.

`String qName`　The qualified name of the element, or an empty string if qualified names are not available.

Returns

void   N/A.

endPrefixMapping Method

Java Signature
public void endPrefixMapping(String prefix)

Visual Basic Signature
N/A.

This method is an implementation of the `ContentHandler.endPrefixMapping()` event method. Override this method to perform custom processing for this event before the client application is notified.
    See `ContentHandler.endPrefixMapping()` for details.

Thrown Exceptions
org.xml.sax.SAXException

See Also
org.xml.sax.ContentHandler.endPrefixMapping(java.lang.String)

Example
See the `ContentHandler.endPrefixMapping()` method documentation for an example.

Parameters
String **prefix**   The namespace prefix.

Returns
void   N/A.

error Method

Java Signature
public void error(SAXParseException e)

Visual Basic Signature
N/A.

This method is an implementation of the `ErrorHandler.error()` event method. Override this method to perform custom processing for this event before the client application is notified.
    See the `ErrorHandler.error()` method documentation for details.

Thrown Exceptions
org.xml.sax.SAXException

See Also
org.xml.sax.ErrorHandler.error(org.xml.sax.SAXParseException)

Example

See the `ErrorHandler.error()` method documentation for an example.

Parameters

`SAXParseException e`   An instance of a SAX parse exception encapsulating the details of the error.

Returns

`void`   N/A.

fatalError Method

Java Signature
```
public void fatalError(SAXParseException e)
```

Visual Basic Signature
N/A.

This method is an implementation of the `ErrorHandler.fatalError()` event method. Override this method to perform custom processing for this event before the client application is notified.
    See the `ErrorHandler.fatalError()` method documentation for details.

Thrown Exceptions
`org.xml.sax.SAXException`

See Also
`org.xml.sax.ErrorHandler.fatalError(org.xml.sax.SAXParseException)`

Example

See the `ErrorHandler.fatalError()` method documentation for an example.

Parameters

`SAXParseException e`   An instance of a SAX parse exception encapsulating the details of the error.

Returns

`void`   N/A.

getContentHandler Method

Java Signature
```
public ContentHandler getContentHandler()
```

Visual Basic Signature
N/A.

This method is part of the `XMLFilterImpl` implementation of the `XMLReader` interface. See the `XMLReader.getContentHandler()` method documentation for details.

See Also
`org.xml.sax.XMLReader.getContentHandler()`

Example

See the XMLReader.getContentHandler() method documentation for an example.

Returns

ContentHandler   The currently registered instance of an object that implements the ContentHandler interface.

getDTDHandler Method

Java Signature
public DTDHandler getDTDHandler()

Visual Basic Signature
N/A.

This method is part of the XMLFilterImpl implementation of the XMLReader interface. See the XMLReader.getDTDHandler() method documentation for details.

See Also
org.xml.sax.XMLReader.getDTDHandler()

Example

See the XMLReader.getDTDHandler() method documentation for an example.

Returns

DTDHandler   The currently registered instance of an object that implements the DTDHandler interface.

getEntityResolver Method

Java Signature
public EntityResolver getEntityResolver()

Visual Basic Signature
N/A.

This method is part of the XMLFilterImpl implementation of the XMLReader interface. See the XMLReader.getEntityResolver() method documentation for details.

See Also
org.xml.sax.XMLReader.getEntityResolver()

Example

See the XMLReader.getEntityResolver() method documentation for an example.

Returns

EntityResolver   The currently registered instance of an object that implements the EntityResolver interface.

getErrorHandler Method

Java Signature
public ErrorHandler getErrorHandler()

Visual Basic Signature
N/A.

This method is part of the XMLFilterImpl implementation of the XMLReader interface. See the XMLReader.getErrorHandler() method documentation for details.

See Also
org.xml.sax.XMLReader.getErrorHandler()

Example
See the XMLReader.getErrorHandler() method documentation for an example.

Returns
ErrorHandler   The currently registered instance of an object that implements the ErrorHandler interface.

getFeature Method

Java Signature
public boolean getFeature(String name)

Visual Basic Signature
N/A.

This method is part of the XMLFilterImpl implementation of the XMLReader interface. See the XMLReader.getFeature() method documentation for details.

Thrown Exceptions
org.xml.sax.SAXNotRecognizedException
org.xml.sax.SAXNotSupportedException

See Also
org.xml.sax.XMLReader.getFeature(java.lang.String)
org.xml.sax.XMLReader.setFeature(java.lang.String, boolean)

Example
See the XMLReader.getFeature() method documentation for an example.

Parameters
String **name**   The feature name.

Returns
boolean   The current Boolean state of the specified feature.

getParent Method

Java Signature
public XMLReader getParent()

Visual Basic Signature
N/A.

This method is part of the `XMLFilterImpl` implementation of the `XMLFilter` interface. See the `XMLFilter.getParent()` method documentation for details.

See Also
org.xml.sax.XMLFilter.getParent()
org.xml.sax.XMLFilter.setParent(org.xml.sax.XMLReader)

Example
See the `XMLFilter.getParent()` method documentation for an example.

Returns
XMLReader   The parent object that implements the XMLReader interface.

getProperty Method

Java Signature
```
public Object getProperty(String name)
```

Visual Basic Signature
N/A.

This method is part of the `XMLFilterImpl` implementation of the `XMLReader` interface. See the `XMLReader.getProperty()` method documentation for details.

Thrown Exceptions
org.xml.sax.SAXNotRecognizedException
org.xml.sax.SAXNotSupportedException

See Also
org.xml.sax.XMLReader.getProperty(java.lang.String)
org.xml.sax.XMLReader.setProperty(java.lang.String, java.lang.Object)

Example
See the `XMLReader.getProperty()` method documentation for an example.

Parameters
String **name**   The property name.

Returns
Object   The value of the specified property as an object.

ignorableWhitespace Method

Java Signature
```
public void ignorableWhitespace(char[] ch, int start, int length)
```

Visual Basic Signature
N/A.

This method is an implementation of the `ContentHandler.ignorableWhitespace()` event method. Override this method to perform custom processing for this event before the client application is notified. See the `ContentHandler.ignorableWhitespace()` method documentation for details.

Thrown Exceptions
org.xml.sax.SAXException

See Also
org.xml.sax.ContentHandler.ignorableWhitespace(char[], int, int)

Example
See the `ContentHandler.ignorableWhitespace()` method documentation for an example.

Parameters

char[] **ch**   An array of characters.

int **start**   The starting position in the array.

int **length**   The number of characters to use from the array.

Returns
void   N/A.

notationDecl Method

Java Signature
public void notationDecl(String name, String publicId, String systemId)

Visual Basic Signature
N/A.

This method is an implementation of the `ContentHandler.notationDecl()` event method. Override this method to perform custom processing for this event before the client application is notified. See the `ContentHandler.notationDecl()` method documentation for details.

Thrown Exceptions
org.xml.sax.SAXException

See Also
org.xml.sax.DTDHandler.notationDecl(java.lang.String, java.lang.String, java.lang.String)

Example
See the `ContentHandler.notationDecl()` method documentation for an example.

Parameters

String **name**   The notation name.

String **publicId**   The notation's public identifier, or null.

String **systemId**   The notation's system identifier, or null.

Returns

void   N/A.

parse Method

Java Signature
public void parse(String systemId)

Visual Basic Signature
N/A.

This method is part of the XMLFilterImpl implementation of the XMLReader interface. See the XMLReader.parse() method documentation for details.

Thrown Exceptions
java.io.IOException
org.xml.sax.SAXException

See Also
org.xml.sax.XMLReader.parse(java.lang.String)

Example
See the XMLReader.parse() method documentation for an example.

Parameters

String **systemId**   The system identifier as a fully qualified URI.

Returns

void   N/A.

parse Method

Java Signature
public void parse(InputSource input)

Visual Basic Signature
N/A.

This method is part of the XMLFilterImpl implementation of the XMLReader interface. See the XMLReader.parse() method documentation for details.

Thrown Exceptions
java.io.IOException
org.xml.sax.SAXException

See Also

org.xml.sax.XMLReader.parse(org.xml.sax.InputSource)

Example

See the XMLReader.parse() method documentation for an example.

Parameters

InputSource **input**   The input source for the document entity.

Returns

void   N/A.

processingInstruction Method

Java Signature
public void processingInstruction(String target, String data)

Visual Basic Signature
N/A.

This method is an implementation of the ContentHandler.processingInstruction() event method. Override this method to perform custom processing for this event before the client application is notified. See the ContentHandler.processingInstruction() method documentation for details.

Thrown Exceptions
org.xml.sax.SAXException

See Also
org.xml.sax.ContentHandler.processingInstruction(java.lang.String, java.lang.String)

Example

See the ContentHandler.processingInstruction() method documentation for an example.

Parameters

String **target**   The processing instruction target.

String **data**   The processing instruction body.

Returns

void   N/A.

resolveEntity Method

Java Signature
public InputSource resolveEntity(String publicId, String systemId)

Visual Basic Signature
N/A.

This method is an implementation of the EntityResolver.resolveEntity() event method. Override this method to perform custom processing for this event before the client application is notified. See the EntityResolver.resolveEntity() method documentation for details.

Thrown Exceptions
java.io.IOException
org.xml.sax.SAXException

See Also
org.xml.sax.EntityResolver.resolveEntity(java.lang.String, java.lang.String)

Example
See the EntityResolver.resolveEntity() method documentation for an example.

Parameters
String **publicId**   The entity's public identifier, or null.

String **systemId**   The entity's system identifier.

Returns
InputSource   An InputSource for the resolved entity.

setContentHandler Method

Java Signature
public void setContentHandler(ContentHandler handler)

Visual Basic Signature
N/A.

This method is part of the XMLFilterImpl implementation of the XMLReader interface. See the XMLReader.setContentHandler() method documentation for details.

See Also
org.xml.sax.XMLReader.setContentHandler(org.xml.sax.ContentHandler)

Example
See the XMLReader.setContentHandler() method documentation for an example.

Parameters
ContentHandler **handler**   An instance of an object that implements the ContentHandler interface.

Returns
void   N/A.

setDocumentLocator Method

Java Signature

public void setDocumentLocator(Locator locator)

Visual Basic Signature

N/A.

This method is an implementation of the `ContentHandler.setDocumentLocator()` event method. Override this method to perform custom processing for this event before the client application is notified. See the `ContentHandler.setDocumentLocator()` method documentation for details.

See Also

org.xml.sax.ContentHandler.setDocumentLocator(org.xml.sax.Locator)

Example

See the `ContentHandler.setDocumentLocator()` method documentation for an example.

Parameters

Locator **locator**   An instance of an object that implements the `Locator` interface.

Returns

void   N/A.

setDTDHandler Method

Java Signature

public void setDTDHandler(DTDHandler handler)

Visual Basic Signature

N/A.

This method is part of the `XMLFilterImpl` implementation of the `XMLReader` interface. See the `XMLReader.setDTDHandler()` method documentation for details.

See Also

org.xml.sax.XMLReader.setDTDHandler(org.xml.sax.DTDHandler)

Example

See the `XMLReader.setDTDHandler()` method documentation for an example.

Parameters

DTDHandler **handler**   An instance of an object that implements the `DTDHandler` interface.

Returns

void   N/A.

setEntityResolver Method

Java Signature
```
public void setEntityResolver(EntityResolver resolver)
```

Visual Basic Signature
N/A.

This method is part of the XMLFilterImpl implementation of the XMLReader interface. See the XMLReader.setEntityResolver() method documentation for details.

See Also
org.xml.sax.XMLReader.setEntityResolver(org.xml.sax.EntityResolver)

Example
See the XMLReader.setEntityResolver() method documentation for an example.

Parameters
EntityResolver **resolver**   An instance of an object that implements the EntityResolver interface.

Returns
void   N/A.

setErrorHandler Method

Java Signature
```
public void setErrorHandler(ErrorHandler handler)
```

Visual Basic Signature
N/A.

This method is part of the XMLFilterImpl implementation of the XMLReader interface. See the XMLReader.setErrorHandler() method documentation for details.

See Also
org.xml.sax.XMLReader.setErrorHandler(org.xml.sax.ErrorHandler)

Example
See the XMLReader.setErrorHandler() method documentation for an example.

Parameters
ErrorHandler **handler**   An object that implements the ErrorHandler interface.

Returns
void   N/A.

setFeature Method

Java Signature
```
public void setFeature(String name, boolean state)
```

Visual Basic Signature
N/A.

This method is part of the `XMLFilterImpl` implementation of the `XMLReader` interface. See the `XMLReader.setFeature()` method documentation for details. This method will fail if the filter's parent reader has not been set.

Thrown Exceptions
org.xml.sax.SAXNotRecognizedException
org.xml.sax.SAXNotSupportedException

See Also
org.xml.sax.XMLReader.setFeature(java.lang.String, boolean)

Example
See the `XMLReader.setFeature()` method documentation for an example.

Parameters
String **name**   The feature name.

boolean **state**   The new Boolean state of the specified feature.

Returns
void   N/A.

setParent Method

Java Signature
public void setParent(XMLReader parent)

Visual Basic Signature
N/A.

This method is part of the `XMLFilterImpl` implementation of the `XMLFilter` interface. See the `XMLFilter.setParent()` method documentation for details.

See Also
org.xml.sax.helpers.XMLFilterImpl.getParent()

Example
See the `XMLFilter.setParent()` method documentation for an example.

Parameters
XMLReader **parent**   The parent object that implements the `XMLReader` interface.

Returns
void   N/A.

setProperty Method

Java Signature
public void setProperty(String name, Object value)

Visual Basic Signature
N/A.

This method is part of the `XMLFilterImpl` implementation of the `XMLReader` interface. See the `XMLReader.setProperty()` method documentation for details. This method will fail if the filter's parent reader has not been set.

Thrown Exceptions
org.xml.sax.SAXNotRecognizedException
org.xml.sax.SAXNotSupportedException

See Also
org.xml.sax.XMLReader.getProperty(java.lang.String)
org.xml.sax.XMLReader.setProperty(java.lang.String, java.lang.Object)

Example
See the `XMLReader.setProperty()` method documentation for an example.

Parameters

String **name**   The property name.

Object **value**   The value of the specified property as an `Object`.

Returns
void   N/A.

skippedEntity Method

Java Signature
public void skippedEntity(String name)

Visual Basic Signature
N/A.

This method is an implementation of the `ContentHandler.skippedEntity()` event method. Override this method to perform custom processing for this event before the client application is notified. See the `ContentHandler.skippedEntity()` method documentation for details.

Thrown Exceptions
org.xml.sax.SAXException

See Also
org.xml.sax.ContentHandler.skippedEntity(java.lang.String)

Example
See the `ContentHandler.skippedEntity()` method documentation for an example.

Parameters

String **name**   The name of the skipped entity.

Returns
void   N/A.

startDocument Method

Java Signature
public void startDocument()

Visual Basic Signature
N/A.

This method is an implementation of the ContentHandler.startDocument() event method. Override this method to perform custom processing for this event before the client application is notified. See the ContentHandler.startDocument() method documentation for details.

Thrown Exceptions
org.xml.sax.SAXException

See Also
org.xml.sax.ContentHandler.startDocument()

Example
See the ContentHandler.startDocument() method documentation for an example.

Returns
void   N/A.

startElement Method

Java Signature
public void startElement(String uri, String localName, String qName, Attributes atts)

Visual Basic Signature
N/A.

This method is an implementation of the ContentHandler.startElement() event method. Override this method to perform custom processing for this event before the client application is notified. See the ContentHandler.startElement() method documentation for details.

Thrown Exceptions
org.xml.sax.SAXException

See Also
org.xml.sax.ContentHandler.startElement(java.lang.String, java.lang.String, java.lang.String, org.xml.sax.Attributes)

Example
See the ContentHandler.startElement() method documentation for an example.

Parameters

String **uri** The element's namespace URI, or an empty string if namespace processing is not being performed or if no namespace was provided.

String **localName** The local name of the element, or an empty string if namespace processing is not being performed.

String **qName** The element's qualified name, or an empty string if qualified names are not available.

Attributes **atts** An implementation of the Attributes interface, representing the attributes associated with the element.

Returns

void   N/A.

startPrefixMapping Method

Java Signature
public void startPrefixMapping(String prefix, String uri)

Visual Basic Signature
N/A.

This method is an implementation of the ContentHandler.startPrefixMapping() event method. Override this method to perform custom processing for this event before the client application is notified. See the ContentHandler.startPrefixMapping() method documentation for details.

Thrown Exceptions
org.xml.sax.SAXException

See Also
org.xml.sax.ContentHandler.startPrefixMapping(java.lang.String, java.lang.String)

Example
See the ContentHandler.startPrefixMapping() method documentation for an example.

Parameters

String **prefix** The namespace prefix.

String **uri** The namespace URI.

Returns

void   N/A.

unparsedEntityDecl Method

Java Signature
public void unparsedEntityDecl(String name, String publicId, String systemId, String notationName)

Visual Basic Signature
N/A.

This method is an implementation of the `DTDHandler.unparsedEntityDecl()` event method. Override this method to perform custom processing for this event before the client application is notified. See the `DTDHandler.unparsedEntityDecl()` method documentation for details.

Thrown Exceptions
org.xml.sax.SAXException

See Also
org.xml.sax.DTDHandler.unparsedEntityDecl(java.lang.String, java.lang.String, java.lang.String, java.lang.String)

Example
See the `DTDHandler.unparsedEntityDecl()` method documentation for an example.

Parameters
String `name`   The entity name.

String `publicId`   The public identifier of the entity, or `null` if no public identifier is available.

String `systemId`   The system identifier of the entity, or `null` if no system identifier is available. If this parameter is a URL, the parser must fully resolve it before calling the `unparsedEntityDecl()` method in the application.

String `notationName`   The name of the associated notation.

Returns
void   N/A.

warning Method

Java Signature
public void warning(SAXParseException e)

Visual Basic Signature
N/A.

This method is an implementation of the `ErrorHandler.warning()` event method. Override this method to perform custom processing for this event before the client application is notified. See the `ErrorHandler.warning()` method documentation for details.

Thrown Exceptions
org.xml.sax.SAXException

See Also
org.xml.sax.ErrorHandler.warning(org.xml.sax.SAXParseException)

Example

See the `ErrorHandler.warning()` method documentation for an example.

Parameters

`SAXParseException` **e**   An instance of a SAX parse exception encapsulating the details of the warning.

Returns

void   N/A.

XMLReader Interface

An object that implements the `XMLReader` interface is the actual XML parser that reads an XML document. Most applications will not implement this interface, but rather will use `org.xml.sax.helpers.XMLReaderFactory` to generate a new object that implements the `XMLReader` interface. The new object can then be configured using its various `set*Handler` methods. Parsing of the XML document is initiated by a call to one of the object's `parse()` methods.

Visual Basic Equivalent
SAXXMLReader30

See Also
org.xml.sax.helpers.ParserAdapter
org.xml.sax.helpers.XMLReaderAdapter
org.xml.sax.XMLFilter

Example
```
import org.xml.sax.helpers.XMLReaderFactory;
import org.xml.sax.helpers.DefaultHandler;
import org.xml.sax.XMLReader;
import org.xml.sax.EntityResolver;
import org.xml.sax.DTDHandler;
import org.xml.sax.ContentHandler;
import org.xml.sax.ErrorHandler;
import org.xml.sax.InputSource;
import org.xml.sax.SAXException;
import org.xml.sax.SAXParseException;
import org.xml.sax.SAXNotRecognizedException;
import org.xml.sax.SAXNotSupportedException;
import java.io.IOException;
. . .
    private XMLReader myReader;
```

Members

getContentHandler Method

Java Signature
```
public ContentHandler getContentHandler()
```

Visual Basic Signature
```
Public Property contentHandler As IVBSAXContentHandler
```

This method returns the object that implements the `ContentHandler` interface and is registered with `XMLReader`. If no `ContentHandler` has been registered, the method returns `null`.

See Also
```
org.xml.sax.XMLReader.setContentHandler(org.xml.sax.ContentHandler)
```

Example
```
import org.xml.sax.helpers.XMLReaderFactory;
import org.xml.sax.helpers.DefaultHandler;
import org.xml.sax.XMLReader;
import org.xml.sax.EntityResolver;
import org.xml.sax.DTDHandler;
import org.xml.sax.ContentHandler;
import org.xml.sax.ErrorHandler;
import org.xml.sax.InputSource;
import org.xml.sax.SAXException;
import org.xml.sax.SAXParseException;
import org.xml.sax.SAXNotRecognizedException;
import org.xml.sax.SAXNotSupportedException;
import java.io.IOException;
. . .
    private XMLReader myReader;
. . .
        myContentHandler = myReader.getContentHandler();
```

Returns

`ContentHandler`   An object that implements the `ContentHandler` interface, or `null` if a `ContentHandler` has not been registered.

getDTDHandler Method

Java Signature
```
public DTDHandler getDTDHandler()
```

Visual Basic Signature
```
Public Property dtdHandler As IVBSAXDTDHandler
```

This method returns the object that implements the `DTDHandler` interface and is registered with `XMLReader`. If no `DTDHandler` has been registered, the method returns `null`.

See Also
```
org.xml.sax.XMLReader.setDTDHandler(org.xml.sax.DTDHandler)
```

Example
```
import org.xml.sax.helpers.XMLReaderFactory;
import org.xml.sax.helpers.DefaultHandler;
import org.xml.sax.XMLReader;
import org.xml.sax.EntityResolver;
import org.xml.sax.DTDHandler;
import org.xml.sax.ContentHandler;
import org.xml.sax.ErrorHandler;
import org.xml.sax.InputSource;
import org.xml.sax.SAXException;
import org.xml.sax.SAXParseException;
import org.xml.sax.SAXNotRecognizedException;
import org.xml.sax.SAXNotSupportedException;
import java.io.IOException;
. . .
    private XMLReader myReader;
. . .
        myDTDHandler = myReader.getDTDHandler();
```

Returns
DTDHandler   An object that implements the DTDHandler interface, or null if no DTDHandler implementation has been registered.

getEntityResolver Method

Java Signature
```
public EntityResolver getEntityResolver()
```

Visual Basic Signature
```
Public Property entityResolver As IVBSAXEntityResolver
```

This method returns the object that implements the EntityResolver interface and is registered with XMLReader. If no EntityResolver has been registered, the method returns null.

See Also
org.xml.sax.XMLReader.setEntityResolver(org.xml.sax.EntityResolver)

Example
```
import org.xml.sax.helpers.XMLReaderFactory;
import org.xml.sax.helpers.DefaultHandler;
import org.xml.sax.XMLReader;
import org.xml.sax.EntityResolver;
import org.xml.sax.DTDHandler;
import org.xml.sax.ContentHandler;
import org.xml.sax.ErrorHandler;
import org.xml.sax.InputSource;
import org.xml.sax.SAXException;
import org.xml.sax.SAXParseException;
```

(continued on next page)

```
import org.xml.sax.SAXNotRecognizedException;
import org.xml.sax.SAXNotSupportedException;
import java.io.IOException;
. . .
    private XMLReader myReader;
. . .
        myEntityResolver = myReader.getEntityResolver();
```

Returns

EntityResolver   An instance of an object that implements the EntityResolver interface, or null if no EntityResolver has been registered.

getErrorHandler Method

Java Signature
```
public ErrorHandler getErrorHandler()
```

Visual Basic Signature
```
Public Property errorHandler As IVBSAXErrorHandler
```

This method returns the current error handler associated with XMLReader. If no ErrorHandler has been registered, the method returns null.

See Also
org.xml.sax.XMLReader.setErrorHandler(org.xml.sax.ErrorHandler)

Example
```
import org.xml.sax.helpers.XMLReaderFactory;
import org.xml.sax.helpers.DefaultHandler;
import org.xml.sax.XMLReader;
import org.xml.sax.EntityResolver;
import org.xml.sax.DTDHandler;
import org.xml.sax.ContentHandler;
import org.xml.sax.ErrorHandler;
import org.xml.sax.InputSource;
import org.xml.sax.SAXException;
import org.xml.sax.SAXParseException;
import org.xml.sax.SAXNotRecognizedException;
import org.xml.sax.SAXNotSupportedException;
import java.io.IOException;
. . .
    private XMLReader myReader;
. . .
        myErrorHandler = myReader.getErrorHandler();
```

Returns

ErrorHandler   An instance of ErrorHandler, or null if no ErrorHandler has been registered.

getFeature Method

Java Signature
public boolean getFeature(String name)

Visual Basic Signature
Public Function getFeature(strName As String) As Boolean

This method returns the value of a feature. A feature name may be any fully qualified URI representing a Boolean value. If the feature is unrecognized by XMLReader, the reader will throw a SAXNotRecognizedException error. The XMLReader object may recognize the requested feature but not support the feature, causing the reader to throw a SAXNotSupportedException. Some features may be unrecognized or unavailable depending on the current context: for example before, during, or after parsing.

There is no fixed set of features; rather, XMLReader implementers are free to define new features as needed. However, since all feature names are fully qualified URIs, implementers should always define feature names based on URIs they control.

All implementations of XMLReader are required to recognize the features http://xml.org/sax/features/namespaces and http://xml.org/sax/features/namespace-prefixes. In addition, any implementation of the XMLReader interface must support a value of true for the http://xml.org/sax/features/namespaces feature, and a value of false for the http://xml.org/sax/features/namespace-prefixes feature. This requirement guarantees that all SAX 2.0 XMLReaders will provide minimal support for namespace processing.

A core reference set of features does exist that XMLReader implementers may choose to support.

http://xml.org/sax/features/namespaces

- If this feature is set to true, XMLReader provides namespace processing.
- If set to false, namespace processing is not performed. Note that a value of false implies a value of true for the feature http://xml.org/sax/features/namespace-prefixes.
- This feature is read-only during parsing but is writable at any other time.
- All classes implementing the XMLReader interface *must* recognize this feature *and* support a value of true for this feature.

http://xml.org/sax/features/namespace-prefixes

- If this feature is set to true XMLReader will *not* perform any namespace processing. Instead, XMLReader reports the original prefixed names used for namespace declarations.
- If this feature is set to false, namespace processing is performed by XMLReader. Note that this implies a value of true for the feature http://xml.org/sax/features/namespaces.
- This feature is read-only during parsing but is writable at any other time.
- All classes implementing the XMLReader interface *must* recognize this feature *and* support a value of false for this feature.

http://xml.org/sax/features/validation

- If this feature is set to true, XMLReader validates the XML document. Note that this also implies a value of true for both features http://xml.org/sax/features/external-general-entities and http://xml.org/sax/features/external-parameter-entities.
- This feature is read-only during parsing but is writable at any other time.

http://xml.org/sax/features/external-general-entities

- If this feature is set to true, XMLReader includes all external general entities.
- If set to false, XMLReader will *not* include any external general entities.
- This feature is read-only during parsing but is writable at any other time.

http://xml.org/sax/features/external-parameter-entities

- If this feature is set to true, XMLReader includes all external parameter entities, including the external DTD.
- If set to false, XMLReader will *not* include any external parameter entities.
- This feature is read-only during parsing but is writable at any other time.

http://xml.org/sax/features/string-interning

- If this feature is set to true, all names (elements, attributes, prefixes, and so on) are interned using java.lang.String.intern.
- If set to false, names are not interned.
- This feature is read-only during parsing but is writable at any other time.

Thrown Exceptions
org.xml.sax.SAXNotRecognizedException
org.xml.sax.SAXNotSupportedException

See Also
org.xml.sax.XMLReader.setFeature(java.lang.String, boolean)

Example
```
import org.xml.sax.helpers.XMLReaderFactory;
import org.xml.sax.helpers.DefaultHandler;
import org.xml.sax.XMLReader;
import org.xml.sax.EntityResolver;
import org.xml.sax.DTDHandler;
import org.xml.sax.ContentHandler;
import org.xml.sax.ErrorHandler;
import org.xml.sax.InputSource;
import org.xml.sax.SAXException;
import org.xml.sax.SAXParseException;
import org.xml.sax.SAXNotRecognizedException;
import org.xml.sax.SAXNotSupportedException;
import java.io.IOException;
. . .
    private XMLReader myReader;
```

```
...
    //Get the value of a feature.
    featureName = "http://xml.org/sax/features/validation";
    try
    {
        System.out.println( "Validation feature value is: " +
                    myReader.getFeature( featureName ) );
    }
    catch( SAXNotRecognizedException e )
    {
        System.err.println("Feature not recognized: " +
                e.getMessage() );
    }
    catch( SAXNotSupportedException e )
    {
        System.err.println( "Feature not supported: " +
                e.getMessage() );
    }
```

Parameters

String **name**   The feature name as a fully qualified URI.

Returns

boolean   The boolean value of the specified feature.

getProperty Method

Java Signature
```
public Object getProperty(String name)
```

Visual Basic Signature
```
Public Function getProperty(strName As String) As Variant
```

This method returns the value of a property. A property name may be any fully qualified URI representing an object value. If the property is unrecognized by XMLReader, the parser will throw a SAXNotRecognizedException. XMLReader may recognize the requested property but not support the property, causing the parser to throw a SAXNotSupportedException error. Some properties may be unrecognized or unavailable depending on the current context: for example before, during, or after parsing.

Implementers of XMLReader are encouraged to invent new properties based upon their own URIs.

Implementers of XMLReader are encouraged, but not required, to support two core properties defined by the SAX 2.0 documentation:

http://xml.org/sax/properties/dom-node

- A org.w3c.dom.Node object.
- During parsing, this property value is the current DOM node being visited. Otherwise, the property value is the root DOM node of the document.
- This property is read-only during parsing but is writable at any other time.

> http://xml.org/sax/properties/xml-string

- A java.lang.String object.
- This property value is the literal string of characters that was the source of the current event.
- This property is read-only.

Thrown Exceptions
org.xml.sax.SAXNotRecognizedException
org.xml.sax.SAXNotSupportedException

See Also
org.xml.sax.XMLReader.setProperty(java.lang.String, java.lang.Object)

Example
```
import org.xml.sax.helpers.XMLReaderFactory;
import org.xml.sax.helpers.DefaultHandler;
import org.xml.sax.XMLReader;
import org.xml.sax.EntityResolver;
import org.xml.sax.DTDHandler;
import org.xml.sax.ContentHandler;
import org.xml.sax.ErrorHandler;
import org.xml.sax.InputSource;
import org.xml.sax.SAXException;
import org.xml.sax.SAXParseException;
import org.xml.sax.SAXNotRecognizedException;
import org.xml.sax.SAXNotSupportedException;
import java.io.IOException;
. . .
    private XMLReader myReader;
. . .
        //Get the value of a property.
        propertyName = "http://bookofsax.com/properties/authors";
        try
        {
            propertyValue =
                myReader.getProperty( propertyName ).toString();
            System.out.println( "Property value is: " +
                                        propertyValue );
        }
        catch( SAXNotRecognizedException e )
        {
            System.err.println("Property not recognized: " +
                    e.getMessage() );
        }
        catch( SAXNotSupportedException e )
        {
            System.err.println( "Property not supported: " +
                    e.getMessage() );
        }
```

Parameters

String **name** A string containing a fully qualified URI representing the property name.

Returns

Object The value of the specified property as an object.

parse Method

Java Signature
```
public void parse(String systemId)
```

Visual Basic Signature
```
Public Sub parseURL(strURL As String)
```

This method causes XMLReader to begin parsing the XML document identified by a system identifier (URI). If the passed system identifier is a URL, it must be fully resolved by the application before it is passed to the parser.

Thrown Exceptions
```
java.io.IOException
org.xml.sax.SAXException
```

See Also
```
org.xml.sax.XMLReader.parse(org.xml.sax.InputSource)
```

Example
```
import org.xml.sax.helpers.XMLReaderFactory;
import org.xml.sax.helpers.DefaultHandler;
import org.xml.sax.XMLReader;
import org.xml.sax.EntityResolver;
import org.xml.sax.DTDHandler;
import org.xml.sax.ContentHandler;
import org.xml.sax.ErrorHandler;
import org.xml.sax.InputSource;
import org.xml.sax.SAXException;
import org.xml.sax.SAXParseException;
import org.xml.sax.SAXNotRecognizedException;
import org.xml.sax.SAXNotSupportedException;
import java.io.IOException;
. . .
    private XMLReader myReader;
. . .
            //Use the system ID for parsing.
            try
            {
                myReader.parse( xmlDocSystemID );
```

(continued on next page)

```
            }
            catch( Exception e )
            {
                System.err.println( "Couldn't parse file " +
                        xmlDocSystemID );
                System.err.println( e.getMessage() );
            }
```

Parameters

String **systemId**   A string containing the system identifier. If the system identifier is a URL, it must be resolved by the application before it is passed to the parser.

Returns

void   N/A.

parse Method

Java Signature
```
public void parse(InputSource input)
```

Visual Basic Signature
```
Public Sub parse(varInput As Variant)
```

This method causes XMLReader to begin parsing the XML document referenced by an InputSource object.

Thrown Exceptions
java.io.IOException
org.xml.sax.SAXException

See Also
org.xml.sax.InputSource
org.xml.sax.XMLReader.parse(java.lang.String)
org.xml.sax.XMLReader.setContentHandler(org.xml.sax.ContentHandler)
org.xml.sax.XMLReader.setDTDHandler(org.xml.sax.DTDHandler)
org.xml.sax.XMLReader.setEntityResolver(org.xml.sax.EntityResolver)
org.xml.sax.XMLReader.setErrorHandler(org.xml.sax.ErrorHandler)

Example
```
import org.xml.sax.helpers.XMLReaderFactory;
import org.xml.sax.helpers.DefaultHandler;
import org.xml.sax.XMLReader;
import org.xml.sax.EntityResolver;
import org.xml.sax.DTDHandler;
import org.xml.sax.ContentHandler;
import org.xml.sax.ErrorHandler;
import org.xml.sax.InputSource;
import org.xml.sax.SAXException;
import org.xml.sax.SAXParseException;
import org.xml.sax.SAXNotRecognizedException;
import org.xml.sax.SAXNotSupportedException;
```

```
import java.io.IOException;
. . .
    private XMLReader myReader;
. . .
        //Use the passed InputSource for parsing.
        try
        {
            myReader.parse( xmlInputSource );
        }
        catch( Exception e )
        {
            System.err.println( "Couldn't parse InputSource " +
                    xmlInputSource.getSystemId() );
            System.err.println( e.getMessage() );
        }
```

Parameters

InputSource **input**   An instance of an InputSource object representing an XML document.

Returns

void   N/A.

setContentHandler Method

Java Signature
```
public void setContentHandler(ContentHandler handler)
```

Visual Basic Signature
```
Public Property contentHandler As IVBSAXContentHandler
```

This method allows a client application to register an object that implements the ContentHandler interface with XMLReader in order to receive content-related events.

Applications may register different ContentHandler implementations at any time, including in the middle of parsing. The parser is required to begin using the new ContentHandler immediately.

If no ContentHandler is registered with the parser, all content events will be silently ignored.

See Also
org.xml.sax.XMLReader.getContentHandler()

Example
```
import org.xml.sax.helpers.XMLReaderFactory;
import org.xml.sax.helpers.DefaultHandler;
import org.xml.sax.XMLReader;
import org.xml.sax.EntityResolver;
import org.xml.sax.DTDHandler;
import org.xml.sax.ContentHandler;
```

(continued on next page)

```
import org.xml.sax.ErrorHandler;
import org.xml.sax.InputSource;
import org.xml.sax.SAXException;
import org.xml.sax.SAXParseException;
import org.xml.sax.SAXNotRecognizedException;
import org.xml.sax.SAXNotSupportedException;
import java.io.IOException;
. . .
    private XMLReader myReader;
. . .
        //Use DefaultHandler for implementations of standard ifcs.
        DefaultHandler myHandlers = new DefaultHandler();
. . .
        myReader.setContentHandler( myHandlers );
```

Parameters

`ContentHandler` **handler**   An object that implements the `ContentHandler` interface.

Returns

void   N/A.

setDTDHandler Method

Java Signature
`public void setDTDHandler(DTDHandler handler)`

Visual Basic Signature
`Public Property dtdHandler As IVBSAXDTDHandler`

This method allows a client application to register an object that implements the `DTDHandler` interface with `XMLReader` in order to receive DTD-related events.

Applications may register different `DTDHandler` implementations at any time, including in the middle of parsing. The parser is required to begin using the new `DTDHandler` immediately.

If no `DTDHandler` is registered with the parser, all DTD events will be silently ignored.

See Also
`org.xml.sax.XMLReader.getDTDHandler()`

Example
```
import org.xml.sax.helpers.XMLReaderFactory;
import org.xml.sax.helpers.DefaultHandler;
import org.xml.sax.XMLReader;
import org.xml.sax.EntityResolver;
import org.xml.sax.DTDHandler;
import org.xml.sax.ContentHandler;
import org.xml.sax.ErrorHandler;
import org.xml.sax.InputSource;
import org.xml.sax.SAXException;
```

```
import org.xml.sax.SAXParseException;
import org.xml.sax.SAXNotRecognizedException;
import org.xml.sax.SAXNotSupportedException;
import java.io.IOException;
...
    private XMLReader myReader;
...
        //Use DefaultHandler for implementations of standard ifcs.
        DefaultHandler myHandlers = new DefaultHandler();
...
        myReader.setDTDHandler( myHandlers );
```

Parameters

DTDHandler **handler**   An object that implements the DTDHandler interface.

Returns

void   N/A.

setEntityResolver Method

Java Signature
```
public void setEntityResolver(EntityResolver resolver)
```

Visual Basic Signature
```
Public Property entityResolver As IVBSAXEntityResolver
```

This method allows a client application to register an object that implements the EntityResolver interface with XMLReader in order to intercept all entity resolution requests.

Applications may register different EntityResolver implementations at any time, including in the middle of parsing. The XMLReader is required to begin using the new EntityResolver immediately.

If an instance of EntityResolver is not registered with XMLReader, the reader will perform its own default resolution.

See Also
org.xml.sax.XMLReader.getEntityResolver()

Example
```
import org.xml.sax.helpers.XMLReaderFactory;
import org.xml.sax.helpers.DefaultHandler;
import org.xml.sax.XMLReader;
import org.xml.sax.EntityResolver;
import org.xml.sax.DTDHandler;
import org.xml.sax.ContentHandler;
import org.xml.sax.ErrorHandler;
import org.xml.sax.InputSource;
import org.xml.sax.SAXException;
import org.xml.sax.SAXParseException;
```

(continued on next page)

```
import org.xml.sax.SAXNotRecognizedException;
import org.xml.sax.SAXNotSupportedException;
import java.io.IOException;
. . .
    private XMLReader myReader;
. . .
        //Use DefaultHandler for implementations of standard ifcs.
        DefaultHandler myHandlers = new DefaultHandler();
. . .
        myReader.setEntityResolver( myHandlers );
```

Parameters

EntityResolver **resolver**   An object that implements the EntityResolver interface.

Returns

void   N/A.

setErrorHandler Method

Java Signature
```
public void setErrorHandler(ErrorHandler handler)
```

Visual Basic Signature
```
Public Property errorHandler As IVBSAXErrorHandler
```

This method allows a client application to register an object that implements the ErrorHandler interface with XMLReader in order to intercept error events.

Applications may register different ErrorHandler implementations at any time, including in the middle of parsing. The parser is required to begin using the new ErrorHandler immediately.

If an ErrorHandler is not registered with XMLReader, all errors will be silently ignored, with unpredictable results; therefore, it is *strongly* recommended that all applications implement the ErrorHandler interface.

See Also
org.xml.sax.XMLReader.getErrorHandler()

Example
```
import org.xml.sax.helpers.XMLReaderFactory;
import org.xml.sax.helpers.DefaultHandler;
import org.xml.sax.XMLReader;
import org.xml.sax.EntityResolver;
import org.xml.sax.DTDHandler;
import org.xml.sax.ContentHandler;
import org.xml.sax.ErrorHandler;
import org.xml.sax.InputSource;
import org.xml.sax.SAXException;
import org.xml.sax.SAXParseException;
import org.xml.sax.SAXNotRecognizedException;
```

```
import org.xml.sax.SAXNotSupportedException;
import java.io.IOException;
. . .
    private XMLReader myReader;
. . .
        //Use DefaultHandler for implementations of standard ifcs.
        DefaultHandler myHandlers = new DefaultHandler();
. . .
        myReader.setErrorHandler( myHandlers );
```

Parameters

ErrorHandler **handler**   An implementation of the ErrorHandler interface.

Returns

void   N/A.

setFeature Method

Java Signature
```
public void setFeature(String name, boolean value)
```

Visual Basic Signature
```
Public Sub putFeature(strName As String, fValue As Boolean)
```

This method allows an application to set the value of a feature. A feature may be any fully qualified URI representing a Boolean value. If the feature is unrecognized by XMLReader, XMLReader will throw a SAXNotRecognizedException error. XMLReader may recognize the requested feature but not support it, causing XMLReader to throw a SAXNotSupportedException error. Some features may be unrecognized or unavailable depending on the current context: for example, before, during, or after parsing.

There is no fixed set of features; rather, XMLReader implementers are free to define new features as needed. However, since all feature names are fully qualified URIs, implementers should always define feature names based on URIs they control.

All implementations of XMLReader are required to recognize the features http://xml.org/sax/features/namespaces and http://xml.org/sax/features/namespace-prefixes. In addition, any implementation of the XMLReader interface must support a value of true for the http://xml.org/sax/features/namespaces feature, and a value of false for the http://xml.org/sax/features/namespace-prefixes feature. This requirement guarantees that all SAX 2.0 XMLReader implementations provide at least minimal support for namespace processing.

A core reference set of features does exist that XMLReader implementers may choose to support.

   http://xml.org/sax/features/namespaces
- If this feature is set to true, XMLReader provides namespace processing.
- If set to false, namespace processing is not performed. Note that a value of false implies a value of true for the feature http://xml.org/sax/features/namespace-prefixes.
- This feature is read-only during parsing but is writable at any other time.

- All classes that implement the XMLReader interface *must* recognize this feature *and* support a value of true for this feature.

http://xml.org/sax/features/namespace-prefixes

- If this feature is set to true, XMLReader will *not* perform any namespace processing. Instead, XMLReader reports the original prefixed names used for namespace declarations.
- If this feature is set to false, namespace processing is performed by XMLReader. Note that this implies a value of true for the feature http://xml.org/sax/features/namespaces.
- This feature is read-only during parsing but is writable at any other time.
- All classes that implement the XMLReader interface *must* recognize this feature *and* support a value of false for this feature.

http://xml.org/sax/features/validation

- If this feature is set to true, XMLReader validates the XML document. Note that this also implies a value of true for both features http://xml.org/sax/features/external-general-entities and http://xml.org/sax/features/external-parameter-entities.
- This feature is read-only during parsing but is writable at any other time.

http://xml.org/sax/features/external-general-entities

- If this feature is set to true, XMLReader includes all external general entities.
- If this feature is set to false, XMLReader will *not* include any external general entities.
- This feature is read-only during parsing but is writable at any other time.

http://xml.org/sax/features/external-parameter-entities

- If this feature is set to true, XMLReader includes all external parameter entities, including the external DTD.
- If this feature is set to false, XMLReader will *not* include any external parameter entities.
- This feature is read-only during parsing but is writable at any other time.

http://xml.org/sax/features/string-interning

- If this feature is set to true, all names (elements, attributes, prefixes, and so on) are interned using java.lang.String.intern.
- If set to false, names are not interned.
- This feature is read-only during parsing but is writable at any other time.

Thrown Exceptions
org.xml.sax.SAXNotRecognizedException
org.xml.sax.SAXNotSupportedException

See Also
org.xml.sax.XMLReader.getFeature(java.lang.String)

Example
```
import org.xml.sax.helpers.XMLReaderFactory;
import org.xml.sax.helpers.DefaultHandler;
import org.xml.sax.XMLReader;
import org.xml.sax.EntityResolver;
import org.xml.sax.DTDHandler;
import org.xml.sax.ContentHandler;
import org.xml.sax.ErrorHandler;
import org.xml.sax.InputSource;
import org.xml.sax.SAXException;
import org.xml.sax.SAXParseException;
import org.xml.sax.SAXNotRecognizedException;
import org.xml.sax.SAXNotSupportedException;
import java.io.IOException;
. . .
    private XMLReader myReader;
```

Parameters

String **name**   The name of the feature as a fully qualified URI.

boolean **value**   The Boolean value of the feature.

Returns

void   N/A.

setProperty Method

Java Signature
```
public void setProperty(String name, Object value)
```

Visual Basic Signature
```
Public Sub putProperty(strName As String, varValue As Variant)
```

This method allows an application to set the value of a property. A property may be any fully qualified URI representing an object value. If the property is unrecognized by XMLReader, the parser will throw a SAXNotRecognizedException error. XMLReader may recognize the requested property but not support it, causing the parser to throw a SAXNotSupportedException error. Some properties may be unrecognized or unavailable depending on the current context: for example, before, during, or after parsing.

Implementers of XMLReader are encouraged to invent new properties based upon their own URIs.

Implementers of XMLReader are also encouraged, but not required, to support two core properties defined by the SAX 2.0 documentation:

> http://xml.org/sax/properties/dom-node

- A org.w3c.dom.Node object.
- During parsing, this property value is the current DOM node being visited. Otherwise, the property value is the root DOM node of the document.
- This property is read-only during parsing but is writable at any other time.

http://xml.org/sax/properties/xml-string
- A java.lang.String object.
- This property value is the literal string of characters that was the source of the current event.
- This property is read-only.

Thrown Exceptions
org.xml.sax.SAXNotRecognizedException
org.xml.sax.SAXNotSupportedException

Example
```
import org.xml.sax.helpers.XMLReaderFactory;
import org.xml.sax.helpers.DefaultHandler;
import org.xml.sax.XMLReader;
import org.xml.sax.EntityResolver;
import org.xml.sax.DTDHandler;
import org.xml.sax.ContentHandler;
import org.xml.sax.ErrorHandler;
import org.xml.sax.InputSource;
import org.xml.sax.SAXException;
import org.xml.sax.SAXParseException;
import org.xml.sax.SAXNotRecognizedException;
import org.xml.sax.SAXNotSupportedException;
import java.io.IOException;
. . .
    private XMLReader myReader;
```

Parameters

String **name**   The property name as a fully qualified URI.

Object **value**   The property's value as an object.

Returns

void   N/A.

XMLReaderAdapter Class

The helper class XMLReaderAdapter wraps a SAX 2.0 XMLReader object, using the Adapter design pattern, making it appear to be a SAX 1.0 Parser object. This class is the inverse of ParserAdapter, allowing SAX 2.0 parsers to be used with legacy applications written to SAX 1.0 interfaces. The class implements both the SAX 2.0 ContentHandler interface and the SAX 1.0 Parser interface. A SAX 1.0 client application uses the SAX 1.0 Parser interface to communicate with the XMLReaderAdapter object. The XMLReaderAdapter implements the SAX 2.0 ContentHandler interface so that it may register itself with the SAX 2.0 XMLReader object to receive notification of parsing events. The XMLReaderAdapter object, in turn, fires SAX 1.0 DocumentHandler events to the SAX 1.0 DocumentHandler object specified by the application.

The wrapped XMLReader object must support a value of true for the http://xml.org/sax/features/namespace-prefixes feature, or parsing will fail, throwing a SAXException error.

As SAX 2.0 becomes ubiquitous, the XMLReaderAdapter class will eventually become obsolete.

Visual Basic Equivalent
N/A.

See Also
org.xml.sax.Parser
org.xml.sax.XMLReader

Example
```
import org.xml.sax.HandlerBase;
import org.xml.sax.DocumentHandler;
import org.xml.sax.DTDHandler;
import org.xml.sax.EntityResolver;
import org.xml.sax.ErrorHandler;
import org.xml.sax.SAXException;
import org.xml.sax.SAXParseException;
import org.xml.sax.XMLReader;
import org.xml.sax.helpers.XMLReaderAdapter;
import org.xml.sax.helpers.XMLReaderFactory;
import java.io.IOException;
. . .
        XMLReaderAdapter SAX1parser = null;
```

Constructors

Java Signature
```
public  XMLReaderAdapter()
```

Visual Basic Signature
N/A.

This constructor method creates a new, empty instance of the XMLReaderAdapter class. The org.xml.sax.parser system property is used to specify the SAX 2.0 XMLReader to embed within this object.

If the org.xml.sax.parser system property is not set, or if the specified reader cannot be instantiated, the SAXException error is thrown.

See Also
org.xml.sax.helpers.XMLReaderAdapter(org.xml.sax.XMLReader)

Example
```
import org.xml.sax.HandlerBase;
import org.xml.sax.DocumentHandler;
import org.xml.sax.DTDHandler;
```

(continued on next page)

```
import org.xml.sax.EntityResolver;
import org.xml.sax.ErrorHandler;
import org.xml.sax.SAXException;
import org.xml.sax.SAXParseException;
import org.xml.sax.XMLReader;
import org.xml.sax.helpers.XMLReaderAdapter;
import org.xml.sax.helpers.XMLReaderFactory;
import java.io.IOException;
. . .
        System.setProperty( "org.xml.sax.parser",
                            "org.apache.xerces.parsers.SAXParser" );
        try
        {
            SAX1parser = new XMLReaderAdapter();
        }
        catch( SAXException e )
        {
            System.out.println( "ERROR:\n\t" +
                                e.getMessage() );
        }
```

Java Signature
```
public  XMLReaderAdapter(XMLReader xmlReader)
```

Visual Basic Signature
N/A.

This method creates a new instance of the XMLReaderAdapter class, wrapping the passed SAX 2.0 XMLReader object. The XMLReader object may not be changed once the XMLReaderAdapter object has been created. The passed XMLReader object cannot be null; otherwise, a java.lang.NullPointerException error is thrown.

See Also
org.xml.sax.helpers.XMLReaderAdapter()

Example
```
import org.xml.sax.HandlerBase;
import org.xml.sax.DocumentHandler;
import org.xml.sax.DTDHandler;
import org.xml.sax.EntityResolver;
import org.xml.sax.ErrorHandler;
import org.xml.sax.SAXException;
import org.xml.sax.SAXParseException;
import org.xml.sax.XMLReader;
import org.xml.sax.helpers.XMLReaderAdapter;
import org.xml.sax.helpers.XMLReaderFactory;
import java.io.IOException;
. . .
        SAX1parser = new XMLReaderAdapter( SAX2xmlReader );
```

Parameters

XMLReader **xmlReader**   The SAX 2.0 XMLReader to wrap.

Members

characters Method

Java Signature
```
public void characters(char[] ch, int start, int length)
```

Visual Basic Signature
N/A.

This method is part of the XMLReaderAdapter implementation of the SAX 2.0 ContentHandler interface.

SAX 1.0 application writers should not concern themselves with the ContentHandler functions; in an ideal world, these functions would be encapsulated and invisible to SAX 1.0 applications. However, XMLReaderAdapter must declare the ContentHandler interface as public so that the wrapped SAX 2.0 XMLReader object has access to the ContentHandler event methods.

Thrown Exceptions
org.xml.sax.SAXException

See Also
org.xml.sax.ContentHandler.characters(char[], int, int)

Example
N/A.

Parameters

char[] **ch**   The characters from the XML document.

int **start**   The starting position in the array.

int **length**   The number of characters to read from the array.

Returns

void   N/A.

endDocument Method

Java Signature
```
public void endDocument()
```

Visual Basic Signature
N/A.

This method is part of the XMLReaderAdapter implementation of the SAX 2.0 ContentHandler interface.

SAX 1.0 application writers should not concern themselves with the
ContentHandler functions; in an ideal world, these functions would be encapsulated
and invisible to SAX 1.0 applications. However, XMLReaderAdapter must declare the
ContentHandler interface as public so that the SAX 2.0 XMLReader object has access to
the ContentHandler event methods.

Thrown Exceptions
org.xml.sax.SAXException

See Also
org.xml.sax.ContentHandler.endDocument()

Example
N/A.

Returns
void   N/A.

endElement Method

Java Signature
public void endElement(String uri, String localName, String qName)

Visual Basic Signature
N/A.

This method is part of the XMLReaderAdapter implementation of the SAX 2.0
ContentHandler interface.

SAX 1.0 application writers should not concern themselves with the
ContentHandler functions; in an ideal world, these functions would be encapsulated
and invisible to SAX 1.0 applications. However, XMLReaderAdapter must declare the
ContentHandler interface as public so that the SAX 2.0 XMLReader object has access to
the ContentHandler event methods.

Thrown Exceptions
org.xml.sax.SAXException

See Also
org.xml.sax.ContentHandler.endElement(java.lang.String, java.lang.String,
java.lang.String)

Example
N/A.

Parameters

String **uri**   The namespace URI of the element, or an empty string if namespace processing is not being performed.

String **localName**   The local name of the element, or an empty string if namespace processing is not being performed.

String **qName**   The qualified name of the element, or an empty string if qualified names are not available.

Returns

void   N/A.

endPrefixMapping Method

Java Signature
public void endPrefixMapping(String prefix)

Visual Basic Signature
N/A.

This method is part of the XMLReaderAdapter implementation of the SAX 2.0 ContentHandler interface.

SAX 1.0 application writers should not concern themselves with the ContentHandler functions; in an ideal world, these functions would be encapsulated and invisible to SAX 1.0 applications. However, XMLReaderAdapter must declare the ContentHandler interface as public so that the SAX 2.0 XMLReader object has access to the ContentHandler event methods.

See Also
org.xml.sax.ContentHandler.endPrefixMapping(java.lang.String)

Example
N/A.

Parameters
String **prefix**   The namespace prefix that went out of scope.

Returns
void   N/A.

ignorableWhitespace Method

Java Signature
public void ignorableWhitespace(char[] ch, int start, int length)

Visual Basic Signature
N/A.

This method is part of the XMLReaderAdapter implementation of the SAX 2.0 ContentHandler interface.

SAX 1.0 application writers should not concern themselves with the ContentHandler functions; in an ideal world, these functions would be encapsulated and invisible to SAX 1.0 applications. However, XMLReaderAdapter must declare the ContentHandler interface as public so that the SAX 2.0 XMLReader object has access to the ContentHandler event methods.

Thrown Exceptions
org.xml.sax.SAXException

See Also
org.xml.sax.ContentHandler.ignorableWhitespace(char[], int, int)

Example
N/A.

Parameters
char[] **ch**   The whitespace character data from the XML document.

int **start**   The start position in the array.

int **length**   The number of characters to read from the array.

Returns
void   N/A.

parse Method

Java Signature
public void parse(String systemId)

Visual Basic Signature
N/A.

This method is part of the XMLReaderAdapter implementation of the SAX 1.0 Parser interface. See the Parser.parse() method documentation for details.

Thrown Exceptions
java.io.IOException
org.xml.sax.SAXException

See Also
org.xml.sax.helpers.XMLReaderAdapter.parse(org.xml.sax.InputSource)
org.xml.sax.Parser.parse(java.lang.String)

Example
```
import org.xml.sax.HandlerBase;
import org.xml.sax.DocumentHandler;
import org.xml.sax.DTDHandler;
import org.xml.sax.EntityResolver;
import org.xml.sax.ErrorHandler;
import org.xml.sax.SAXException;
import org.xml.sax.SAXParseException;
import org.xml.sax.XMLReader;
import org.xml.sax.helpers.XMLReaderAdapter;
import org.xml.sax.helpers.XMLReaderFactory;
import java.io.IOException;
    . . .
        try
        {
```

```
            SAX1parser.parse( xmlFile );
        }
        catch( SAXParseException e )
        {
            System.out.println( xmlFile + " is not well formed." );
            System.out.println( e.getMessage() +
                                " at line " + e.getLineNumber() +
                                ", column " + e.getColumnNumber() );
        }
        catch( SAXException e )
        {
            System.out.println( e.getMessage() );
        }
        catch( IOException e )
        {
            System.out.println( "Could not report on " + xmlFile +
                                " because of the IOException " + e );
        }
```

Parameters

String **systemId**   The absolute URL of the document.

Returns

void   N/A.

parse Method

Java Signature
```
public void parse(InputSource input)
```

Visual Basic Signature
N/A.

This method is part of the XMLReaderAdapter implementation of the SAX 1.0 Parser interface. See the Parser.parse() documentation for details.

Thrown Exceptions
java.io.IOException
org.xml.sax.SAXException

See Also
org.xml.sax.helpers.XMLReaderAdapter.parse(java.lang.String)
org.xml.sax.Parser.parse(org.xml.sax.InputSource)

Example

See the Parser.parse() method documentation for an example.

Parameters

InputSource **input**   An input source for the document.

Returns

void   N/A.

processingInstruction Method

Java Signature
public void processingInstruction(String target, String data)

Visual Basic Signature
N/A.

This method is part of the XMLReaderAdapter implementation of the SAX 2.0 ContentHandler interface.

SAX 1.0 application writers should not concern themselves with the ContentHandler functions; in an ideal world, these functions would be encapsulated and invisible to SAX 1.0 applications. However, XMLReaderAdapter must declare the ContentHandler interface as public so that the SAX 2.0 XMLReader object has access to the ContentHandler event methods.

Thrown Exceptions
org.xml.sax.SAXException

See Also
org.xml.sax.ContentHandler.processingInstruction(java.lang.String, java.lang.String)

Example
N/A.

Parameters

String **target**   The processing instruction target.

String **data**   The processing instruction data, or null if none was supplied. The data does not include any whitespace separating the data from the target.

Returns

void   N/A.

setDocumentHandler Method

Java Signature
public void setDocumentHandler(DocumentHandler handler)

Visual Basic Signature
N/A.

This method is part of the XMLReaderAdapter implementation of the SAX 1.0 Parser interface. See the Parser.setDocumentHandler() method documentation for details.

See Also
org.xml.sax.Parser.setDocumentHandler(org.xml.sax.DocumentHandler)

Example

See the `Parser.setDocumentHandler()` method documentation for an example.

Parameters

`DocumentHandler` **handler**   An instance of an object that implements the `DocumentHandler` interface.

Returns

void   N/A.

setDocumentLocator Method

Java Signature
```
public void setDocumentLocator(Locator locator)
```

Visual Basic Signature
N/A.

This method is part of the `XMLReaderAdapter` implementation of the SAX 2.0 `ContentHandler` interface.

   SAX 1.0 application writers should not concern themselves with the `ContentHandler` functions; in an ideal world, these functions would be encapsulated and invisible to SAX 1.0 applications. However, `XMLReaderAdapter` must declare the `ContentHandler` interface as public so that the SAX 2.0 `XMLReader` object has access to the `ContentHandler` event methods.

See Also

org.xml.sax.ContentHandler.setDocumentLocator(org.xml.sax.Locator)

Example

N/A.

Parameters

`Locator` **locator**   A instance of an object that implements the `Locator` interface capable of returning the location of any document-related event.

Returns

void   N/A.

setDTDHandler Method

Java Signature
```
public void setDTDHandler(DTDHandler handler)
```

Visual Basic Signature
N/A.

This method is part of the `XMLReaderAdapter` implementation of the SAX 1.0 `Parser` interface. See the `Parser.setDTDHandler()` method documentation for details.

See Also

org.xml.sax.Parser.setDTDHandler(org.xml.sax.DTDHandler)

Example

See the `Parser.setDTDHandler()` method documentation for an example.

Parameters

`DTDHandler` **handler**   An instance of an object that implements the `DTDHandler` interface.

Returns

void   N/A.

setEntityResolver Method

Java Signature
`public void setEntityResolver(EntityResolver resolver)`

Visual Basic Signature
N/A.

This method is part of the `XMLReaderAdapter` implementation of the SAX 1.0 `Parser` interface. See the `Parser.setEntityResolver()` method documentation for details.

See Also

org.xml.sax.Parser.setEntityResolver(org.xml.sax.EntityResolver)

Example

See the `Parser.setEntityResolver()` method documentation for an example.

Parameters

`EntityResolver` **resolver**   An instance of an object that implements the `EntityResolver` interface.

Returns

void   N/A.

setErrorHandler Method

Java Signature
`public void setErrorHandler(ErrorHandler handler)`

Visual Basic Signature
N/A.

This method is part of the `XMLReaderAdapter` implementation of the SAX 1.0 `Parser` interface. See the `Parser.setErrorHandler()` documentation for details.

See Also

org.xml.sax.Parser.setErrorHandler(org.xml.sax.ErrorHandler)

Example

See the `Parser.setErrorHandler()` method documentation for an example.

Parameters

ErrorHandler **handler**   An instance of an object that implements the `ErrorHandler` interface.

Returns

void   N/A.

setLocale Method

Java Signature
```
public void setLocale(Locale locale)
```

Visual Basic Signature
N/A.

This method is part of the `XMLReaderAdapter` implementation of the SAX 1.0 `Parser` interface. See the `Parser.setLocale()` documentation for details. The notion of an error-reporting locale is not supported in SAX 2.0; therefore, this method will always fail, throwing a `SAXException` error.

Thrown Exceptions
org.xml.sax.SAXException

See Also
org.xml.sax.Parser.setLocale(java.util.Locale)

Example

See the `Parser.setLocale()` method documentation for an example.

Parameters

Locale **locale**   A Locale object.

Returns

void   N/A.

skippedEntity Method

Java Signature
```
public void skippedEntity(String name)
```

Visual Basic Signature
N/A.

This method is part of the `XMLReaderAdapter` implementation of the SAX 2.0 `ContentHandler` interface.

SAX 1.0 application writers should not concern themselves with the ContentHandler functions; in an ideal world, these functions would be encapsulated and invisible to SAX 1.0 applications. However, XMLReaderAdapter must declare the ContentHandler interface as public so that the SAX 2.0 XMLReader object has access to the ContentHandler event methods.

Thrown Exceptions

org.xml.sax.SAXException

See Also

org.xml.sax.ContentHandler.skippedEntity(java.lang.String)

Example

N/A.

Parameters

String **name**   The name of the skipped entity. If it is a parameter entity, the name will begin with %. If the entity is an external DTD subset, it will be the string [dtd].

Returns

void   N/A.

startDocument Method

Java Signature
```
public void startDocument()
```

Visual Basic Signature
N/A.

This method is part of the XMLReaderAdapter implementation of the SAX 2.0 ContentHandler interface.

SAX 1.0 application writers should not concern themselves with the ContentHandler functions; in an ideal world, these functions would be encapsulated and invisible to SAX 1.0 applications. However, XMLReaderAdapter must declare the ContentHandler interface as public so that the SAX 2.0 XMLReader object has access to the ContentHandler event methods.

Thrown Exceptions

org.xml.sax.SAXException

See Also

org.xml.sax.ContentHandler.startDocument()

Example

N/A.

Returns

void   N/A.

startElement Method

Java Signature
public void startElement(String uri, String localName, String qName, Attributes atts)

Visual Basic Signature
N/A.

This method is part of the XMLReaderAdapter implementation of the SAX 2.0 ContentHandler interface.

SAX 1.0 application writers should not concern themselves with the ContentHandler functions; in an ideal world, these functions would be encapsulated and invisible to SAX 1.0 applications. However, XMLReaderAdapter must declare the ContentHandler interface as public so that the SAX 2.0 XMLReader object has access to the ContentHandler event methods.

Thrown Exceptions
org.xml.sax.SAXException

See Also
org.xml.sax.ContentHandler.endDocument()

Example
N/A.

Parameters

String uri   The element's namespace URI, or an empty string if namespace processing is not being performed.

String localName   The local name of the element, or an empty string if namespace processing is not being performed.

String qName   The element's qualified name, or an empty string if qualified names are not available.

Attributes atts   An instance of an object that implements the Attributes interface representing the list of the attributes attached to the element.

Returns
void   N/A.

startPrefixMapping Method

Java Signature
public void startPrefixMapping(String prefix, String uri)

Visual Basic Signature
N/A.

This method is part of the XMLReaderAdapter implementation of the SAX 2.0 ContentHandler interface.

SAX 1.0 application writers should not concern themselves with the ContentHandler functions; in an ideal world, these functions would be encapsulated and invisible to SAX 1.0 applications. However, XMLReaderAdapter must declare the ContentHandler interface as public so that the SAX 2.0 XMLReader object has access to the ContentHandler event methods.

See Also

org.xml.sax.ContentHandler.startPrefixMapping(java.lang.String, java.lang.String)

Example

N/A.

Parameters

String **prefix**   The namespace prefix coming into scope.

String **uri**   The namespace URI to which the prefix is mapped.

Returns

void   N/A.

XMLReaderFactory Class

The helper class XMLReaderFactory dynamically creates, using the Factory design pattern, instances of objects that implement the XMLReader interface. Instances of XMLReader may be created using either an explicit class name or the value of the system property org.xml.sax.driver.

Visual Basic Equivalent
N/A.

See Also
org.xml.sax.XMLReader

Example
```
import org.xml.sax.helpers.XMLReaderFactory;
import org.xml.sax.XMLReader;
import org.xml.sax.SAXException;
. . .
      XMLReader myReader;
  . . .
          myReader = XMLReaderFactory.createXMLReader();
```

Members

createXMLReader Method

Java Signature
```
public XMLReader createXMLReader()
```

Visual Basic Signature
N/A.

This method creates an instance of an object that implements the XMLReader interface using the value of the system property org.xml.sax.driver. The property value must be an explicit, fully qualified name, such as org.apache.xerces.parsers.SAXParser.

Thrown Exceptions
org.xml.sax.SAXException

See Also
org.xml.sax.helpers.XMLReaderFactory.createXMLReader(java.lang.String)

Example
```
import org.xml.sax.helpers.XMLReaderFactory;
import org.xml.sax.XMLReader;
import org.xml.sax.SAXException;
. . .
      XMLReader myReader;
. . .
         myReader = XMLReaderFactory.createXMLReader();
```

Returns
XMLReader   An object that implements the XMLReader interface.

createXMLReader Method

Java Signature
public XMLReader createXMLReader(String className)

Visual Basic Signature
N/A.

This method creates an instance of an object that implements the XMLReader interface using the passed class name. The passed class name must be an explicit, fully qualified name, such as org.apache.xerces.parsers.SAXParser.

Thrown Exceptions
org.xml.sax.SAXException

See Also
org.xml.sax.helpers.XMLReaderFactory.createXMLReader()

Example
```
import org.xml.sax.helpers.XMLReaderFactory;
import org.xml.sax.XMLReader;
import org.xml.sax.SAXException;
. . .
      XMLReader myReader;
      String parserClass = "org.apache.xerces.parsers.SAXParser";
. . .
         myReader = XMLReaderFactory.createXMLReader( parserClass );
```

Parameters

String **className**   The fully qualified class name of the parser to use (for example, org.apache.xerces.parsers.SAXParser)

Returns

XMLReader   An object that implements the XMLReader interface.

11

DEPRECATED SAX 1.0 API

This chapter details the deprecated SAX 1.0 interfaces and classes. New application development should use only the SAX 2.0 interfaces and classes. With its addition of namespace support and explicit support for filters, SAX 2.0 offers two significant enhancements over SAX 1.0. This chapter is primarily targeted at those developers tasked with maintaining SAX 1.0 applications and those developers curious (or bored) enough to be interested in the evolution of SAX.

AttributeList Interface

The AttributeList interface is a SAX 1.0 interface that has been deprecated in favor of the SAX 2.0 Attributes interface to provide support for namespace-related information. The use of this interface is *strongly* discouraged; nevertheless, it is documented here.

With the implementation of the AttributeList interface, an object may represent a list of attributes on a start tag. The most common use of an AttributeList is as an argument to the SAX 1.0 DocumentHandler.startElement() event handler.

Individual attributes within the AttributeList collection may be accessed in two ways:

- By index
- By name

The order of attributes in the list is not guaranteed to match the order in the XML document.

Only attributes that have been specified or defaulted will be included in the attribute list; #IMPLIED attributes will not appear in the list.

Visual Basic Equivalent
N/A.

See Also
org.xml.sax.Attributes
org.xml.sax.helpers.AttributeListImpl
org.xml.sax.DocumentHandler.startElement(java.lang.String, org.xml.sax.AttributeList)

Example
```
import org.xml.sax.HandlerBase;
import org.xml.sax.AttributeList;
import org.xml.sax.SAXException;
public class AttributeListSample extends HandlerBase
{
    public void startElement( String name,
                        AttributeList atts )
                        throws SAXException
    {
. . .
    }
}
```

Members

getLength Method

Java Signature
```
public int getLength()
```

Visual Basic Signature
```
Public Function getLength() As Long
```

This method returns the number of attributes in the `AttributeList`. If there are no attributes, the number of attributes returned will be zero.

See Also
org.xml.sax.Attributes.getLength()

Example
```
import org.xml.sax.HandlerBase;
import org.xml.sax.AttributeList;
import org.xml.sax.SAXException;
. . .
        int i;
        String attName = "", attType = "", attValue = "";
        // Get attribute properties by index.
```

```
            for( i=0 ; i<atts.getLength() ; i++ )
            {
. . .
            }
```

Returns

int   The number of attributes in the list.

getName Method

Java Signature
```
public String getName(int i)
```

Visual Basic Signature
```
Public Function getName(ByVal i As Long) As String
```

This method returns the name of the attribute specified by the passed index. If the specified index is out of range, the method will return `null`.

See Also
org.xml.sax.AttributeList.getLength()
org.xml.sax.Attributes.getLocalName(int)
org.xml.sax.Attributes.getQName(int)

Example
```
import org.xml.sax.HandlerBase;
import org.xml.sax.AttributeList;
import org.xml.sax.SAXException;
. . .
            attName = atts.getName(i);
```

Parameters
int i   The index into the list of attributes.

Returns
String   The name of the specified attribute, or `null` if the passed index is out of range.

getType Method

Java Signature
```
public String getType(int i)
```

Visual Basic Signature
```
Public Function getType(ByVal i As Long) As String
```

The method returns a string representing the type of the attribute specified by the passed index. The type is one of these strings:

- CDATA
- ID
- IDREF
- IDREFS
- NMTOKEN
- ENTITY
- ENTITIES
- NOTATION

In accordance with the XML 1.0 specification, if the parser does not report attribute types or has not parsed a declaration for the attribute, the parser must return CDATA.

If the specified index is out of range, the function returns null.

See Also
org.xml.sax.AttributeList.getLength()
org.xml.sax.AttributeList.getType(java.lang.String)
org.xml.sax.Attributes.getType(int)

Example
```
import org.xml.sax.HandlerBase;
import org.xml.sax.AttributeList;
import org.xml.sax.SAXException;
. . .
        attType = atts.getType(i);
```

Parameters
int i   An index into the list of attributes.

Returns

String   The type of the specified attribute, or null if the passed index is out of range.

getType Method

Java Signature
public String getType(String name)

Visual Basic Signature
Public Function getType(ByVal name As String) As String

The method returns a string representing the type of the attribute specified by the passed name. The type is one of these strings:

- CDATA
- ID
- IDREF
- IDREFS
- NMTOKEN
- ENTITY
- ENTITIES
- NOTATION

In accordance with the XML 1.0 specification, if the parser does not report attribute types or has not parsed a declaration for the attribute, the parser must return CDATA.

If a corresponding attribute is not found in the list, the function returns null.

See Also
org.xml.sax.AttributeList.getType(int)
org.xml.sax.Attributes.getType(java.lang.String)
org.xml.sax.Attributes.getType(java.lang.String, java.lang.String)

Example
```
import org.xml.sax.HandlerBase;
import org.xml.sax.AttributeList;
import org.xml.sax.SAXException;
. . .
        attType = atts.getType( attName );
        System.out.println("\tName: " + attName +
                            " Type: " + attType );
```

Parameters
String **name**   A string containing the name of an attribute.

Returns
String   The type of the specified attribute, or null if no matching attribute was found.

getValue Method

Java Signature
public String getValue(int i)

Visual Basic Signature
`Public Function getValue(ByVal i As Long) As String`

The method returns the value of the attribute specified by the passed index. If the attribute is of a type (`ENTITIES, IDREFS, NMTOKENS`) such that its value is a list of tokens, the tokens are concatenated into a single space-delimited string.

If the specified index is out of range, the function returns `null`.

See Also
`org.xml.sax.AttributeList.getLength()`
`org.xml.sax.AttributeList.getValue(java.lang.String)`
`org.xml.sax.Attributes.getValue(int)`

Example
```
import org.xml.sax.HandlerBase;
import org.xml.sax.AttributeList;
import org.xml.sax.SAXException;
. . .
        attValue = atts.getValue(i);
```

Parameters
`int i`   The index of the attribute in the list (starting at 0).

Returns
`String`   The value of the specified attribute, or `null` if the passed index is out of range.

getValue Method

Java Signature
`public String getValue(String name)`

Visual Basic Signature
`Public Function getValue(ByVal name As String) As String`

The method returns the value of the attribute specified by the passed name. If the attribute is of a type (`ENTITIES, IDREFS, NMTOKENS`) such that its value is a list of tokens, the tokens are concatenated into a single space-delimited string.

If a corresponding attribute is not found in the list, the function returns `null`.

See Also
`org.xml.sax.AttributeList.getValue(int)`
`org.xml.sax.Attributes.getValue(java.lang.String)`
`org.xml.sax.Attributes.getValue(java.lang.String, java.lang.String)`

Example
```
import org.xml.sax.HandlerBase;
import org.xml.sax.AttributeList;
import org.xml.sax.SAXException;
. . .
        attValue = atts.getValue( attName );
        System.out.println("\tName: " + attName +
                        " Value: " + attValue );
```

Parameters

String **name**   A string containing the name of an attribute in the AttributeList.

Returns

String   The value of the specified attribute, or null if no matching attribute is found.

AttributeListImpl Class

The AttributeListImpl class is a SAX 1.0 class that has been deprecated in favor of the SAX 2.0 AttributesImpl class to provide support for namespace-related information. The use of this class is *strongly* discouraged; nevertheless, it is documented here.

The helper class AttributeListImpl exposes two areas of functionality to the SAX 1.0 application developer. First, the class provides a default implementation of the org.xml.sax.AttributeList interface. Second, the class provides additional methods (over and above the AttributeList interface set of methods) to create and modify a list of attributes.

The two most common uses of this class are to make a copy of an object implementing the AttributeList interface in the startElement() method of a DocumentHandler implementation and to create and modify an object implementing the AttributeList interface for use in a SAX driver.

Since AttributesListImpl contains unique methods not declared as part of the AttributeList interface, you should never assume that a passed AttributeList was instantiated via the AttributeListImpl class. Java developers should use the instanceof keyword to verify that an object is an instantiation of AttributeListImpl before attempting to use any of the extended methods not declared in the AttributeList interface.

Visual Basic Equivalent

N/A.

See Also

org.xml.sax.AttributeList
org.xml.sax.Attributes
org.xml.sax.helpers.AttributesImpl
org.xml.sax.DocumentHandler.startElement(java.lang.String, org.xml.sax.AttributeList)

Example
```
import org.xml.sax.HandlerBase;
import org.xml.sax.AttributeList;
import org.xml.sax.helpers.AttributeListImpl;
import org.xml.sax.SAXException;
. . .
        AttributeListImpl attListImpl = null;
```

Constructors

Java Signature
```
public AttributeListImpl()
```

Visual Basic Signature
```
Public AttributeListImpl()
```

This constructor method creates a new, empty instance of the `AttributeListImpl` class. Parser writers will find this method useful for creating a single instance of the `AttributeList` class that is reused throughout the processing of an XML document by resetting the list via invocations of the `clear()` method.

See Also
org.xml.sax.helpers.AttributeListImpl.addAttribute(java.lang.String, java.lang.String, java.lang.String)
org.xml.sax.helpers.AttributeListImpl.clear()
org.xml.sax.helpers.AttributesImpl()

Example
```
import org.xml.sax.HandlerBase;
import org.xml.sax.AttributeList;
import org.xml.sax.helpers.AttributeListImpl;
import org.xml.sax.SAXException;
. . .
        attListImpl = new AttributeListImpl();
```

Java Signature
```
public AttributeListImpl(AttributeList atts)
```

Visual Basic Signature
```
Public AttributeListImpl(ByVal atts As AttributeList)
```

This constructor method creates a new instance of an `AttributeListImpl` object, copying the contents of the passed `AttributeList` object. This constructor method is often used by application developers to make a copy of an existing attribute list.

See Also
org.xml.sax.DocumentHandler.startElement(java.lang.String, org.xml.sax.AttributeList)
org.xml.sax.helpers.AttributesImpl(org.xml.sax.Attributes)

Example
```
import org.xml.sax.HandlerBase;
import org.xml.sax.AttributeList;
import org.xml.sax.helpers.AttributeListImpl;
import org.xml.sax.SAXException;
. . .
    public void startElement( String name,
                              AttributeList atts )
                          throws SAXException
    {
        AttributeListImpl attListImpl = null;
. . .
            attListImpl = new AttributeListImpl( atts );
```

Parameters

AttributeList atts   An object to copy that implements the AttributeList interface.

Members

addAttribute Method

Java Signature
`public void addAttribute(String name, String type, String value)`

Visual Basic Signature
`Public Sub addAttribute(ByVal name As String, ByVal type As String, ByVal value As String)`

This method adds an attribute to the end of the list. For performance reasons, the method does not check for name conflicts, leaving that task to the calling application.

See Also
org.xml.sax.DocumentHandler.startElement(java.lang.String, org.xml.sax.AttributeList)
org.xml.sax.helpers.AttributeListImpl.removeAttribute(java.lang.String)
org.xml.sax.helpers.AttributesImpl.addAttribute(java.lang.String, java.lang.String, java.lang.String, java.lang.String, java.lang.String)

Example
```
import org.xml.sax.HandlerBase;
import org.xml.sax.AttributeList;
import org.xml.sax.helpers.AttributeListImpl;
import org.xml.sax.SAXException;
. . .
    public void startElement( String name,
```

(continued on next page)

```
                        AttributeList atts )
                        throws SAXException
    {
        AttributeListImpl attListImpl = null;
        int i;

        // Copy the passed attribute list by hand.
        for( i=0 ; i<atts.getLength() ; i++ )
        {
            attListImpl.addAttribute(   atts.getName(i),
                                        atts.getType(i),
                                        atts.getValue(i) );
        }
```

Parameters

String **name**   The attribute's name.

String **type**   The attribute's type (NMTOKEN for an enumeration) as a string.

String **value**   The attribute's value. The value cannot be null.

Returns

void   N/A.

clear Method

Java Signature
```
public void clear()
```

Visual Basic Signature
```
Public Sub clear()
```

This method clears an attribute list; however, to enhance performance, it does not actually free the memory in use by the list.

Parser writers will find this method useful for clearing the attribute list in order to reuse the list between DocumentHandler.startElement() events. It is more efficient to reuse a single instance of an AttributeList rather than create and destroy an AttributeList with each encountered element.

See Also
org.xml.sax.DocumentHandler.startElement(java.lang.String, org.xml.sax.AttributeList)
org.xml.sax.helpers.AttributesImpl.clear()

Example
```
import org.xml.sax.HandlerBase;
import org.xml.sax.AttributeList;
import org.xml.sax.helpers.AttributeListImpl;
import org.xml.sax.SAXException;
. . .
```

```
        AttributeListImpl attListImpl = null;
...
        // Clear the list.
        attListImpl.clear();
```

Parameters

Returns

void   N/A.

getLength Method

Java Signature
```
public int getLength()
```

Visual Basic Signature
```
Public Function getLength() As Long
```

This method returns the number of attributes in the list. If there are no attributes, the number of attributes returned will be zero.

Note that this method is part of the implementation of the `AttributeList` interface.

See Also
```
org.xml.sax.AttributeList.getLength()
org.xml.sax.helpers.AttributesImpl.getLength()
```

Example
See the `AttributeList.getLength()` method documentation for an example.

Parameters

Returns

int   The number of attributes in the `AttributeList`.

getName Method

Java Signature
```
public String getName(int i)
```

Visual Basic Signature
```
Public Function getName(ByVal i As Long) As String
```

This method returns the name of the attribute specified by the passed index. If the specified index is out of range, the method will return `null`.

Note that this method is part of the implementation of the `AttributeList` interface.

See Also

org.xml.sax.AttributeList.getName(int)
org.xml.sax.helpers.AttributesImpl.getLocalName(int)
org.xml.sax.helpers.AttributesImpl.getQName(int)

Example

See the AttributeList.getName() method documentation for an example.

Parameters

int i   The position of the attribute in the list.

Returns

String   The name of the specified attribute, or null if the passed index is out of range.

getType Method

Java Signature
public String getType(int i)

Visual Basic Signature
Public Function getType(ByVal i As Long) As String

The method returns a string that represents the type of the attribute specified by the passed index. The type is one of these strings:

- CDATA
- ID
- IDREF
- IDREFS
- NMTOKEN
- ENTITY
- ENTITIES
- NOTATION

In accordance with the XML 1.0 specification, if the parser does not report attribute types or has not parsed a declaration for the attribute, the parser must return CDATA.

If the specified index is out of range, the function returns null.

Note that this method is part of the implementation of the AttributeList interface.

See Also

org.xml.sax.AttributeList.getType(int)
org.xml.sax.helpers.AttributesImpl.getType(int)

Example

See the `AttributeList.getType()` method documentation for an example.

Parameters

int **i**   The position of the attribute in the list.

Returns

String   The type of the specified attribute, or `null` if the passed index is out of range.

getType Method

Java Signature
```
public String getType(String name)
```

Visual Basic Signature
```
Public Function getType(ByVal name As String) As String
```

The method returns a string that represents the type of the attribute specified by the passed name. The type is one of these strings:

- CDATA
- ID
- IDREF
- IDREFS
- NMTOKEN
- ENTITY
- ENTITIES
- NOTATION

In accordance with the XML 1.0 specification, if the parser does not report attribute types or has not parsed a declaration for the attribute, the parser must return CDATA.

If a corresponding attribute is not found in the list, the function returns `null`.

Note that this method is part of the implementation of the `AttributeList` interface.

See Also
```
org.xml.sax.AttributeList.getType(java.lang.String)
org.xml.sax.helpers.AttributesImpl.getType(java.lang.String)
org.xml.sax.helpers.AttributesImpl.getType(java.lang.String, java.lang.String)
```

Example

See the `AttributeList.getType()` method documentation for an example.

Parameters

String **name**   The attribute name.

Returns

String   The type of the specified attribute, or null if no matching attribute is found.

getValue Method

Java Signature
public String getValue(int i)

Visual Basic Signature
Public Function getValue(ByVal i As Long) As String

The method returns the value of the attribute specified by the passed index. If the attribute is of a type (ENTITIES, IDREFS, NMTOKENS) such that its value is a list of tokens, the tokens are concatenated into a single space-delimited string.

If the specified index is out of range, the method returns null.

Note that this method is part of the implementation of the AttributeList interface.

See Also
org.xml.sax.AttributeList.getValue(int)
org.xml.sax.helpers.AttributesImpl.getValue(int)

Example
See the AttributeList.getValue() method documentation for an example.

Parameters
int i   The position of the attribute in the list.

Returns
String   The value of the specified attribute, or null if the passed index is out of range.

getValue Method

Java Signature
public String getValue(String name)

Visual Basic Signature
Public Function getValue(ByVal name As String) As String

The method returns the value of the attribute specified by the passed name. If the attribute is of a type (ENTITIES, IDREFS, NMTOKENS) such that its value is a list of tokens, the tokens are concatenated into a single space-delimited string.

If a corresponding attribute is not found in the list, the method
returns null.

Note that this method is part of the implementation of the AttributeList interface.

See Also
org.xml.sax.AttributeList.getValue(java.lang.String)
org.xml.sax.helpers.AttributesImpl.getValue(java.lang.String)
org.xml.sax.helpers.AttributesImpl.getValue(java.lang.String, java.lang.String)

Example
See the `AttributeList.getValue()` method documentation for an example.

Parameters
String **name**   The attribute name.

Returns
String   The value of the specified attribute, or `null` if no matching attribute is found.

removeAttribute Method

Java Signature
```
public void removeAttribute(String name)
```

Visual Basic Signature
```
Public Sub removeAttribute(ByVal name As String)
```

This method removes the attribute with the specified name from the list. Invoking this method changes the length of the attribute list and possibly the position of other attributes in the list.

If the specified attribute is not found in the list, no operation is performed.

See Also
org.xml.sax.helpers.AttributeListImpl.addAttribute(java.lang.String, java.lang.String, java.lang.String)
org.xml.sax.helpers.AttributesImpl.removeAttribute(int)

Example
```
import org.xml.sax.HandlerBase;
import org.xml.sax.AttributeList;
import org.xml.sax.helpers.AttributeListImpl;
import org.xml.sax.SAXException;
. . .
      AttributeListImpl attListImpl = null;
      int i;
. . .
      // Now let's remove all the attributes from our list.
      // Note that we delete from the end so we don't have any
      // worries with respect to the changing length of the list.
      while( (i=attListImpl.getLength()) > 0 )
         attListImpl.removeAttribute( attListImpl.getName(i-1) );
```

Parameters

String **name**   The name of the attribute to remove from the list.

Returns

void   N/A.

setAttributeList Method

Java Signature
```
public void setAttributeList(AttributeList atts)
```

Visual Basic Signature
```
Public Sub setAttributeList(ByVal atts As AttributeList)
```

The method copies all of the attribute elements from an `AttributeList` object into this object. The same functionality may be achieved by either iterating the elements of an object that implements the `AttributeList` interface and calling `AttributeListImpl.addAttribute()` for each iteration or creating the `AttributeListImpl` object using the `AttributeListImpl( AttributeList )` constructor method.

Note that this method is not a member of the `AttributeList` interface.

Example
```
import org.xml.sax.HandlerBase;
import org.xml.sax.AttributeList;
import org.xml.sax.helpers.AttributeListImpl;
import org.xml.sax.SAXException;
. . .
    public void startElement( String name,
                        AttributeList atts )
                        throws SAXException
    {
        AttributeListImpl attListImpl = null;
. . .
            attListImpl = new AttributeListImpl();
            attListImpl.setAttributeList( atts );
```

Parameters

AttributeList **atts**   The implementation of the `AttributeList` interface to be copied.

Returns

void   N/A.

DocumentHandler Interface

The DocumentHandler interface is a SAX 1.0 interface that has been deprecated in favor of the SAX 2.0 ContentHandler interface to provide support for namespace-related information. The use of this interface is *strongly* discouraged; nevertheless, it is documented here.

The DocumentHandler interface is the heart of SAX 1.0; almost all SAX 1.0 applications implement this callback interface to receive notification of parsing events. The application registers an instance of the DocumentHandler interface with the parser using the setDocumentHandler() method of Parser. As the XML document is processed, the parser calls methods in the registered DocumentHandler, thereby triggering events in the application.

Applications that do not want to implement the entire DocumentHandler interface, may derive a class from HandlerBase. The HandlerBase class provides a default implementation of the DocumentHandler interface. Applications can then override the event methods for which the application writer wants to perform custom processing.

Visual Basic Equivalent
N/A.

See Also
org.xml.sax.ContentHandler
org.xml.sax.DTDHandler
org.xml.sax.ErrorHandler
org.xml.sax.HandlerBase
org.xml.sax.Locator
org.xml.sax.Parser
org.xml.sax.Parser.setDocumentHandler(org.xml.sax.DocumentHandler)

Example
```
import org.xml.sax.AttributeList;
import org.xml.sax.DocumentHandler;
import org.xml.sax.Locator;
import org.xml.sax.SAXException;
public class DocumentHandlerSample implements DocumentHandler
{
...
}
```

Members

characters Method

Java Signature
```
public void characters(char[] ch, int start, int length)
```

Visual Basic Signature
```
Public Sub characters(ByVal ch() As char, ByVal start As Long, ByVal length As Long)
```

The parser calls this method as it finds character data. The character data may be passed to this method in one contiguous chunk, or the parser may split the data into several chunks using multiple notifications.

Validating parsers will report ignorable whitespace using the DocumentHandler.ignorableWhitespace() method instead of the characters() method.

Thrown Exceptions
org.xml.sax.SAXException

See Also
org.xml.sax.ContentHandler.characters(char[], int, int)
org.xml.sax.DocumentHandler.ignorableWhitespace(char[], int, int)

Example
```
import org.xml.sax.AttributeList;
import org.xml.sax.DocumentHandler;
import org.xml.sax.Locator;
import org.xml.sax.SAXException;
. . .
    public void characters( char[] ch, int start, int length )
                        throws SAXException
    {
        String data = "";
        System.out.println("SAX1 characters event fired.  " +
                        "Number of chars: " + length);
        data = String.copyValueOf( ch, start, length);
        System.out.println( "\t" + data );
    }
```

Parameters

char[] **ch**   The characters from the XML document.

int start   The start position in the character array.

int length   The number of characters to read from the array.

Returns

void   N/A.

endDocument Method

Java Signature
public void endDocument()

Visual Basic Signature
Public Sub endDocument()

This method is the last notification received from the parser during the processing of a document. The method is called when the parser discovers the end of the XML document, or abandons parsing due to a fatal error.

This method is the logical place for the application to perform any needed document postprocessing, such as the clean up of allocated resources.

Thrown Exceptions
org.xml.sax.SAXException

See Also
org.xml.sax.ContentHandler.endDocument()

Example
```
import org.xml.sax.AttributeList;
import org.xml.sax.DocumentHandler;
import org.xml.sax.Locator;
import org.xml.sax.SAXException;
. . .
    public void endDocument() throws SAXException
    {
        System.out.println( "SAX1 endDocument event fired." );
    }
```

Returns
void   N/A.

endElement Method

Java Signature
public void endElement(String name)

Visual Basic Signature
Public Sub endElement(ByVal name As String)

The parser invokes this method for every element end tag encountered in an XML document. Obviously, a corresponding startElement() notification should have already been received.

For an empty element, the application will receive both startElement() and endElement() notifications.

Thrown Exceptions
org.xml.sax.SAXException

See Also
org.xml.sax.ContentHandler.endElement(java.lang.String, java.lang.String, java.lang.String)

Example
```
import org.xml.sax.AttributeList;
import org.xml.sax.DocumentHandler;
import org.xml.sax.Locator;
import org.xml.sax.SAXException;
. . .
    public void endElement( String name )
```

(continued on next page)

```
                    throws SAXException
{
        System.out.println( "SAX1 End element event fired.\n\t" +
                            "name: " + name );
}
```

Parameters

String **name**   The element's name including any namespace prefix.

Returns

void   N/A.

ignorableWhitespace Method

Java Signature
```
public void ignorableWhitespace(char[] ch, int start, int length)
```

Visual Basic Signature
```
Public Sub ignorableWhitespace(ByVal ch() As char, ByVal start As Long, ByVal length As Long)
```

The parser calls this method when it finds ignorable whitespace data. The whitespace data may be passed to this method in one contiguous chunk, or the parser may split the data into several chunks using multiple notifications.

Validating parsers *must* use this method to report ignorable whitespace encountered during parsing. The event is optional for other parsers.

Thrown Exceptions
org.xml.sax.SAXException

See Also
org.xml.sax.ContentHandler.ignorableWhitespace(char[], int, int)
org.xml.sax.DocumentHandler.characters(char[], int, int)

Example
```
import org.xml.sax.AttributeList;
import org.xml.sax.DocumentHandler;
import org.xml.sax.Locator;
import org.xml.sax.SAXException;
. . .
    public void ignorableWhitespace(    char[] ch,
                                        int start,
                                        int length )
                                        throws SAXException
    {
        System.out.println( "SAX1 ignorableWhitespace event fired." +
                            "\t" + length +
                            " whitespace chars ignored." );
    }
```

Parameters

char[] **ch**   The characters from the XML document.

int start   The start position in the array.

int length   The number of characters to read from the array.

Returns

void   N/A.

processingInstruction Method

Java Signature
```
public void processingInstruction(String target, String data)
```

Visual Basic Signature
```
Public Sub processingInstruction(ByVal target As String, ByVal data As String)
```

This method is invoked when the parser finds a processing instruction in the XML document. Note that processing instructions may occur before and/or after the startElement() and endElement() events for the root element.

According to the W3C XML specification, a parser must never report a text or XML declaration.

Thrown Exceptions
org.xml.sax.SAXException

See Also
org.xml.sax.ContentHandler.processingInstruction(java.lang.String, java.lang.String)

Example
```
import org.xml.sax.AttributeList;
import org.xml.sax.DocumentHandler;
import org.xml.sax.Locator;
import org.xml.sax.SAXException;
...
    public void processingInstruction( String target, String data )
                    throws SAXException
    {
        System.out.println( "SAX1 processingInstruction event fired.\n\t" +
                        "target: " + target + "\n\t" +
                        "data: " + data );
    }
```

Parameters

String **target**   The processing instruction target.

String **data**   The processing instruction data, or null if no data was supplied. The data does not include any whitespace separating the data from the target.

Returns

void   N/A.

setDocumentLocator Method

Java Signature
public void setDocumentLocator(Locator locator)

Visual Basic Signature
Public Sub setDocumentLocator(ByVal locator As Locator)

This event method supplies the application with a `Locator` object reference; a Locator allows the application to determine the document location of any event. If a SAX parser supplies `Locator` objects, this method will be invoked at the start of XML document parsing, before any other events. Parsers are strongly encouraged, but not required, to supply `Locator` objects to applications.

Thrown Exceptions

See Also
org.xml.sax.Locator
org.xml.sax.ContentHandler.setDocumentLocator(org.xml.sax.Locator)

Example
```
import org.xml.sax.AttributeList;
import org.xml.sax.DocumentHandler;
import org.xml.sax.Locator;
import org.xml.sax.SAXException;
. . .
    public void setDocumentLocator( Locator locator )
    {
        System.out.println( "SAX1 setDocumentLocator event fired.\n\t" +
                            "Parser Locator support = " +
                            (locator != null) );
        myLocator = locator;
    }
```

Parameters

Locator **locator**   A Locator object capable of returning the location of any document-related event.

Returns

void   N/A.

startDocument Method

Java Signature
public void startDocument()

Visual Basic Signature
```
Public Sub startDocument()
```

This event is invoked by the parser at the beginning of a XML document. With the possible exception of `setDocumentLocator()`, this method will be the first event fired by the parser; thus, this method is the logical place for the application to perform any needed preprocessing such as resource allocation.

Thrown Exceptions
org.xml.sax.SAXException

See Also
org.xml.sax.ContentHandler.startDocument()

Example
```
import org.xml.sax.AttributeList;
import org.xml.sax.DocumentHandler;
import org.xml.sax.Locator;
import org.xml.sax.SAXException;
. . .
    public void startDocument() throws SAXException
    {
        System.out.println( "SAX1 startDocument event fired." );
    }
```

Parameters

Returns
void   N/A.

startElement Method

Java Signature
```
public void startElement(String name, AttributeList atts)
```

Visual Basic Signature
```
Public Sub startElement(ByVal name As String, ByVal atts As AttributeList)
```

The parser invokes this method for every element start tag encountered in an XML document. Every `startElement()` event will be matched by an `endElement()` event, even for empty elements.

Thrown Exceptions
org.xml.sax.SAXException

See Also
org.xml.sax.AttributeList
org.xml.sax.ContentHandler.startElement(java.lang.String, java.lang.String, java.lang.String, org.xml.sax.Attributes)
org.xml.sax.DocumentHandler.endElement(java.lang.String)

Example
```
import org.xml.sax.AttributeList;
import org.xml.sax.DocumentHandler;
import org.xml.sax.Locator;
import org.xml.sax.SAXException;
. . .
    public void startElement( String name,
                              AttributeList atts )
                        throws SAXException
    {
        System.out.println( "SAX1 Start element event fired.\n\t" +
                            "name: " + name );
    }
```

Parameters

String **name** The element's name including any namespace prefix.

AttributeList **atts** An instance of an object that implements the AttributeList interface that contains the attributes attached to the element.

Returns

void   N/A.

HandlerBase Class

The HandlerBase class is a SAX 1.0 class that has been deprecated in favor of the SAX 2.0 DefaultHandler class to provide support for namespace-related information. The use of this class is *strongly* discouraged; nevertheless, it is documented here.

The helper class, HandlerBase, provides a default implementation of the SAX 1.0 DocumentHandler event handler interface along with default implementations of the DTDHandler, EntityResolver, and ErrorHandler interfaces. The default event methods provided by the HandlerBase class are, for the most part, empty methods, meaning they do not perform any processing. SAX 1.0 applications may inherit from this class and override only the event methods for which the application needs to perform custom processing, leaving the parent HandlerBase class to handle any events the application does not care about.

Parsers will also use this class to assign default event handlers. This allows the parser to perform its processing even if applications do not implement and assign event handlers.

Visual Basic Equivalent

N/A.

See Also

org.xml.sax.DocumentHandler
org.xml.sax.DTDHandler
org.xml.sax.EntityResolver
org.xml.sax.ErrorHandler
org.xml.sax.helpers.DefaultHandler

Example
```
import org.xml.sax.HandlerBase;
import org.xml.sax.AttributeList;
import org.xml.sax.SAXException;
public class HandlerBaseSample extends HandlerBase
{
    // Override the HandlerBase.startElement() method.
    public void startElement( String name,
                              AttributeList atts )
                    throws SAXException
    {
        System.out.println( "Start element event fired.\n\t" +
                            "Do some custom processing here." );
    }
}
```

Constructors

Java Signature
```
public  HandlerBase()
```

Visual Basic Signature
```
Public HandlerBase()
```

This constructor method creates a HandlerBase object. Most SAX 1.0 applications will inherit from HandlerBase as it provides default implementations of the DocumentHandler, DTDHandler, EntityResolver, and ErrorHandler interfaces, allowing the application developer to concentrate on implementing only custom processing.

Example
```
HandlerBase myHandler = new HandlerBase();
```

Parameters

Members

characters Method

Java Signature
```
public void characters(char[] ch, int start, int length)
```

Visual Basic Signature
```
Public Sub characters(ByVal ch() As char, ByVal start As Long, ByVal length As Long)
```

This method is an implementation of the characters() method of the deprecated DocumentHandler interface. This default implementation does nothing. Applications may override this method to perform custom processing.

See DocumentHandler.characters() for further details.

Thrown Exceptions

org.xml.sax.SAXException

See Also

org.xml.sax.DocumentHandler.characters(char[], int, int)
org.xml.sax.helpers.DefaultHandler.characters(char[], int, int)

Example

See DocumentHandler.characters() method documentation for an example.

Parameters

char[] ch   The characters from the XML document.

int start   The start position in the character array.

int length   The number of characters to read from the array.

Returns

void   N/A.

endDocument Method

Java Signature
public void endDocument()

Visual Basic Signature
Public Sub endDocument()

This method is an implementation of the endDocument() method of the deprecated DocumentHandler interface. This default implementation does nothing. Applications may override this method to perform custom processing.

See DocumentHandler.endDocument() for further details.

Thrown Exceptions
org.xml.sax.SAXException

See Also
org.xml.sax.DocumentHandler.endDocument()
org.xml.sax.helpers.DefaultHandler.endDocument()

Example

See DocumentHandler.endDocument() method documentation for an example.

Returns

void   N/A.

endElement Method

Java Signature
public void endElement(String name)

Visual Basic Signature
```
Public Sub endElement(ByVal name As String)
```

This method is an implementation of the `endElement()` method of the deprecated `DocumentHandler` interface. This default implementation does nothing. Applications may override this method to perform custom processing.
   See `DocumentHandler.endElement()` for further details.

Thrown Exceptions
org.xml.sax.SAXException

See Also
org.xml.sax.DocumentHandler.endElement(java.lang.String)
org.xml.sax.helpers.DefaultHandler.endElement(java.lang.String, java.lang.String, java.lang.String)

Example
See `DocumentHandler.endElement()` method documentation for an example.

Parameters
String **name**   The element's name, including any namespace prefix.

Returns
void   N/A.

error Method

Java Signature
```
public void error(SAXParseException e)
```

Visual Basic Signature
```
Public Sub error(ByVal e As SAXParseException)
```

This method is an implementation of the `error()` method of the `ErrorHandler` interface. This default implementation does nothing. Applications may override this method to perform custom processing.
   See `ErrorHandler.error()` for further details.

Thrown Exceptions
org.xml.sax.SAXException

See Also
org.xml.sax.SAXParseException
org.xml.sax.ErrorHandler.error(org.xml.sax.SAXParseException)
org.xml.sax.helpers.DefaultHandler.error(org.xml.sax.SAXParseException)

Example
See `ErrorHandler.error()` method documentation for an example.

Parameters
SAXParseException **e**   The error information encoded as an exception.

Returns

void   N/A.

fatalError Method

Java Signature
public void fatalError(SAXParseException e)

Visual Basic Signature
Public Sub fatalError(ByVal e As SAXParseException)

This method is an implementation of the fatalError() method of the ErrorHandler interface. This default implementation throws a SAXParseException error. Applications may override this method to perform custom processing.
   See ErrorHandler.fatalError() for further details.

Thrown Exceptions
org.xml.sax.SAXException

See Also
org.xml.sax.SAXParseException
org.xml.sax.ErrorHandler.fatalError(org.xml.sax.SAXParseException)
org.xml.sax.helpers.DefaultHandler.fatalError(org.xml.sax.SAXParseException)

Example
See ErrorHandler.fatalError() method documentation for an example.

Parameters
SAXParseException e   The error information encoded as an exception.

Returns
void   N/A.

ignorableWhitespace Method

Java Signature
public void ignorableWhitespace(char[] ch, int start, int length)

Visual Basic Signature
Public Sub ignorableWhitespace(ByVal ch() As char, ByVal start As Long, ByVal length As Long)

This method is an implementation of the ignorableWhitespace() method of the deprecated DocumentHandler interface. This default does nothing. Applications may override this method to perform custom processing.
   See DocumentHandler.ignorableWhitespace() for further details.

Thrown Exceptions
org.xml.sax.SAXException

See Also
org.xml.sax.DocumentHandler.ignorableWhitespace(char[], int, int)
org.xml.sax.helpers.DefaultHandler.ignorableWhitespace(char[], int, int)

Example
See DocumentHandler.ignorableWhitespace() method documentation for an example.

Parameters
char[] ch   The characters from the XML document.

int start   The start position in the character array.

int length   The number of characters to read from the array.

Returns
void   N/A.

notationDecl Method

Java Signature
public void notationDecl(String name, String publicId, String systemId)

Visual Basic Signature
Public Sub notationDecl(ByVal name As String, ByVal publicId As String, ByVal systemId As String)

This method is an implementation of the notationDecl() method of the DTDHandler interface. This default does nothing. Applications may override this method to perform custom processing.
  See DTDHandler.notationDecl() for details.

Thrown Exceptions

See Also
org.xml.sax.DTDHandler.notationDecl(java.lang.String, java.lang.String, java.lang.String)
org.xml.sax.helpers.DefaultHandler.notationDecl(java.lang.String, java.lang.String, java.lang.String)

Example
See DTDHandler.notationDecl() method documentation for an example.

Parameters
String name   The notation name.

String publicId   The public identifier of the notation, or null if no public identifier was given.

String systemId   The system identifier of the notation, or null if no system identifier was given. If this parameter is a URL, the parser must fully resolve it before calling the notationDecl() method in the application.

Returns

void   N/A.

processingInstruction Method

Java Signature
public void processingInstruction(String target, String data)

Visual Basic Signature
Publicy Sub processingInstruction(ByVal target As String, ByVal data As String)

This method is an implementation of the processingInstruction() method of the deprecated DocumentHandler interface. This default implementation does nothing. Applications may override this method to perform custom processing.
   See DocumentHandler.processingInstruction() for details.

Thrown Exceptions
org.xml.sax.SAXException

See Also
org.xml.sax.DocumentHandler.processingInstruction(java.lang.String, java.lang.String)
org.xml.sax.helpers.DefaultHandler.processingInstruction(java.lang.String, java.lang.String)

Example
See DocumentHandler.processingInstruction() method documentation for an example.

Parameters
String **target**   The processing instruction target.

String **data**   The processing instruction data, or null if no data was supplied.

Returns
void   N/A.

resolveEntity Method

Java Signature
public InputSource resolveEntity(String publicId, String systemId)

Visual Basic Signature
Public Function resolveEntity(ByVal publicId As String, ByVal systemId As String) As InputSource

This method is an implementation of the resolveEntity() method of the EntityResolver interface. This default implementation always returns null, forcing the parser to use the system identifier in the XML document. Applications may override this method to perform custom processing.
   See EntityResolver.resolveEntity() for details.

Thrown Exceptions

org.xml.sax.SAXException

See Also

org.xml.sax.EntityResolver.resolveEntity(java.lang.String, java.lang.String)
org.xml.sax.helpers.DefaultHandler.resolveEntity(java.lang.String, java.lang.String)

Example

See EntityResolver.resolveEntity() method documentation for an example.

Parameters

String publicId   The public identifier of the external entity being referenced, or null if no public identifier was supplied.

String systemId   The system identifier of the external entity being referenced. If the system identifier is a URL, the parser must fully resolve the reference before triggering this event.

Returns

InputSource   An InputSource for the external entity. For this default implementation, null will always be returned.

setDocumentLocator Method

Java Signature
```
public void setDocumentLocator(Locator locator)
```

Visual Basic Signature
```
Public Sub setDocumentLocator(ByVal locator As Locator)
```

This method is an implementation of the setDocumentLocator() method of the deprecated DocumentHandler interface. This default implementation does nothing. Applications may override this method to perform custom processing.
   See DocumentHandler.setDocumentLocator() for details.

Thrown Exceptions

See Also

org.xml.sax.Locator
org.xml.sax.DocumentHandler.setDocumentLocator(org.xml.sax.Locator)
org.xml.sax.helpers.DefaultHandler.setDocumentLocator(org.xml.sax.Locator)

Example

See DocumentHandler.setDocumentLocator() method documentation for an example.

Parameters

Locator **locator**   A Locator object capable of returning the location of any document-related event.

Returns

void   N/A.

startDocument Method

Java Signature
```
public void startDocument()
```

Visual Basic Signature
```
Public Sub startDocument()
```

This method is an implementation of the startDocument() method of the deprecated DocumentHandler interface. This default implementation does nothing. Applications may override this method to perform custom processing.

See DocumentHandler.startDocument() for details.

Thrown Exceptions
org.xml.sax.SAXException

See Also
org.xml.sax.DocumentHandler.startDocument()
org.xml.sax.helpers.DefaultHandler.startDocument()

Example
See DocumentHandler.startDocument() method documentation for an example.

Returns
void   N/A.

startElement Method

Java Signature
```
public void startElement(String name, AttributeList attributes)
```

Visual Basic Signature
```
Public Sub startElement(ByVal name As String, ByVal attributes As AttributeList)
```

This method is an implementation of the startElement() method of the deprecated DocumentHandler interface. This default implementation does nothing. Applications may override this method to perform custom processing.

See the DocumentHandler.startElement() method documentation for details.

Thrown Exceptions
org.xml.sax.SAXException

See Also
org.xml.sax.DocumentHandler.startElement(java.lang.String, org.xml.sax.AttributeList)
org.xml.sax.helpers.DefaultHandler.startElement(java.lang.String, java.lang.String, java.lang.String, org.xml.sax.Attributes)

Example
See the DocumentHandler.startElement() method documentation for an example.

Parameters

String **name**   The element's name, including any namespace prefix.

AttributeList **attributes**   An object that implements the AttributeList interface that contains the attributes attached to the element.

Returns

void   N/A.

unparsedEntityDecl Method

Java Signature
public void unparsedEntityDecl(String name, String publicId, String systemId, String notationName)

Visual Basic Signature
Public Sub unparsedEntityDecl(ByVal name As String, ByVal publicId As String, ByVal systemId As String, ByVal notationName As String)

This method is an implementation of the unparsedEntityDecl() method of the DTDHandler interface. This default implementation does nothing. Applications may override this method to perform custom processing.
   See DTDHandler.unparsedEntityDecl() for further details.

Thrown Exceptions

See Also
org.xml.sax.DTDHandler.unparsedEntityDecl(java.lang.String, java.lang.String, java.lang.String, java.lang.String)
org.xml.sax.helpers.DefaultHandler.unparsedEntityDecl(java.lang.String, java.lang.String, java.lang.String, java.lang.String)

Example
See the DTDHandler.unparsedEntityDecl() method documentation for an example.

Parameters

String **name**   The unparsed entity's name.

String **publicId**   The public identifier of the entity, or null if no public identifier was given.

String **systemId**   The system identifier of the entity, or null if no system identifier was given. If this parameter is a URL, the parser must fully resolve it before calling the unparsedEntityDecl() method in the application.

String **notationName**   The name of the notation corresponding to a notationDecl() event.

Returns

void   N/A.

warning Method

Java Signature
```
public void warning(SAXParseException e)
```

Visual Basic Signature
```
Public Sub warning(ByVal e As SAXParseException)
```

This method is an implementation of the `warning()` method of the `ErrorHandler` interface. This default implementation does nothing. Applications may override this method to perform custom processing.

See `ErrorHandler.warning()` for further details.

Thrown Exceptions
org.xml.sax.SAXException

See Also
org.xml.sax.SAXParseException
org.xml.sax.ErrorHandler.warning(org.xml.sax.SAXParseException)
org.xml.sax.helpers.DefaultHandler.warning(org.xml.sax.SAXParseException)

Example
See the `ErrorHandler.warning()` method documentation for an example.
Parameters

`SAXParseException e`   An instance of a SAX parse exception that encapsulates the details of the warning.

Returns
void   N/A.

Parser Interface

The `Parser` interface is a SAX 1.0 interface that has been deprecated in favor of the SAX 2.0 `XMLReader` interface to provide support for namespace-related information. The use of this interface is *strongly* discouraged; nevertheless, it is documented here.

An object implementing the `Parser` interface is the actual XML parser that reads an XML document. This interface should not be implemented directly; instead, the `org.xml.sax.helpers.ParserFactory` class should be used to generate a new implementation of `Parser`. The new object can then be configured using its various `set*()` methods. Parsing of the XML document is initiated by a call to one of the object's `parse()` methods.

Visual Basic Equivalent
N/A.

See Also
org.xml.sax.DocumentHandler
org.xml.sax.DTDHandler
org.xml.sax.EntityResolver
org.xml.sax.ErrorHandler
org.xml.sax.HandlerBase
org.xml.sax.InputSource
org.xml.sax.XMLReader

Example
```
import org.xml.sax.helpers.ParserFactory;
import org.xml.sax.Parser;
import org.xml.sax.EntityResolver;
import org.xml.sax.DTDHandler;
import org.xml.sax.DocumentHandler;
import org.xml.sax.ErrorHandler;
import org.xml.sax.InputSource;
import org.xml.sax.SAXException;
import org.xml.sax.SAXParseException;
import org.xml.sax.SAXNotRecognizedException;
import org.xml.sax.SAXNotSupportedException;
import java.io.IOException;
import java.util.Locale;
. . .
    private Parser myParser;
```

Members

parse Method

Java Signature
```
public void parse(String systemId)
```

Visual Basic Signature
N/A.

This method causes the `Parser` to begin parsing the XML document identified by a system identifier (URI). If the passed system identifier is a URL, it must be fully qualified.

Thrown Exceptions
java.io.IOException
org.xml.sax.SAXException

See Also
org.xml.sax.Parser.parse(org.xml.sax.InputSource)
org.xml.sax.XMLReader.parse(java.lang.String)

Example

```
import org.xml.sax.helpers.ParserFactory;
import org.xml.sax.Parser;
import org.xml.sax.EntityResolver;
import org.xml.sax.DTDHandler;
import org.xml.sax.DocumentHandler;
import org.xml.sax.ErrorHandler;
import org.xml.sax.InputSource;
import org.xml.sax.SAXException;
import org.xml.sax.SAXParseException;
import org.xml.sax.SAXNotRecognizedException;
import org.xml.sax.SAXNotSupportedException;
import java.io.IOException;
import java.util.Locale;
. . .
        try
        {
            myParser.parse( systemID );
        }
        catch( SAXParseException e )
        {
            System.err.println( systemID + " is not well formed." );
            System.err.println( e.getMessage() +
                                " at line " + e.getLineNumber() +
                                ", column " + e.getColumnNumber() );
        }
        catch( SAXException e )
        {
            System.err.println( e.getMessage() );
        }
        catch( IOException e )
        {
            System.err.println( "Could not report on " + systemID +
                                " because of the IOException " + e );
        }
```

Parameters

String systemId   The system identifier (URI) of the XML document to be parsed.

Returns

void   N/A.

parse Method

Java Signature

```
public void parse(InputSource source)
```

Visual Basic Signature
N/A.

This method causes the Parser to begin parsing the XML document contained in an InputSource object.

Thrown Exceptions
java.io.IOException
org.xml.sax.SAXException

See Also
org.xml.sax.InputSource
org.xml.sax.Parser.parse(java.lang.String)
org.xml.sax.XMLReader.parse(org.xml.sax.InputSource)

Example
```java
import org.xml.sax.helpers.ParserFactory;
import org.xml.sax.Parser;
import org.xml.sax.EntityResolver;
import org.xml.sax.DTDHandler;
import org.xml.sax.DocumentHandler;
import org.xml.sax.ErrorHandler;
import org.xml.sax.InputSource;
import org.xml.sax.SAXException;
import org.xml.sax.SAXParseException;
import org.xml.sax.SAXNotRecognizedException;
import org.xml.sax.SAXNotSupportedException;
import java.io.IOException;
import java.util.Locale;
...
    try
    {
        myParser.parse( input );
    }
    catch( SAXParseException e )
    {
        System.err.println( "Document is not well formed." +
                        e.getMessage() +
                        " at line " + e.getLineNumber() +
                        ", column " + e.getColumnNumber() );
    }
    catch( SAXException e )
    {
        System.err.println( e.getMessage() );
    }
    catch( IOException e )
    {
        System.err.println( "Could not report on document" +
                        " because of the IOException " + e );
```

Parameters

InputSource **source**   An instance of an `InputSource` object that represents an XML document.

Returns

void   N/A.

setDocumentHandler Method

Java Signature
```
public void setDocumentHandler(DocumentHandler handler)
```

Visual Basic Signature
N/A.

Using this method, a client application can register an object that implements the `DocumentHandler` interface in order to receive content-related events.

Applications can register different implementations of `DocumentHandler` at any time, including in the middle of parsing. The parser is required to begin using the new `DocumentHandler` immediately.

If no `DocumentHandler` is registered with the parser, all content events will be silently ignored.

See Also
org.xml.sax.DocumentHandler
org.xml.sax.HandlerBase
org.xml.sax.XMLReader.setContentHandler(org.xml.sax.ContentHandler)

Example
```java
import org.xml.sax.helpers.ParserFactory;
import org.xml.sax.Parser;
import org.xml.sax.EntityResolver;
import org.xml.sax.DTDHandler;
import org.xml.sax.DocumentHandler;
import org.xml.sax.ErrorHandler;
import org.xml.sax.InputSource;
import org.xml.sax.SAXException;
import org.xml.sax.SAXParseException;
import org.xml.sax.SAXNotRecognizedException;
import org.xml.sax.SAXNotSupportedException;
import java.io.IOException;
import java.util.Locale;
. . .
    public void setDocumentHandler( DocumentHandler handler )
    {
        myParser.setDocumentHandler( handler );
    }
```

Parameters

DocumentHandler **handler**   An object that implements the DocumentHandler interface.

Returns

void   N/A.

setDTDHandler Method

Java Signature
```
public void setDTDHandler(DTDHandler handler)
```

Visual Basic Signature
N/A.

This method allows a client application to register an object that implements the DTDHandler interface in order to receive DTD-related events.

Applications can register different implementations of DTDHandler at any time, including in the middle of parsing. The parser is required to begin using the new DTDHandler immediately.

If no DTDHandler is registered with the parser, all DTD events will be silently ignored.

See Also
org.xml.sax.DTDHandler
org.xml.sax.HandlerBase
org.xml.sax.XMLReader.setDTDHandler(org.xml.sax.DTDHandler)

Example
```
import org.xml.sax.helpers.ParserFactory;
import org.xml.sax.Parser;
import org.xml.sax.EntityResolver;
import org.xml.sax.DTDHandler;
import org.xml.sax.DocumentHandler;
import org.xml.sax.ErrorHandler;
import org.xml.sax.InputSource;
import org.xml.sax.SAXException;
import org.xml.sax.SAXParseException;
import org.xml.sax.SAXNotRecognizedException;
import org.xml.sax.SAXNotSupportedException;
import java.io.IOException;
import java.util.Locale;
. . .
    public void setDTDHandler( DTDHandler handler )
    {
        myParser.setDTDHandler( handler );
    }
```

Parameters

`DTDHandler` **`handler`**   An object that implements the `DTDHandler` interface.

Returns

void   N/A.

setEntityResolver Method

Java Signature
```
public void setEntityResolver(EntityResolver resolver)
```

Visual Basic Signature
N/A.

Using this method, a client application can register an object that implements the `EntityResolver` interface in order to intercept all entity resolution requests.

Applications can register different implementations of `EntityResolver` at any time, including in the middle of parsing. The parser is required to begin using the new `EntityResolver` immediately.

If an implementation of `EntityResolver` is not registered with the `Parser`, the parser will perform its own default resolution.

See Also
org.xml.sax.EntityResolver
org.xml.sax.HandlerBase
org.xml.sax.XMLReader.setEntityResolver(org.xml.sax.EntityResolver)

Example
```
import org.xml.sax.helpers.ParserFactory;
import org.xml.sax.Parser;
import org.xml.sax.EntityResolver;
import org.xml.sax.DTDHandler;
import org.xml.sax.DocumentHandler;
import org.xml.sax.ErrorHandler;
import org.xml.sax.InputSource;
import org.xml.sax.SAXException;
import org.xml.sax.SAXParseException;
import org.xml.sax.SAXNotRecognizedException;
import org.xml.sax.SAXNotSupportedException;
import java.io.IOException;
import java.util.Locale;
. . .
    public void setEntityResolver( EntityResolver resolver )
    {
        myParser.setEntityResolver( resolver );
    }
```

Parameters

EntityResolver **resolver**   An object that implements the EntityResolver interface.

Returns

void   N/A.

setErrorHandler Method

Java Signature
```
public void setErrorHandler(ErrorHandler handler)
```

Visual Basic Signature
N/A.

Using this method, a client application can register an object that implements the ErrorHandler interface in order to intercept all error reporting events.

Applications can register different implementations of ErrorHandler at any time, including in the middle of parsing. The parser is required to begin using the new ErrorHandler immediately.

If an implementation of ErrorHandler is not registered with the Parser, all errors will be silently ignored, with unpredictable results; therefore, it is *strongly* recommended all applications implement the ErrorHandler interface.

See Also
org.xml.sax.ErrorHandler
org.xml.sax.HandlerBase
org.xml.sax.SAXException
org.xml.sax.XMLReader.setErrorHandler(org.xml.sax.ErrorHandler)

Example
```
import org.xml.sax.helpers.ParserFactory;
import org.xml.sax.Parser;
import org.xml.sax.EntityResolver;
import org.xml.sax.DTDHandler;
import org.xml.sax.DocumentHandler;
import org.xml.sax.ErrorHandler;
import org.xml.sax.InputSource;
import org.xml.sax.SAXException;
import org.xml.sax.SAXParseException;
import org.xml.sax.SAXNotRecognizedException;
import org.xml.sax.SAXNotSupportedException;
import java.io.IOException;
import java.util.Locale;
. . .
    public void setErrorHandler( ErrorHandler handler )
    {
        myParser.setErrorHandler( handler );
    }
```

Parameters

ErrorHandler **handler**   An object that implements the ErrorHandler interface.

Returns

void   N/A.

setLocale Method

Java Signature
```
public void setLocale(Locale locale)
```

Visual Basic Signature
N/A.

This method allows an application to request that the Parser use the specified locale for error reporting. Parsers are not required to support localization for error messages; however, if they do not support the requested locale, they must throw a SAXException error.

A locale may *not* be changed in the middle of parsing.

Note that Parser.setLocale() does not have a corresponding method in the SAX 2.0 XMLReader interface.

Thrown Exceptions
org.xml.sax.SAXException

See Also
org.xml.sax.SAXException
org.xml.sax.SAXParseException

Example
```
import org.xml.sax.helpers.ParserFactory;
import org.xml.sax.Parser;
import org.xml.sax.EntityResolver;
import org.xml.sax.DTDHandler;
import org.xml.sax.DocumentHandler;
import org.xml.sax.ErrorHandler;
import org.xml.sax.InputSource;
import org.xml.sax.SAXException;
import org.xml.sax.SAXParseException;
import org.xml.sax.SAXNotRecognizedException;
import org.xml.sax.SAXNotSupportedException;
import java.io.IOException;
import java.util.Locale;
 . . .
        try
        {
            myParser.setLocale( locale );
        }
        catch( SAXException e )
        {
```

```
            String errMsg;
            errMsg = "Requested Locale is not supported.";
            System.out.println( errMsg + "\n\t" +
                                e.toString() );
        }
```

Parameters

Locale **locale**   A Java Locale object.

Returns

void   N/A.

ParserFactory Class

The ParserFactory class is a SAX 1.0 class that has been deprecated in favor of the SAX 2.0 XMLReaderFactory class to provide support for namespace-related information. The use of this class is *strongly* discouraged; nevertheless, it is documented here.

The ParserFactory class creates SAX 1.0 parsers dynamically at run-time using either the value of the org.xml.sax.parser system property or a passed string containing the parser's class name.

This class is designed specifically for Java developers and is not included as part of the platform-independent SAX specification. However, SAX implementations in languages other than Java may choose to include this class as a convenience to application developers.

Visual Basic Equivalent

N/A.

See Also

org.xml.sax.helpers.XMLReaderFactory
org.xml.sax.Parser

Example

```
import org.xml.sax.helpers.ParserFactory;
import org.xml.sax.Parser;
import java.lang.Exception;
public class ParserFactorySample
{
    public ParserFactorySample()
    {
        Parser myParser;
        String parserClass = "org.apache.xerces.parsers.SAXParser";
        try
        {
            myParser = ParserFactory.makeParser();
        }
        catch( Exception e )
        {
```

(continued on next page)

```
            try
            {
                myParser = ParserFactory.makeParser( parserClass );
            }
            catch( Exception ee )
            {
                System.err.println( "Couldn't create parser! " +
                                    ee.getMessage() );
                return;
            }
        }
    }
}
```

Members

makeParser Method

Java Signature
```
public Parser makeParser()
```

Visual Basic Signature
N/A.

This method creates a new SAX 1.0 `Parser` object using the parser specified by the value of the `org.xml.sax.parser` system property. The `Parser` class specified by `org.xml.sax.parser` must exist and must implement the SAX 1.0 `Parser` interface.

If no value is set for the `org.xml.sax.parser` property, the method throws a `java.lang.NullPointerException` error. If the specified `Parser` class cannot be found, the method throws a `java.lang.ClassNotFoundException` error. If the specified `Parser` class is found but does not implement the SAX 1.0 `Parser` interface, the method throws a `java.lang.ClassCastException` error.

Thrown Exceptions
java.lang.ClassCastException
java.lang.ClassNotFoundException
java.lang.IllegalAccessException
java.lang.InstantiationException
java.lang.NullPointerException

See Also
org.xml.sax.Parser
org.xml.sax.helpers.ParserFactory.makeParser(java.lang.String)

Example
```
import org.xml.sax.helpers.ParserFactory;
import org.xml.sax.Parser;
import java.lang.Exception;
. . .
        Parser myParser;
```

```
        String parserClass = "org.apache.xerces.parsers.SAXParser";
        try
        {
            myParser = ParserFactory.makeParser();
        }
        catch( Exception e )
        {
            try
            {
                myParser = ParserFactory.makeParser( parserClass );
            }
            catch( Exception ee )
            {
                System.err.println( "Couldn't create parser! " +
                                    ee.getMessage() );
                return;
            }
        }
```

Returns

Parser   An object implementing the SAX 1.0 Parser interface.

makeParser Method

Java Signature
```
public Parser makeParser(String className)
```

Visual Basic Signature
N/A.

This method creates a new SAX 1.0 Parser object using the passed Parser class name. The specified Parser class must exist and must implement the SAX 1.0 Parser interface.

If the specified Parser class cannot be found, the method throws a java.lang.ClassNotFoundException error. If the specified Parser class is found but does not implement the SAX 1.0 Parser interface, the method throws a java.lang.ClassCastException error.

Thrown Exceptions
java.lang.ClassCastException
java.lang.ClassNotFoundException
java.lang.IllegalAccessException
java.lang.InstantiationException

See Also
org.xml.sax.Parser
org.xml.sax.helpers.ParserFactory.makeParser()

Example

```
import org.xml.sax.helpers.ParserFactory;
import org.xml.sax.Parser;
import java.lang.Exception;
```
. . .
```
    Parser myParser;
    String parserClass = "org.apache.xerces.parsers.SAXParser";
    try
    {
        myParser = ParserFactory.makeParser();
    }
    catch( Exception e )
    {
        try
        {
            myParser = ParserFactory.makeParser( parserClass );
        }
        catch( Exception ee )
        {
            System.err.println( "Couldn't create parser! " +
                                ee.getMessage() );
            return;
        }
    }
```

Parameters

`String className`   A string containing the name of the SAX 1.0 `Parser` class.

Returns

`Parser`   An object implementing the SAX 1.0 `Parser` interface.

INDEX

Note: Italicized numbers indicate illustrations.

A

Apache Foundation's XML Project, 6
APIs (application program interfaces), 2–3. *See also* SAX
application-specific objects, 7
ASCII encoding, 28
`<!ATTLIST>` declaration, 35
`AttributeList` interface, 50
attributes
   See also namespaces
   getting information about, 15–16
   names, prefixes of, 41
   `path`, 31
   preserving, 13
   `src`, 35, 37
   `xmlns`, 41, 60
`AttributesImpl` object, 14

B

binary numbers, mapping to characters, 28
Borland JBuilder Foundation 3.0 IDE, 6, 7
Borland Web site, 7
BufferedReader member (m_brIn), 59

building SAX application, 7–16
   accessing attribute values using Attributes Interface, 15–16
   basic application flow, 7
   configuring environment, 7
   implementing ContentHandler Interface, 10–11
   parsing and processing, 11–15
   `XMLReader` interface, 9–10
   `XShell` sample application, 8–9

C

`catch( )` block, of `doBatch( )` method, 21
chaining filters, 48
character data, notification of found, 10
character encoding, 28
`characters( )` notification method, 13, 14
classes
   deprecation in SAX 2.0, 53
   `EntityResolver`, 26
   helper classes
      as class factory for `XMLReader` instances, 9
      `DefaultHandler`, 10, 20, 56–57
      defined by SAX application, 9
      `LocatorImpl`, 61
   locating at runtime, 7
   `NamespaceSupport`, 43, 60–61

classes *(continued)*
    NewSAXApp, 54
    OldSAXApp, 51, 53
    org.apache.xerces.parsers.
        SAXParser, 9
    SAXParser, 9
CLASSPATH environment
        variable, 7, 18
code, replacing deprecated, 53-54
column number, retrieval during
        parsing, 31
com.bookofsax.SAXAnimate
        utility, 11-12
configuring environment, 7
ContentHandler interface
    implementing, 10-11
    setDocumentLocator( ) callback
        method of, 31
ContentHandler notification
        methods, 43
Cp1252 character set, 28
custom entity resolvers, 28-30

D

declarePrefix( ) method, 61
DefaultHandler helper class, 10, 20,
        56, 56-57
default namespace, 41
<dir> command, 31
directory listing, of invalid path,
        31-32
doBatch( ) method, 11, 21
doCD( ) method, 15
<!DOCTYPE> declaration, 22, 34
DocumentHandler interface, 50
Document Object Model (DOM), 2
document type definitions. *See*
        DTDs

doDir( ) method, 15, 18-19, 31
doEcho( ) method, 15, 37
DOM (Document Object Model), 2
downloading simple SAX
        application, 16
DTDHandler interface, 34, 35
DTDs (document type definitions)
    capturing information from,
        33-37
    conformance to rules of, 19, 21
<dump> element, 44
dumpEntity( ) method, 37

E

<echo> element, 35, 37
element tags
    open/unmatched, 19
    start and end, notification for
        recognition, 10
encoding
    character, 28
    MIME type as public ID, 34
endElement( ) notification method
    in catching SAXExceptions, 19
    example of, 14-15
    in namespace prefix tracking, 44
    in namespace recognition, 42
ending documents, notification for,
        10
endPrefixMapping( ) notification
        method, 43
entities
    external, 28-30, 34
    processing references to, 37
    unparsed, 35, 36-37
entity declarations, 29, 34, 35,
        36-37
entity references, undeclared, 35

entityResolver( ) method, 29
EntityResolver class, 26
entity resolvers, custom, 28–30
environment, configuring, 7
error( ) notification method, 19, 22
ErrorHandler interface, 19–21
errors, handling, 17–23
    See also validation
    application-specific, 31
    ErrorHandler interface, 19–21
    fatal errors, 19, 21, 62
    misspellings, 35
    multiple errors, 22–23
    parse-time errors, 62
    SAXExceptions, 18–19
    SAX property and feature exceptions, 21–22
    testing for, 18
    undeclared entity references, 35
event-driven APIs, 2–3
ext-command.xml file, 29
extending XMLFilter, 48
extensibility, 26, 60
eXtensible Markup Language (XML)
    popularity of, 1
    violation of rules, 19
external entities, 28–30, 34

F

fatal errors, 19, 21, 62
feature exceptions, 21–22
feature methods, 60
feature names, 21
file: protocol, 27, 29
filters, chaining, 48

G

getByteStream( ) InputSource method, 59
getCharacterStream( ) InputSource method, 59
getContentHandler( ) method, 57
getDeclaredPrefixes( ) method, 61
getFeature( ) method, 60
getIndex( ) method, 15–16
getLength( ) method, 16
getQName( ) method, 16
getType( ) method, 15
getValue( ) method, 15, 54

H

handler methods, setting, 56–57
HashMap object, 36
helper classes
    as class factory for XMLReader instances, 9
    DefaultHandler, 10, 20, 56, 56–57
    defined by SAX application, 9
    LocatorImpl, 61
http: protocol, 27, 29

I

IDEs (Integrated Development Environments), 6–7
IDs, system, 26, 27, 29, 30
ignorable whitespace, 10
images, referenced from XML document, 34
index, accessing attribute values by, 16

InputSource, 25–32
    character encoding, 28
    constructing, 26–27
    custom entity resolvers, 28–30
    locator interface, 31–32
    overview, 26
    primary uses, 26
    public and system IDs, 26, 27–28
    working with, 57–59
Integrated Development Environments (IDEs), 6–7
interfaces
    AttributeList, 50
    ContentHandler
        implementing, 10–11
        setDocumentLocator( ) callback method of, 31
    deprecation in SAX 2.0, 50, 53
    DocumentHandler, 50
    ErrorHandler, 19–21
    locator interface, 31–32
    XMLFilter, 46–47
    XMLReader interface
        and NamespaceSupport class, 61
        setDTDHandler( ) method of, 35
        using, 9–10

J

java.exe (the JDK Java runtime), 7
java.util.Stack object, 13
Java 2 SDK (JDK), 6

L

LetterOrDigit( ) method, 56
line numbers, retrieval during parsing, 31
local part, of tag name, 40
LocatorImpl helper class, 61
locator interface, 31–32
Locator object, 31

M

m_hmNotations HashMap, 37
m_stChars stack, 14
main( ) method, 8, 52
methods
    See also names of specific methods
    for creating new XMLReader object instance, 9
    for getting attribute information, 15–16
    replacing deprecated, 51, 52
migrating SAX 1.0 applications, 49–54
    replacing deprecated code, 53–54
    strategies, 50–52
    using old parsers, 54
    XMLReaderAdapter class, 52–53
MIME type, encoding as public ID, 34
misspellings, 35
multiple errors, 22–23
multiple filters, chaining, 48
my_msg.txt file, 34

N

names
  accessing attribute values by, 15
  feature name, 21
  qualified, 40
namespace prefixes
  defined, 40
  going in and out of scope,
    notification of, 10
  mapping notification, 12
  tracking, 43–44
  URI for, 41
namespaces, 39–44
  default, 41
  recognizing at parse time, 42–43
  support for
    added in SAX 2.0, 50
    checking, 41–42
    implementing, 60–61
  terminology, 40–41
  tracking, 60–61
NamespaceSupport.pushContext( )
  method, 44
NamespaceSupport class, 43, 60–61
NDATA keyword, 34, 36
NewSAXApp.java file, 54
NewSAXApp class, 54
nonfatal errors, 21
notationDecl( ) method, 35, 36
notations, 35–37
notifications
  characters( ) method, 13, 14
  ContentHandler methods, 10, 43
  endElement( ) method, 13,
    14–15, 42
    calling doDir( ) method, 19
    in catching SAXException, 19
  example of, 14–15
  in namespace prefix
    tracking, 44
  in namespace recognition, 42
  endPrefixMapping( ) method,
    43
  error( ) method, 19, 22
  fatalError( ) method, 19, 21,
    62
  processing, 12–13
  sequencing by SAX, 11–12
  startElement( ) method, 13–14
  unregistered, 56
  warning( ) method, 19
NullPointerException, 57

O

obtaining SAX, 6–7
OldSAXApp class, 51, 53
org.apache.xerces.parsers.
  SAXParser class, 9
org.xml.sax.helpers package, 7
org.xml.sax package, 7
<other:echo> element, 43

P

parse( ) method, 11, 26, 57–59
parsers
  namespace support, 41
  using old, 54
  writing, 55–62
    error handling, 62
    feature and property
      methods, 60

parsers *(continued)*
    `LocatorImpl` class, 61
    namespace tracking, 60–61
    using `DefaultHandler`
        class, 56–57
    working with `InputSource`
        class, 57–59
    Xerces, 6
parsing, 11–15
    Cp1252 document, 28
    problems with. *See* errors,
        handling
    recognizing namespaces during,
        42–43
    retrieving current URL, line, and
        column number during, 31
    of system ID, 29
path attribute, 31
picoSAX
    error handling, 62
    feature and property
        methods, 60
    `LocatorImpl` class, 61
    namespace tracking, 60–61
    performance of and
        shortcuts, *56*
    using `DefaultHandler`
        class, 56–57
    working with `InputSource`
        class, 57–59
`popContext( )` method, 44, 61
prefixes, namespace
    defined, 40
    going in and out of scope,
        notification of, 10
    mapping notification, 12
    tracking, 43–44
processing instructions, notification
    of found, 10

processing XML document, 11–15
`processName( )` method, 61
program output, display of in this
    book, 19
property exceptions, 21–22
protocols, 27, 29, 30
public IDs, 26, 27–28, 34
`pushback( )` method, 61
`pushContext( )` method, 61

Q

qualified names, 40

R

`readChar( )` method, 61
registering
    to receive DTD event
        notifications, 35
    to receive notifications on
        ErrorHandler interface, 20
`resolveEntity( )` method, 30

S

SAX (Simple API for XML)
    building application, 7–16
        accessing attribute values
            using Attributes Interface,
            15–16
        basic application flow, 7
        configuring environment, 7
        implementing
            ContentHandler Interface,
            10–11
        parsing and processing, 11–15
        XMLReader interface, 9–10

SAX (Simple API for XML)
  (continued)
    XShell sample application, 8–9
    obtaining, 6–7
    overview, 2–3
    specifications for, 6
    version numbers, *6*
    what it is, 6
SAX 1.0
    differences from SAX 2.0, 50
    migrating applications, 49–54
        replacing deprecated code, 53–54
        strategies, 50–52
        using old parsers, 54
        XMLReaderAdapter class, 52–53
SAX 2.0, 50
SAX ErrorHandler interface, 62
SAXExceptions, 18–19
    feature exceptions, 21–22
    property exceptions, 21–22
    SAXNotRecognizedException, 21
    SAXNotSupportedException, 21
    SAXParseException, 19, 31
SAX Locator object, 31
SAXNotRecognizedException, 21
SAXNotRecognized exception, 60
SAXNotSupportedException, 21
SAXParseException, 19, 31, 62
SAXParser class, 9
sequencing notifications, 11–12
set*( ) methods, 27
setContentHandler( ) method, 57
setDocumentLocator( ) method, 31, 61
setDTDHandler( ) method, 35

setEncoding( ) method, 27
setEntityResolver( ) method, 30
setErrorHandler( ) method, 20
setFeature( ) method, 42, 60
Simple API for XML. *See* SAX
specifications for SAX, 6
src attribute, 35, 37
startElement( ) notification method, 13–14, 44
starting documents, notification for, 10
startPrefixMapping( ) notification method, 43, 44
String arrays, 36
StringBuffer object, 14
System.in InputStream, 8
system IDs, 26, 27, 29, 30
SYSTEM keyword, 29

T

<table> elements, 51
tags
    comparison of names, 41
    local part of name, 40
    open, unmatched, 19
Tokenizer helper class, 58–59
tracking
    namespace declarations, 43
    namespaces, 60–61
    notation and entity declarations, 36–37
transition to SAX 2.0. *See* migrating SAX 1.0 applications
tree-based APIs, 2
try . . . catch block, 18, 21, 62

U

undeclared entity references, 35
Unicode characters, 28
Uniform Resource Identifiers (URIs), 27, 30, 41
Uniform Resource Locators (URLs), 27, 28, 29, 31
unmatched open element tags, 19
unparsed entities
   external, 34
   how notations work with, 35
   tracking entity declarations, 36-37
unparsedEntityDecl( ) method, 35, 37
unzipping programs, 6
URIs (Uniform Resource Identifiers), 27, 30, 41
URLs (Uniform Resource Locators), 27, 28, 29, 31
user input, display of in this book, 19
UTF-8 encoding, 28

V

validation
   See also errors, handling
   to DTD rules, 21
   src attributes of <echo> elements, 35
version numbers, SAX, *6*

W

warning( ) notification method, 19
Web site, for this book, 8
whitespace, ignorable, 10
Windows ANSI character set, 28

X

x-env: protocol, 29
xerces.jar file, 7
Xerces parser, 6, 8, 21
XML (eXtensible Markup Language)
   popularity of, 1
   violation of rules, 19
XML-DEV mailing list, 2
XMLFilter, 46-48
xmlns attributes, 41, 60
XML Project, Apache Foundation's, 6
XMLReader.parse( ) method, 26
XMLReader.setErrorHandler( ) method, 20
XMLReader.setFeature( ) method, 21, 41-42
XMLReaderAdapter helper class, 50, 52-53
XMLReaderAdapter instance, 53
XMLReaderFactory.createXMLReader( ) method, 9
XMLReader interface
   and NamespaceSupport class, 61
   setDTDHandler( ) method of, 35
   using, 9-10
XMLReader object, 53
XShell.doBatch( ) method, 18-19
XShell.java source file, 44
XShell application, 8-9

XShell class, 10
XShell constructor, 10
   adding call to, 20
   call to setDTDHandler( )
      method, 35
   call to XMLReader.setFeature( )
      method, 41–42
   enabling validation, 21
   modifying to call
      setEntityResolver( )
      method, 30
XShellScript.dtd, 22
XShellTestScript.xml, *22*

Z

zipping programs, 6

More No-Nonsense Books from no starch press

THE BOOK OF VMWARE
The Complete Guide to the VMware Workstation

by BRIAN WARD

This comprehensive guide to installing and running VMware includes sections on device emulation; configuring the guest operating system; networking and file transfers; and troubleshooting common questions and answers.

2002, 264 PP., $39.95 ($55.95 CDN)
ISBN 1-886411-72-7

JIN SATO'S LEGO® MINDSTORMS™
The Master's Technique

by JIN SATO

When it comes to LEGO MINDSTORMS, few are as creative or inspired as Jin Sato, creator of MIBO, the Lego Hall of Fame robotic dog. In his landmark book, Sato teaches the basic principles of robotics engineering, including how to plan and build robots with tires, legs, and grasping hands.

2002, 312 PP., $24.95 ($37.95 CDN)
ISBN 1-886411-56-5

THE BOOK OF VB .NET
.NET Insight for VB Developers

by MATTHEW MACDONALD

Built on the Microsoft .NET framework, Visual Basic .NET allows programmers to create everything from Internet applications to sophisticated Windows programs with the latest eye-catching interfaces. This comprehensive guide to .NET development is organized into a series of lightning tours and real-world examples, covering everything from Web Services to migrating to .NET.

2002, 488 PP., $39.95 ($55.95 CDN)
ISBN 1-886411-82-4

THE BOOK OF ZOPE
How to Build and Deliver Web Applications

by BEEHIVE

Zope, the leading Open Source web application server, helps teams of developers create and manage dynamic, web-based business applications like Intranets and portals. The Book of Zope is a complete introduction, covering installation; DTML programming; users, roles, and permissions; ZClasses; ZCatalog; databases; programming Zope with Python; debugging; and the use of external data sources.

2001, 400 PP., $39.95 ($59.95 CDN)
ISBN 1-886411-57-3

THE LINUX COOKBOOK
Tips and Techniques for Everyday Use

by MICHAEL STUTZ

This is a complete reference to all of the free software that comes with Linux, with sections on printing, converting and managing files, editing and formatting text; working with digital audio; creating and manipulating graphics, and connecting to the Internet.

2001, 396 PP., $29.95 ($44.95 CDN)
ISBN 1-886411-48-4

Phone:

1 (800) 420-7240 OR
(415) 863-9900
MONDAY THROUGH FRIDAY,
9 A.M. TO 5 P.M. (PST)

Fax:

(415) 863-9950
24 HOURS A DAY,
7 DAYS A WEEK

Email:

SALES@NOSTARCH.COM

Web:

HTTP://WWW.NOSTARCH.COM

Mail:

NO STARCH PRESS
555 DE HARO STREET, SUITE 250
SAN FRANCISCO, CA 94107
USA

Distributed in the U.S. by Publishers Group West

UPDATES

This book was carefully reviewed for technical accuracy, but it's inevitable that some things will change after the book goes to press. Visit **http://www.nostarch.com/sax_updates.htm** for updates, errata, and other information.